DEMOCRACY IS
A GOOD THING

THE THORNTON CENTER CHINESE THINKERS SERIES

The John L. Thornton China Center at Brookings develops timely, independent analysis and policy recommendations to help U.S. and Chinese leaders address key long-standing challenges, both in terms of Sino-U.S. relations and China's internal development. As part of this effort, the Thornton Center Chinese Thinkers Series aims to shed light on the ongoing scholarly and policy debates in China.

China's momentous socioeconomic transformation has not taken place in an intellectual vacuum. Chinese scholars have actively engaged in fervent discussions about the country's future trajectory and its ever-growing integration with the world. This series introduces some of the most influential recent works by prominent thinkers from the People's Republic of China to English language readers. Each volume, translated from the original Chinese, contains writings by a leading scholar in a particular academic field (for example, political science, economics, law, or sociology). This series offers a much-needed intellectual forum promoting international dialogue on various issues that confront China and the world.

DEMOCRACY IS A GOOD THING

Essays on Politics, Society, and Culture in Contemporary China

YU KEPING

BROOKINGS INSTITUTION PRESS
Washington, D.C.

Copyright © 2009
THE BROOKINGS INSTITUTION
1775 Massachusetts Avenue, N.W., Washington, D.C. 20036
www.brookings.edu

Library of Congress Cataloging-in-Publication data

Yu, Keping.
 Democracy is a good thing : essays on politics, society, and culture in contemporary China / Yu Keping.
  p. cm.
 Includes bibliographical references and index.
 Summary: "Presents selections of works of Yu Keping, a Chinese intellectual and figure in official think tanks, on politics and democracy that reveal the ongoing debates in Chinese political and intellectual circles on democratic reform and where China's political development is heading"—Provided by publisher.
 ISBN 978-0-8157-9694-7 (cloth : alk. paper)
 1. Democracy—China. 2. China—Politics and government. I. Title.

JQ1516.Y8 2008
320.951—dc22   2008041977

9 8 7 6 5 4 3 2 1

The paper used in this publication meets minimum requirements of the American National Standard for Information Sciences—Permanence of Paper for Printed Library Materials: ANSI Z39.48-1992.

Typeset in Adobe Garamond

Composition by Cynthia Stock
Silver Spring, Maryland

Printed by R. R. Donnelley
Harrisonburg, Virginia

Contents

Foreword by John L. Thornton   vii

Acknowledgments   xiii

Introduction by Cheng Li   xvii

PART I
POLITICAL DEVELOPMENT IN REFORM-ERA CHINA

1   *Democracy Is a Good Thing*   3

2   *The Study of Political Science and Public Administration in China: An Overview*   6

3   *The Seventeenth Party Congress and the Agenda for China's Political Reforms*   27

PART II
SOCIAL TRANSFORMATION AND CIVIL SOCIETY

4   *China's Civil Society: Conceptual Definitions, Types, and Background*   37

5   *The Characteristics of Chinese Civil Society: Administrative Regulations and Institutional Environment*   52

6   *Civil Society Organizations: Challenges and Responses*   75

PART III
CULTURE, MODERNITY, AND SUSTAINABILITY

7 Culture and Modernity in the Chinese Intellectual
   Discourse: A Historical Perspective   93

8 The Transformation of Chinese Culture since the
   Launching of Reform: A Historical Perspective   113

9 China's Economic Modernization and Sustainability   134

10 Harmony between Man and Nature: China's
   Environmental Practices and Challenges   140

PART IV
GLOBALIZATION AND GOVERNANCE

11 Preserving China's Autonomy in the Era of Globalization   149

12 Federalism in Modern China: Concepts and Experiments   157

13 A Harmonious World and Global Governance:
   A Chinese Perspective   168

Notes   181

Further Reading: The Writings of Yu Keping   199

Index   207

FOREWORD

This volume and the Brookings series it launches share an origin, an explanation of which may help readers place in context the essays that follow. Five and a half years ago, I began teaching a seminar on leadership at Tsinghua University in Beijing and spending a good part of the year in China. It was a choice that would change and deepen my view of the country in many ways. I thought I knew something about China during the years I spent in finance, when I traveled there frequently to work with its government and business leaders. What impressed me now, however, as a part-time resident of the Chinese capital, was just how narrow my knowledge and insight actually were. All countries and cultures are not equally complex. China, with its sheer size, history, culture, the pace of change in its economy, the opacity of its politics, and the extent of its interactions with the outside world, is one of the most complicated of all.

As I went about trying to understand my new subject in some systematic fashion, it also became clear to me that many of the trends reshaping the world's most populous country—the concerns foremost on the minds of my students—rarely seemed to find their way into a Western newspaper. Over the past year, largely due to its hosting of the Beijing Olympics, China has received more attention than usual. But for the most part the increased coverage has been (much) more of the same, and the China portrayed through the Western media rarely broke through the boundaries of well-known story lines and themes: its extraordinary economic growth, the trade imbalance with the United States, human rights issues (especially after the March riots in Tibet), its role in international challenges such as North Korea and Sudan, environmental disasters, the safety of Chinese food, toys, and other manufactured goods—and, of course, the Olympics themselves. Each of these issues is worthy of attention, to be sure, but even put together they still represent an incomplete picture of a vast and rapidly evolving country.

In an effort to fill this gap in our common knowledge, Brookings established a China Center in 2006, led by Ambassador Jeffrey Bader, to bring together some of the West's most discerning observers of China and give them the resources to investigate the forces shaping the country. Senior Fellow Cheng Li, for instance, who is the principal editor of this volume, has done innovative work analyzing the characteristics of China's current and next generation of leaders. We at Brookings also realized that we needed a permanent presence in China if we wanted to stay relevant; today's China is a place where you can feel out of touch after having been away just a few months. Accordingly, we established the Brookings-Tsinghua Center at Tsinghua University, becoming the first American think tank to have a research capability in China. The Center acts as a forum to bring together leading Chinese thinkers, policymakers, and other stakeholders to discuss the vital issues, domestic and international, of the day. Among its activities, the Center produced a report for senior Chinese officials containing policy recommendations for the next stage of China's financial system reform. It has also played a role in advancing the U.S.-China Strategic Economic Dialogue by organizing a series of informal exchanges between senior U.S. officials and leading Chinese opinion leaders.

The "Chinese Thinkers" series, of which Yu Keping's book is the inaugural volume, is a part of this multipronged effort to promote a more nuanced view of China in the West. There is no longer much debate about China's importance; it is commonly accepted that, along with the United States, China will be one of a handful of countries that will play a disproportionate role in setting the course of the current century. The Chinese understand this too, and one encounters there new thinking and debate in almost every field, sector, business, and endeavor about what kind of nation China should aspire to be and the proper role it should play in the world. Unfortunately, much of that discussion is invisible to the Westerner who does not live in China or read Chinese. This series is meant to help address that deficiency by selecting and translating into English the works of some of China's most original thinkers. Yu Keping is a natural place to start. We expect future volumes to include figures such as the economist Hu Angang (a major proponent of Green GDP) and the legal scholar He Weifang (a trenchant observer of China's judicial system).

Why Yu Keping?

In the fall of 2006, in another attempt to deepen our experiential understanding of China, Brookings President Strobe Talbott and I led a delegation on a three-week visit to the country. Our group, which included Brookings trustees and accomplished individuals from a range of disciplines (including three former deputy secretaries of state), began in the far west region of Xinjiang, with stops in Chongqing and Shanghai, and included a series of discussions with senior Chinese in Beijing. In a ninety-minute meeting with Premier Wen Jiabao in the Zhongnanhai leadership compound, we asked how he saw prospects for democratization in his country. Wen spent the next forty-five minutes on the topic. He defined democracy as having three pillars: elections, an independent judiciary, and effective oversight of government. He spoke of the advances China had made in each area over the past three decades and the serious challenges that remained. His conclusion: "We have to move toward democracy. We have many problems, but we know the direction in which we are going."

Realizing from Wen's reply that this was an issue to which he—and no doubt other Chinese—had given considerable thought, I decided to look into the subject in a more serious way and spent the next fourteen months researching and writing an essay published in *Foreign Affairs* in January 2008. I began my research by asking a broad range of Chinese for their recommendations of the most thoughtful thinkers on the subject of their country's political evolution. Yu Keping's name came up repeatedly. Then one day a friend forwarded me an article Yu had published in China around the same time as our meeting with Premier Wen. The four-page essay had a deceptively simple title, "Democracy Is a Good Thing." Reading it was a revelation. (The essay lends its title to this volume and is reprinted as the first chapter.)

Over the next year, Yu Keping and I spent many hours together discussing the past, present, and future of China's political evolution. These sessions helped refine the intellectual framework for my own thinking and the article

I would eventually write. Much of what Yu taught me can be found in the essays that follow in his own words. Yu is a learned but modest man—a scholar-official in the traditional Chinese sense. In our numerous meetings, I found him to be intellectually open and non-ideological—qualities that permeate his writing.

Democracy in China

One of the lessons that Yu Keping taught me was that China's political evolution can only be understood in the context of the country's struggle for democracy dating back to the second half of the nineteenth century. Many of the turning points of modern Chinese history were triggered by popular surges demanding greater democracy that ended ultimately in tragedy or disillusionment. Sun Yat-sen's short-lived Republic, the May Fourth Movement, the early years of the People's Republic of China, the Democracy Wall movement, and Tiananmen Square are all points on this timeline. The hope of Yu Keping and like-minded Chinese thinkers is that an incremental building-block approach toward democratic development—including the development of rule of law and strengthening of civil society—while perhaps less dramatic than earlier movements, will leave a more permanent legacy.

My own view is that the next decade will be a telling one for political evolution in China. One particular trend to watch will be the development of "intra-party democracy"—or more democratic processes within the Chinese Communist Party itself. President Hu Jintao has made this a pillar of his second, five-year term. One motivation for the push is the realization that the country has grown too complex to be managed by a group of leaders at the top: more institutionalized forms of decisionmaking are essential to governing in a complicated world. Another rationale, implied by Hu and others, is that democratization in China cannot hope to succeed without democratic habits first taking root in the ruling CCP itself, since the Party still dominates many aspects of political and economic life. Hu has called on the Party to "unleash (its) creative energies" and "emancipate the mind" through measures such as injecting greater transparency in decisions and fielding multiple candidates for positions. One intriguing possibility mentioned by some knowledgeable Chinese, which would represent an important advance, would be for the 371-member Central Committee to elect directly the next Politburo—and perhaps even the Standing Committee—in 2012, when Hu and his comrades are expected to retire and transfer power to the next generation of China's leaders.

Another question debated among Chinese intellectuals is what Chinese democracy will look like when it is ultimately achieved. Views run the gamut from those who favor a system akin to the liberal model prevalent in the West to those who support a more limited form of "guided democracy." China's neighbors confirm that democracy can take many shapes: from the decades-long domination of the Liberal Democratic Party in Japan (perhaps finally coming to a close) to the free-wheeling multiparty system of South Korea. Whatever its elements and influences, most Chinese I know insist that their country will develop a political system that is distinctive and reflects Chinese society, traditions, and values.

Yu Keping's writings provide non-Chinese with a path to enter the discourse on China's political evolution through the eyes of one of the country's most thoughtful commentators. In addition, I hope that the essays contained here will give Western readers a sense of this important scholar's mind and character, which in their vitality and ambition reflect the signature qualities of China today.

JOHN L. THORNTON

Acknowledgments

I have published a number of books now and for each of them I have always started out planning to convey my sincere gratitude to the many people who helped me along the way. However, each time I find that the list of my benefactors is so long that I have to give up the idea of thanking each one individually and instead issue a blanket statement of appreciation. When I finished this book, my first to be published in English, I felt an even greater debt of gratitude to those who supported me and thus want to express my thanks to those without whose contributions this volume would not have come to fruition.

The year 2008 is the thirtieth anniversary of China's inauguration of the reform and opening policies. Since 1978 these policies not only have brought China dramatic economic achievements that have enabled the country to become an economic powerhouse but have also fueled great social and political progress toward democracy and the rule of law. I have been a witness and a participant in these great transformations—and also a beneficiary of them. The reforms enabled me to transform my life; once little more than a young farmer in a village in Zhejiang Province in the late 1970s, I have risen to become a scholar in Beijing. Thus, first of all, I would like to dedicate this book to the thirtieth anniversary of the reform and opening policies.

John L. Thornton, the chairman of the board of the Brookings Institution, encouraged me to publish my writings in English and persuaded me to undertake this project. He also helped bring the book to a successful conclusion by contributing the foreword to this volume. It would be fair to say that this book would not have come about without his encouragement and support. I want to thank Brookings president Strobe Talbott, vice president and director of foreign policy Carlos Pascual, and director of the John L. Thornton China Center Jeffrey Bader for their support in bringing this project to press. I am also grateful to Woo Lee, managing director of JL Thornton & Company, for his tremendous help in making sure that the book project proceeded promptly.

This book comprises a number of my previously published articles from recent years. All are presented here in an entirely new format and have been edited to be more readable and understandable to the English audience. Indeed, after participating in the translation and editing of this book, it seems to me that the job of editing is almost one of creation. To those who worked with me so diligently to transform my writings into the final form that appears here, I would like to express my deepest gratitude. At the John L. Thornton China Center, Dr. Cheng Li made a large number of extremely helpful suggestions on how best to restructure the book from its original manuscript form. I am also grateful to Dr. Li for taking time out of his busy schedule to write the introductory chapter. Dr. Scott W. Harold waded through each of the chapters, painstakingly correcting minor grammar points while also posing challenging questions and giving big-picture feedback that improved the readability of the volume. Henry Fung and Robert O'Brien then gave it an additional careful proofreading.

I also want to thank Robert L. Faherty, vice president and director of the Brookings Institution Press, and Christopher Kelaher, senior acquisitions editor, for their interest in my work. At the Brookings Institution Press, managing editor Janet Walker and copy editor Marty Gottron put in long hours reviewing the product and giving it a final once-over.

I would like to extend special thanks to my personal assistant, Yan Jian, who patiently and carefully handled much of the proofreading and editing work and took the time to double check all of the footnotes and other citations. Many people were involved in the English translation of my original Chinese essays. I am unable to acknowledge them individually, but my gratitude to each of them is profound.

Last, but not least, I would like to give my special thanks to my parents, my wife, and my daughter. All of my academic work has been made possible by their love, encouragement, and assistance, but they never let me mention them in the acknowledgements sections of my Chinese publications. Therefore, I want to take this opportunity to express my deep love and affection for them in the English version of my book.

YU KEPING

Beijing
August 2008

INTRODUCTION

Making Democracy Safe for China

CHENG LI

"A merican discourse about China," observed Richard Madsen, a distin-guished sinologist in the United States, "has long been as much about ourselves as about China."[1] Far too often we American analysts evaluate China according to our own preconceived notion of what the country is like rather than paying much attention to the Chinese mentality and reality. Throughout history, American views, values, and interests have shaped our assessments of and debates on China's political trajectory, especially the pos-sibility and desirability of democracy in the world's most populous country. Optimists often envision the promotion of democratic principles in China as the best way to fulfill President Woodrow Wilson's century-old idealistic appeal that "the world must be made safe for democracy."[2] A democratic China, they believe, would not only mollify ideological and political ten-sions between China and the West, but also inspire Chinese policymakers to abide by international norms and standards. In contrast, pessimists are cyni-cal about any discussion regarding China's political progress toward democ-racy in the foreseeable future. In their view, China's remarkable economic

The author thanks Elizabeth Brooks, Sally Carman, Christina Culver, and Robert O'Brien for suggesting ways in which to clarify this chapter.

development makes the one-party-state system more resilient and thus more capable of resisting any significant political change.[3] According to these pessimists, this resilient Chinese authoritarian regime, with its rapid economic and military modernization, inevitably constitutes a significant threat to the United States.

What is largely absent in the English-speaking communities of contemporary China studies, however, is a knowledge and understanding of the Chinese discourse about the country's political future. In fact, since the late 1990s, and even more so in recent years, Chinese public intellectuals have engaged in heated discourse on various aspects of China's political reform. Since 2005 Chinese scholars and the official media have fostered a nationwide public discussion about democracy, something that American political scientist David Shambaugh has called the "democracy wave" debates.[4] This Chinese discourse reflects some new thinking about democracy, governance, and civil society in the scholarly communities of the People's Republic of China (PRC). But unfortunately, as noted recently by a Singapore-based scholar, "most leading social scientists in China do not write in English and most of their work has not been translated."[5] As a result, their work goes largely unread by members of the Western academic and policymaking communities.

It is critically important, however, for the outside world to understand the ongoing Chinese intellectual and political discourse. Although foreign pressure or influence may have played an important role from time to time in the political development of China, ultimately only the Chinese leaders and their people can decide the course of the country's political trajectory. The following three interrelated questions are crucial to any analysis of China's political future. First, what incentives do Chinese leaders have for pursuing political reforms? Second, what factors or obstacles will prevent them from doing so? And third, what measures should China adopt to help overcome these obstacles?

Arguably no one has been more articulate in addressing these three questions than Yu Keping, the author of this volume. In fact, the aforementioned "democracy wave" debates in China began with Yu's now well-known article entitled "Democracy is a Good Thing" (chapter 1). The article, which was based on Yu's interview with the Hong Kong–based *Dagong Daily* in 2005, was reprinted first in the *Beijing Daily* in the fall of 2006 and since then has appeared in almost all of the country's major newspapers.[6] In 2007 the *Southern Daily,* a leading liberal newspaper in China, ranked "Democracy Is a Good Thing" as one of the most influential articles in the country during that year.[7] That same year, Yu himself was selected by the Chinese media as one of the most influential public intellectuals in China. In 2008 Yu was named by the Chinese media as one of the top fifty people who have been most influential for China's development in the past three decades.[8]

In a way, Yu's thesis is similar to Winston Churchill's famous witty remark that "democracy is the worst form of government except all the others that have been tried." Using simple and explicit words, Yu directly addresses a profound suspicion and concern that is deeply rooted in the minds of many Chinese nationals: why is democracy good for China? The public discourse on the desirability of democracy that Yu's article has stimulated is much needed for the country, currently in the midst of a far-reaching socioeconomic transformation. If democracy will lead to chaos, or even the dissolution of the country, there is no incentive for the Chinese leaders and people to pursue it. In addition, if democracy is perceived by the country's political, economic, and cultural elites as something that will undermine, rather than enhance, their interests, there will be no strong consensus for such a political future in China. Therefore, the greatest intellectual challenge for Yu and other like-minded scholars is to make democracy safe for China both conceptually and procedurally.

The Book's Objective, Organization, and Outlook

This book aims to help those in the English-speaking communities of China studies better understand some of the dynamic new thinking occurring in the PRC around Chinese political reforms and democracy. It features translations of some of Yu Keping's most important essays on politics, society, and culture in contemporary China. These essays, selected by Yu himself, were all originally published in Chinese; most of them appeared in prominent academic journals and magazines in China between 2006 and 2008. With a couple of exceptions, they were translated into English exclusively for this volume.

The book is organized into four thematic parts. Part one highlights political changes in post-Mao China, especially in the wake of the agenda for political reforms announced at the recent Seventeenth National Congress of the Chinese Communist Party (CCP). It also includes an overview of the groundbreaking developments in the academic disciplines of political science and public administration in reform-era China, illustrating how these developments contribute to the diffusion of international norms throughout the country. Part two focuses on China's emerging civil society. In this section, the author provides comprehensive information about, and a thorough analysis of, the types, status, and characteristics of China's civil society organizations, as well as the government's administrative regulations that both guide and restrict them. Part three examines various challenging dichotomies that the country faces. Among them are culture and modernity, economic growth and sustainability, and human society and environmental protection. The final part places China's ongoing socioeconomic and political transformation within the context of the broader issue of global governance. The author argues for a delicate balance between the need to preserve the Chinese cultural and sociopolitical identity in the era of globalization and the imperative for the country to participate more actively in the construction of a harmonious world.

All four of these parts not only present multidimensional political changes occurring in Chinese state and society but also serve to reinforce the book's central thesis about the feasibility of democracy in China. While acknowledging many of the potential problems that democracy may cause, Yu argues that there is a way by which China can make a transition to democracy with "minimum political and social costs."[9] Yu calls this approach "incremental democracy" and suggests that China's political reforms should be incremental over time and manageable in scale. These political reforms include intraparty democracy, grassroots elections, and legal reforms. Yu believes that these reforms will ultimately result in a "democratic breakthrough" when various existing political forces are ready for such a drastic change. This approach, in Yu's view, is the best way to achieve a political "soft landing" in China.[10]

Universal Values of Democracy

A frequently raised question is whether Yu Keping's conception of democracy is similar to that of most people in the world, especially those in the West. Conceptual clarity is essential in the political and intellectual dialogue between the Chinese and the outside world. At the same time, however, foreign analysts need to understand the political context in which Chinese leaders and their advisors, such as Yu Keping, address this question. Like Chinese leaders, Yu Keping does not argue that China should experiment with a multiparty democratic competition, nor does he believe that the country should move toward an American-style system based on a tripartite division between the executive, legislative, and judicial branches of government. In fact, while stating unambiguously that China should draw some positive elements from the Western political culture and system, Yu maintains that "Westernization of the Chinese political system" should not be a political objective for China.

Yu's position is understandable. Even those who are most optimistic about the potential democratization of China do not expect the country to develop a multiparty system in the near future. Chinese thinkers such as Yu have every reason to argue that the PRC's version of democracy will, and should, have its own unique features. After all, British democracy, Australian democracy, Japanese democracy, Mexican democracy, and American democracy all differ from each other in some important ways. They all, however, feature institutional checks and balances, political choice, constitutionalism, the independence of the media, and certain civil liberties. China's political system can have its own unique characteristics, but it must include these same elements if it wishes to be considered democratic in nature.

Throughout his writings, Yu Keping clearly and consistently advocates the universal values of democracy (*minzhu de pushijiazhi*). When Yu states that "democracy is a good thing," he means that it is good for all of human society, not just for the Americans or the Chinese. In his discussion of cultural developments in the era of globalization, Yu observes, "globalization not only makes people realize that they share a common fate but also helps them identify with such basic values as freedom, equality, justice, security, welfare, and dignity. Pursuit of such basic values is the core principle, as well as the ultimate destination, of cultural globalization" (chapter 8).

It is interesting to note that China's leaders are also speaking about the universal values of democracy. In a meeting with a delegation from the Brookings Institution in Beijing in October 2006, Premier Wen Jiabao spent a substantial amount of time explaining China's objectives for political democracy.[11] He defined democracy in largely the same way as many in the West would explain it. "When we talk about democracy," Premier Wen said, "we usually refer to the three most important components: elections, judicial independence, and supervision based on checks and balances."[12] In addition to expressing such sentiments in private forums, Wen and President Hu Jintao have repeatedly announced publicly the importance of democracy in building an ever-stronger Chinese state. Indeed, the word *democracy* has become a mainstay in the political speeches of many among the Chinese leadership.

Both Yu's thesis about democracy and Wen's remarks about China's road map for political development reflect new thinking in the liberal wing of the Chinese political establishment. For a long time, the party doctrine has portrayed Western democracy as a system that represents only the interests of a small number of the rich and powerful. To Chinese critics, politics in the West has particular problems that result from the way in which campaigns are financed. At the same time, Chinese leaders and scholars have tended to overemphasize the uniqueness of China's conditions and the Chinese characteristics in their economic and political system. Make no mistake, not all Chinese leaders or public intellectuals agree with the enthusiastic views regarding democracy articulated by Premier Wen and Professor Yu. One may even reasonably assume that Wen and Yu represent a minority view in both the Chinese leadership and scholarly communities.

As some Chinese scholars have observed, the fact that Yu argues that "democracy is a good thing" implies that many in the country hold the opposite view that "democracy is a bad thing."[13] According to Shi Tianjian, a political scientist at Duke University, Yu's thesis does not necessarily reflect an ideological breakthrough in the CCP establishment, but it does reflect a new trend or a new school of thought emerging from the Chinese leadership. "It is a major change as one previously considered a thing as bad, but now views the same thing as good," observed Shi.[14] All these observations highlight the originality and importance of Yu's thesis in the Chinese political discourse. The following pages provide a more detailed description of Yu's professional career, his main scholarly contributions, and how he differs from other prominent Chinese thinkers on the issue of democracy.

Yu Keping: A Thinker from a New Generation

The Chinese media often identify Yu Keping as a "rising star of the new generation of CCP theoreticians" (*Zhonggong lilun xinxiu*).[15] His scholarly accomplishments have earned him a reputation in the field of political science in China. This is evident in the fact that he concurrently serves as a guest professor in about a dozen of the country's most prestigious universities including Peking, Tsinghua, Renmin, Beijing Normal, Nankai, Fudan, Shanghai Jiaotong, Zhejiang, Xiamen, Sichuan, Jilin, the Harbin Institute of Technology, and China National School of Administration. Very few political scientists, Chinese or foreign, have received the academic honor of teaching at so many top schools in the PRC.

In addition to being actively engaged in academic research and theoretical thinking, Yu is also an insider in the Chinese political establishment. Since 2001 he has served as deputy director of the Central Compilation and Translation Bureau (CCTB) under the Central Committee of the CCP. This is a ministry-level official position. Therefore, Yu has a dual identity as a scholar-official (*xuezhexing guanyuan*). The CCTB is a major research institution responsible for four important tasks: translating the classic foreign language works of Marxist theoreticians into Chinese; translating the works of the top Chinese leaders into foreign languages; conducting research on Chinese socialism in both theory and practice; and conducting research on new theoretical developments in social sciences and philosophy around the world.[16] Although much smaller than the Central Party School (CPS), the CCTB also serves as a major think tank for the Chinese leadership, especially in the area of theoretical research. Yu currently also serves as director of the China Center for Comparative Politics and Economics and of the Center for Chinese Government Innovations at Peking University. These two university-based think tanks have been active in keeping abreast of both the global trends in social science research and China's domestic political changes.

During the reform era, a number of CCP establishment theoreticians have played an important role in attaining ideological breakthroughs. For example, in 1978 Hu Fuming, then an instructor of philosophy at Nanjing University, published an article entitled "Practice Is the Sole Criterion for Testing Truth" in the *Guangming Daily*, challenging the orthodox view of the CCP leadership abiding by the tenets of Maoism. Not long thereafter the party jettisoned Maoism in favor of the policies of reform and opening the country to the outside world. In 1991, when party conservatives criticized Deng Xiaoping's bold market reforms, Zhou Ruijin, then deputy editor in chief of the *Liberation Daily*, wrote an article that was very controversial at the time, rejecting the simplistic and dichotomist way of thinking about socialism and capitalism. Both theoretically and practically, the article justified the acceleration of market liberalization in the country, especially in the pacesetter city of Shanghai. In 2003 Zheng Bijian, then vice president of the Central Party School, gave a keynote speech at the Boao Forum in Hainan, outlining the reasons why China's rise would not be a threat to the rest of the world.[17] Zheng's work has since been used extensively by Hu Jintao in his formulation of the "theory of China's peaceful rise." It should be noted that Hu Fuming, Zhou Ruijin, and Zheng Bijian were all born in the 1930s and belong to a generation of CCP theoreticians who had their formative experiences in the Communist revolution and the first decade of the PRC. Yu's generation of CCP theoreticians, on the other hand, came of age during the Cultural Revolution and became actively engaged in intellectual discourse in the reform era. Thus, in many ways, their views differ profoundly from those of this preceding generation.

Yu Keping was born into a humble family in Zhuji County, Zhejiang Province, in 1959. He grew up during the Cultural Revolution. In 1976, at the age of seventeen, he began to work as a farmer and later a village cadre at Huashan Village in his home county. This experience was similar to that of many prominent leaders of the so-called fifth generation including Vice President Xi Jinping, Vice Premier Li Keqiang, Vice Premier Wang Qishan, and Director of the CCP Organization Department Li Yuanchao, as well as of distinguished public intellectuals and artists such as economist Hu Angang, sociologist Li Yinhe, historian Qin Hui, movie director Zhang Yimou, and artist Chen Danqing. The hardships these people experienced in the countryside have fostered some valuable traits in the generation such as endurance, critical thought, and humility as well as an intimate knowledge of rural China.[18]

As a result of Deng Xiaoping's policy initiatives, China resumed the use of college entrance exams in 1978. Yu was among the first group of students to enter college after passing the most competitive entrance exams in the history of the PRC. He enrolled in a three-year program in the Department of Political Science and History at Shaoxing Normal College in his native province. Following graduation, Yu spent the next ten years in Chinese educational institutions, first as a graduate student and then as an instructor. He received a master's degree in philosophy at Xiamen University in 1985 and then became one of the first two doctoral recipients in political science in the PRC when he was awarded a PhD degree in 1988 by Peking University.[19] Yu's doctoral advisor was Professor Zhao Baoxu, who is often regarded, in both China and abroad, as a founder of the academic field of political science in the PRC.

Throughout Yu's time in school, China was undergoing a series of phenomenal social and economic changes. Indeed, the decade between 1978 and 1988 was an exciting period marked by an enthusiasm among Chinese youths for drawing lessons from the Cultural Revolution and absorbing all sorts of new knowledge, including Western liberal ideas. According to Li Jingpeng, a political science professor at Peking University who taught Yu in the late 1980s, in his student years Yu not only showed enormous interest in Western intellectual history and recent trends but also paid particular attention to the selective application of Western theories to China's political development.[20] Yu's doctoral thesis was entitled "An Analytical Framework for Contemporary Chinese Politics."

Like many prominent social scientists in his generation, Yu has spent much time overseas. In the mid-1990s, as a visiting professor, he taught at schools such as Duke University in the United States and the Free University in Germany. Over the years, Yu has developed a wide-ranging intellectual interest in Western thought through a voracious reading of Western social science writings. He was particularly influenced by the work of prominent Western thinkers such as Jürgen Habermas, Harold Laski, and Lester M. Salamon. Yu has also collaborated with some distinguished American and European scholars including Arif Dirlik, Anthony Saich, and Thomas Heberer. He served as consultant for a government innovation project organized by the United Nations Development Programme and currently is a board member for some international journals such as *Global Studies* in Great Britain and *New Political Science* in the United States.[21] In 2008 Yu was awarded an honorary PhD degree at the University of Duisburg-Essen in the German federal state of North Rhine-Westphalia; he was the tenth Chinese national in German history to be awarded such an honorary degree.

Since the beginning of his academic career, Yu has been known for his unconventional thinking and bold ideas. In 1990, for example, Yu argued in a scholarly article that human rights should be considered fundamental values of human society.[22] At the time, the Chinese media and mainstream scholarly communities still rejected the concept of human rights and often characterized it as a hypocritical Western idea or a term used in anti-China rhetoric. To a great extent, Yu's view of human rights challenged the ideological status quo of the time.

Yu was also among the first group of Chinese scholars in the PRC to study civil society and nongovernmental organizations (NGOs). According to Yu, civil society and NGOs are not the "patents of the West." As he articulates in his section on China's social transformation and civil society in this volume, the multiple and dynamic roles of NGOs could share the burden of governance and contribute to a harmonious society. In Yu's view, the rapid rise of Chinese NGOs has profoundly changed state-society relations in the country. Yu believes that under the current conditions the objective for the Chinese government and the public should be "good governance" (*shanzhi*) instead of the traditional way of "good government" (*shanzheng*). Probably earlier than anyone else in China, Yu applied these Western concepts to contemporary Chinese political values.

For Yu, the basis of good governance is cooperation between the public and the government with the aim of maximizing public interest in the process of societal management. This does not mean that no conflict should be allowed but that both sides should be willing to negotiate and compromise. Changes in state-society relations will naturally put more pressure on the government, which needs to constantly adjust its policies to meet the demands of an ever-changing society. Yu lists ten basic components of good governance: legitimacy, transparency, efficiency, stability, responsibility, responsiveness, rule of law, justice, participation, and cleanness.

Yu's research has also contributed a great deal to central-local relations in terms of good governance. To help local officials improve their leadership skills and search for local government reforms and innovations, Yu initiated the program of China Local Government Innovation Awards, which is jointly administrated by the Central Compilation and Translation Bureau, the Central Party School, and Peking University. Three rounds of competition have been completed. More than 1,100 local governments applied for the awards; forty of them became final winners. In this regard, Yu is not only a thinker but also a doer.

It should be noted that several leading public intellectuals in Yu's generation who once had the dual identity of scholar-official recently became full-time officials. Examples include Wang Huning, Cao Jianming, and Xia Yong. All of them are in their late forties and early fifties, all are well-accomplished scholars in the fields of political science and law, and all spent several years as visiting scholars in the leading universities of the United States and Europe. Wang served as dean of the law school at Fudan; Cao was president of the East China University of Political Science and Law; and Xia worked as director of the Institute of Law at the Chinese Academy of Social Sciences. Currently, Wang is a member of the secretariat and director of the Policy Research Office of the CCP Central Committee, serving as one of the top aids to Secretary General Hu Jintao; Cao is procurator general of the Supreme People's Procuratorate; and Xia holds the position of director of the Central Bureau of Secrecy of the CCP Central Committee. Their current high-ranking official positions do not allow them to participate in intellectual discourse or to publish their scholarly work.

In contrast, Yu Keping has actively engaged in academic research and debate. His remarkably long list of scholarly publications in the past decade, which can be found at the end of this volume, shows his many professional interests and his ardent commitment to his field of expertise. A prolific writer, Yu, who is still in his forties, has already written twelve monographs, coauthored four books, edited fourteen volumes, and published numerous articles. His most famous works include *Liberation of Thoughts and Political Progress* (2008), *Democracy Is a Good Thing* (2006), *The Institutional Environment of Chinese Civil Society* (2006), *Globalization and Sovereignty* (2004), and *Incremental Democracy and Good Governance* (2003). These widely circulated and respected publications are transforming the Chinese view of political reforms, civil society, governance, and cultural modernization in the era of globalization. His most important contribution, however, is his painstaking endeavor to offer a road map for China's democratic future.

Mapping a Chinese Path to Democracy

For many political and cultural elites in present-day China, the idea of democracy probably generates more fear than hope. Fear regarding a democratic transition is deeply rooted in the mindset of the Chinese, who believe it could lead to one of several disastrous futures. Among them are possible prolonged domestic chaos (*luan*), another 1989 Tiananmen-like tragedy, the loss of privilege or power on the part of the establishment, vicious political conflicts among leaders, the rise of demagogues, an anti-China conspiracy by foreign powers, the breakdown of the multiethnic nation, and the uprising of a large number of poor and resentful social groups such as migrant laborers. From the perspective of the political establishment, China cannot afford the tensions and possible frictions generated by that fear.

In a recent interview with the Chinese media, Yu Keping pointed out three major obstacles for governmental reforms and democratic experiments in the country. First, there is no strong incentive for government officials to experiment with democratic reforms. Second, government reforms involve big political risk, and officials worry that the current political environment has a low degree of tolerance for any mistakes. Consequently, officials are not willing to take the risk. Third, "institutional inertia" does not encourage bold political experiments. To a great extent, political reforms involve the readjustment of interests and redistribution of power. Understandably, no institution or interest group is eager to experience heavy losses in power and privilege as a result of political reforms.[23]

A survey of 200 Chinese officials and scholars conducted in 2005 showed that 50 percent believed that China's economic and political reforms have been constrained by "some elite groups with vested economic interests" (*jide liyi jituan*).[24] A good example of how government officials and business interest groups have formed a "wicked coalition" can be found in the realm of real estate development.[25] Some Chinese observers believe that the various players associated with property development have emerged as one of the most powerful special interest groups in the present-day PRC.[26] According to

Sun Liping, a sociology professor at Tsinghua University, the real estate interest group has accumulated tremendous economic and social capital since the mid-1990s.[27] The group includes not only property developers, real estate agents, bankers, and housing market speculators but also some government officials and public intellectuals (economists and journalists) who promote and protect the interests of the property developers and investors.[28] Not surprisingly, another recent survey of Chinese local officials conducted by the Central Party School showed that 90 percent of the officials were not willing to pursue large-scale political reforms.[29]

Despite, or perhaps because of, these obstacles to political reforms, Yu believes that democracy should be seen as a solution for China rather than a problem. He argues that democracy provides answers to some of the daunting challenges that China now faces. Although democracy can possibly undermine legal institutions, cause political divisions within the country, and is generally less efficient than a dictatorship because of the time involved in negotiation and compromise in the policymaking process, Yu believes that it provides more political legitimacy and long-term stability than an authoritarian regime. In his view, the social and cultural changes fostered by successful economic development since 1978 have also generated political pressures for the increased autonomy of civil society. In addition, public concern about the elite groups with vested economic interests, and especially public grievances regarding official corruption, should be seriously addressed rather than suppressed. In Yu's words, "all power must be effectively balanced; otherwise, it inevitably leads to arbitrary rule and corruption" (chapter 3).

Recognition of these obstacles leads Yu Keping to pay a great deal of attention to charting a road map for China's democratic development. According to Yu, a premature rush to democracy or "the unconditional promotion of democracy will bring disastrous consequences to the nation and its people" (chapter 1). In accordance with this line of thinking, Yu has developed three important concepts. First is the "price of democracy" (*minzhu de daijia*) that the country has to pay. This price is sometimes so high as to be unacceptable. "It requires the wisdom of the politicians and the people to determine," as Yu argues, "how to pay the minimum political and social price in order to obtain the maximum democratic effects" (chapter 1). Reducing "political and administrative costs" in China's democratic pursuits, therefore, should be the central concern. Whether or not Chinese citizens will achieve strong public consensus about democracy largely depends on their calculation of these perceived costs.

The second concept that Yu has developed is "incremental democracy" (*jianjin minzhu*). Under the current sociopolitical circumstances, in Yu's view, China's transition to democracy should not, and will not, be achieved through radical means. Instead, it should be carried out in multiple dimensions and through an incremental process. These dimensions include intraparty democracy, grassroots elections, administrative reforms, and the growth of civil society. Yu has particularly emphasized intraparty democracy. In his view, "without intraparty democracy," it will be "difficult to attain democracy in China" (chapter 3). According to Yu, "if grassroots democracy means pushing forward democracy from the bottom up, intraparty democracy entails doing so from the inside out." As he describes in chapter 3, the focus of improving intraparty democracy "lies in the reform of intraparty election, decisionmaking and policymaking, and in revamping oversight systems."

Yu goes into great detail on why incremental democracy is the optimal strategy for Chinese political reform. He believes that gradual changes are conducive to China's own historical experiences. Democracy requires sufficient political, economic, social, and legal capital; and the attainment of positive improvement in all of these areas not only will quantitatively increase democratic feasibility but will also eventually result in a fundamental qualitative "breakthrough." Meanwhile, incremental political development will gain momentum when an increasingly large portion of the public benefits from socioeconomic reforms. Yu, however, does not offer a timetable regarding when "the democratic breakthrough" will take place.

Third, Yu has developed the notion of "dynamic stability" (*dongtai wending*) to characterize the new approach used by the CCP to deal with sociopolitical tensions in the country. While Chinese political and cultural elites may have valid reasons to be concerned about the need for social stability, their obsession over stability may be counterproductive in the new demographic and political environment (chapter 6). Yu refers to the Chinese authorities' traditional approach toward attaining stability as a strategy for "static stability" (*jingtai wending*) based on "holding everything in place" (*yi du wei zhu*).[30] In contrast, Yu advocates dynamic stability based on "channeling everything into its proper place" (*yi shu wei zhu*). Some new mechanisms such as public hearings, opinion surveys, letter petitions, and group protests are good examples. In his words, "'dynamic stability' aims to maintain order through negotiation instead of repression."[31]

According to Yu, the Chinese authorities should negotiate with social forces and should constantly adjust policies to meet the needs of the general public in order to maintain dynamic stability. In present-day China, the CCP holds power, but power does not necessarily mean legitimate authority or good governance. With regard to dynamic stability, legitimate authority is more important than power because good governance can lead to stability, order, trust, and efficiency.[32] Yu believes that the best way to prevent social unrest or revolution is to promote good governance rather than rely on strict control.

As a whole, these three concepts—the price of democracy, incremental democracy, and dynamic stability—aim to draw a road map for a new phase of China's sociopolitical development. Of course, Yu Keping has not been alone in advocating democracy in today's China. Distinguished scholars such as Jiang Ping (former president of China University of Law and Political Science), Xie Tao (former vice president of Renmin University), Zhou Ruijin (former deputy editor in chief of *People's Daily*), Li Rui (former personal secretary to Mao), Cao Siyuan (a prominent scholar in the field of bankruptcy law), He Weifang (a law professor at Zhejiang University and a leading scholar on constitutionalism in China), Liu Junning (a long-time leading advocate for political reforms), and Mao Shoulong (a professor of public administration at People's University) have all actively participated in the political and intellectual discourse about democracy in China.

Xie Tao, for example, has recently argued that the assessment of a political system is not just a theoretical question but in fact should be a practical one that can affect the lives of millions of Chinese people. In an article widely circulated in the Chinese media, Xie asked pointedly: "How is it possible that China's political system is a good one, when it could not prevent the national madness of the Great Leap Forward and the Cultural Revolution, and could not protect basic human rights?"[33] Some scholars, such as He Weifang and Cao Siyuan, even argue that China should make the transition from a Leninist party-state political system to a constitutional state. In that regard, their proposed democratic transition for China seems far more radical than Yu's.

Some overseas Chinese dissidents argue that Yu's democratic road map for China is no more than an empty promise to the Chinese people and the outside world. For example, Hu Ping, the author of "On Freedom of Speech," one of the first and most comprehensive papers on the democratic movement in the PRC and one that shaped intellectual discourse during the Democracy Wall Movement in Beijing in 1979, criticized Yu for creating a "false notion" in the outside world that the CCP is interested in democracy.[34] Hu believes that any discussion of democracy that does not seriously consider a multiparty system will go nowhere. In addition, Hu argues that Yu's proposed mechanisms for dynamic stability fundamentally differ from democratic principles such as the freedoms of speech and assembly.

Criticism of Yu's thesis emanates not only from those of the "New Right" who advocate a more radical path for China's democratic future but also from those "New Left" public intellectuals who challenge the desirability and feasibility of democracy for the country. They believe that any serious effort to move toward political democracy in China may release long-restrained social tensions and quickly undermine the CCP's capacity to allocate social and economic resources. Pan Wei, a Berkeley-educated political science professor at Peking University, favors legalistic political reforms instead of democratic elections and is more interested in a Singaporean-style rule of law rather than Western-style democracy. He bluntly criticizes what he calls "democracy worship and election obsession" among his Chinese colleagues. Pan is cynical about Yu's concept of incremental democracy. In his view, both intraparty elections and grassroots democracy are currently primarily "political shows."[35] Pan argues that in a country such as China without the rule of law, it would be a disaster to move toward democratic elections. In his words, "the CCP will split if the party adopts elections; and the PRC will disintegrate if the country adopts elections."[36]

The new wave of the intellectual and political discourse about China's future democracy initiated by Yu Keping and other Chinese thinkers will likely continue in the years to come. This wave can probably best be characterized by the intriguing and thoughtful idea of making democracy safe for China. Each reader, of course, can make his or her own judgment about the significance and implications of this Chinese intellectual discourse about democracy. It is reasonable to assume, however, that ideas matter in China as well as elsewhere in the world. As an emerging economic power, China is in the midst of searching for its new international image and core political values. The information and insights offered by Yu in the following pages may not only reveal Chinese perspectives, anxieties, and dilemmas, but also be indicative of the future political trajectory of the country.

PART I

POLITICAL DEVELOPMENT IN REFORM-ERA CHINA

CHAPTER ONE

DEMOCRACY IS A GOOD THING

Democracy is a good thing. This is true not only for individuals or certain officials but also for the entire nation and for all the people of China.[1] Simply put, for those officials who care more about their own interests than about the national interest, democracy is not a good thing; in fact, it is a troublesome thing, even a bad thing. Under conditions of democratic rule, officials must be elected by the citizens, gaining the endorsement and support of the majority of the people. Officials' powers can be curtailed by the citizens; officials cannot simply do whatever they want. They must sit along with the citizens and negotiate with them. Just these two points alone already make many officials dislike democracy. Therefore, democracy cannot operate on its own; it requires citizens themselves and government officials who represent the interests of the people to promote and implement it.

Democracy is a good thing, but that does not mean that everything about democracy is good. Democracy is definitely not 100 percent perfect; it has many internal inadequacies and contradictions. Democracy allows the citizens to go into the streets, hold assemblies, and engage in actions that can fuel political instability. Democracy can make certain matters that are very simple under undemocratic conditions overly complicated and frivolous, thereby increasing the political and administrative costs. Democracy often involves repeated negotiations and discussions, occasionally causing a delay in making timely decisions and thereby decreasing administrative efficiency. Democracy often affords opportunities for certain sweet-talking politicians to mislead the people, and so on. But among all the political systems that have been invented and implemented, democracy is the one with the fewest number of flaws. Relatively speaking, democracy is the best political system for humankind.

Democracy is a good thing, but this does not mean that democracy can do everything. Democracy is a political system that holds that sovereignty belongs to the people, but it is only one of many systems that govern human societies. Democracy mainly regulates the political lives of people, but it cannot replace the other systems and it cannot regulate everything in people's lives. Democracy has its internal limitations; it is not a panacea and it cannot solve all of humankind's problems. But democracy guarantees basic human rights, offers equal opportunity to all people, and represents a basic human value. Not only is democracy a means for solving people's livelihood issues, but it is also a goal of human development. A tool for achieving other goals, democracy is also in accord with human nature. Even if food and housing are widely available or even guaranteed to all, the human character is incomplete without democratic rights.

Democracy is a good thing, but that does not mean that democracy comes without a price. Democracy can destroy the legal system, cause the social and political order to go out of control, and even prevent economic development during certain periods. Democracy can disrupt international peace and cause political divisions within the nation; the democratic process can also propel dictators onto the political stage. All of these have already occurred in human history, and they will likely continue to occur. Therefore, the price of democracy is sometimes high to the point of being unacceptable. At their roots, however, these faults are not the faults of democracy as a system but rather the faults of the politicians and statesmen in particular democracies. Certain politicians do not understand the objective rules of democratic government; they ignore the social and historical conditions of the times in which they live; they go beyond the stage of historical development and promote democracy in an impractical manner; and therefore they end up with the opposite consequences. Certain politicians treat democracy as their tool for seizing power, using the idea of "democracy" to win popularity only to end up misleading the people. With them, democracy is only a cover for populism and dictatorship; democracy is the pretense and power is the substance.

Democracy is a good thing, but this is not to say that democracy comes unconditionally. Implementing democracy requires the presence of economic, cultural, and political preconditions; the unconditional promotion of democracy will bring disastrous consequences to the nation and its people. Political democracy is the trend of history, and it is the inevitable trend for all nations of the world to move toward democracy. But the timing and speed of the development of democracy and the choice of the form and system of democracy are conditional. An ideal democratic system must be related to the economic level of development of society, the regional politics, and the international environment, and it must also be intimately related to the national tradition of political culture, the quality of the politicians and the people, and the daily customs of the people. It requires the wisdom of the politicians and the people to determine how to pay the minimum political and social price in order to obtain the maximum democratic effects. In that sense, democratic politics is a political art. To promote democratic politics, one should have an elaborate system design and excellent political techniques.

Democracy is a good thing, but that does not mean that democracy can force the people to do things. The most concrete meaning of democracy is that it is government by the people who get to make choices. Even though democracy is a good thing, no person or political organization has the right to regard itself as the embodiment of democracy and therefore able to force the people to do this and not to do that in the name of democracy. Democracy requires enlightenment; it requires the rule of law, authority, and sometimes even coercion to maintain social order. The basic approach to developing democracy is not the forceful imposition of a democratic order by the government, but rather the emergence of such an order from among the people. Since democracy is rule by the people, it should respect the people's own choice. If a national government employs forceful means to make the people accept a system that they did not choose, then this is national autocracy and national tyranny masquerading as democracy. When one country uses mostly violent methods to force the people in other countries to accept their so-called democratic system, then this is international autocracy and international tyranny. National tyranny and international tyranny are both contrary to the nature of democracy.

We Chinese are presently building a strong, modern socialist nation with unique Chinese characteristics. For us, democracy is not only a good thing but an essential one. The classical authors of Marxism said, "There is no socialism without democracy." Recently Chairman Hu Jintao pointed out further, "There is no modernization without democracy." Of course, we are building a socialist democracy with unique Chinese characteristics. On the one hand, we want to absorb the best aspects of human political culture from around the world, including the best of democratic politics; on the other hand, we will not import wholesale an overseas political model. Our construction of political democracy must be closely integrated with the history, culture, traditions, and existing social conditions in our nation. Only in this way can the people of China truly enjoy the sweet fruits of political democracy.

CHAPTER TWO

THE STUDY OF POLITICAL SCIENCE AND PUBLIC ADMINISTRATION IN CHINA

An Overview

A famous saying by Mao Zedong states: "Politics is the commander, the soul, and the lifeline of economic work."[1] Intimately familiar with the traditions of Chinese culture and history, Mao shaped the political and economic life of post-1949 China in accordance with his own understanding of politics. Under Mao's leadership, China placed special stress on the role and influence that production played in determining political and economic life and emphasized the importance of historical development in determining social relations. No matter how people judge the political practices of Mao Zedong, they must remember one thing: compared with Western countries, politics carries much more significance in the social life of the people of China than do the economy and society, an insight that is still valid today. As a result, the field of political science in China has certain unique characteristics, whether the discipline is seen as a part of history, a science, a system of knowledge, a profession, or a cause.

This chapter examines the distinctive characteristics and disciplinary development of political science in China and then discusses the birth and growth of the field of public administration in the country. As a sister discipline to political science, the study of public administration has contributed to the continuing transformation of the Chinese government. Both political science and public administration, as two important fields in the social sciences, have been and will continue to be extremely valuable for China's political and administrative reforms in the years to come.

Political Science as Part of History

There is a distinction between political science in the narrow sense and political science in the broad sense. Political science in the broad sense is politics. It is the common knowledge that comes from inquiring about the causes of political phenomena in human society and the accompanying patterns of political development. It is one of the oldest and most important knowledge systems in human history. Since the emergence of the state, there has always been political life, and thus political theory and political philosophy were developed to explain politics. In the course of human history, politics has always been interlinked with law, philosophy, ethics, and literature and has always been given high attention by the ruling class. In history, nearly all of the greatest philosophers have inquired into theoretical questions of politics, and many philosophers themselves were outstanding political scientists or political philosophers.

Political science in the narrow sense refers to an independent discipline of science, which began to develop within the last hundred years or so. It uses scientific research methods to study principles and patterns of political development, and it obtains support from empirical fact and evidence. The field of political science employs a strict logical structure, special paradigms, concepts, and disciplinary norms. In the broad sense, political science has existed in China since ancient times. However, political science as an independent subset of scientific inquiry emerged at the end of the Qing dynasty and the beginning of the Republican period in early twentieth century. It started with the introduction and translation of modern works of Western political science. The intellectual reformers of the late Qing dynasty sought theoretical support from Western political science for undertaking political reform in China. While introducing and translating works from Western political science, they began to undertake their own independent research and teaching activities in the field of political science. A large number of Western political classics were introduced and translated into Chinese at this time, including such important works as *The Social Contract* by Jean-Jacques Rousseau and *On Liberty* by John Stuart Mill.

In the three years from 1901 to 1904, as many as sixty-six classic Western political texts were translated and published in Chinese. In 1899 Shixue Guan (the Training Center for Government Officials) was officially established at Jingshi Daxue Tang (Metropolitan University, the predecessor of Peking University). In fact, Shixue Guan can fairly be seen as the predecessor to the departments of political science or public administration in contemporary universities in China. In 1903 Metropolitan University offered, for the first time, in its curriculum "the course of politics," which was the first political science course developed in a university in China. Most of the comprehensive universities established after the founding of the Republic of China created departments of political science or the major of political science. According to statistics by Professor Zhao Baoxu at Peking University, by 1948 more than forty of the one hundred plus universities in China at the time had departments of political science.[2]

The volatile circumstances that existed from the outbreak of the Anti-Japanese War in 1937 to the end of Kuomintang rule over mainland China left the discipline of political science in a state of limbo. After 1949, when the People's Republic of China (PRC) was founded, the model of political science used in the Soviet Union was borrowed and duplicated in China wholesale. Thus political science as practiced in the pre-PRC era was regarded as a "fake science" and was completely replaced with the theories of Marxism-Leninism. Moreover, the position of political science as an independent discipline was increasingly weakened and minimized. In 1952, with the reform and readjustment of the universities and institutes for higher education, the departments of political science in all universities or institutes were formally abolished. In the long span from the early 1950s to the late 1970s, the field of political science as an independent discipline no longer truly existed (although some universities continued to have a "department of political science" or "department of international politics"). Indeed, it would be fair to say that political science as a discipline effectively disappeared from Chinese academia for almost thirty years.

The revitalization of political science in China occurred after the reform and opening to the outside world in late 1978. In 1979, at the National Conference on Theoretical Exchange and Discussion, Deng Xiaoping called for a revitalization of the discipline of political science. "In the past, for many years we have ignored the study of political science, law, sociology, and world politics," he said. "Now it is time for us to catch up in these areas."[3] From that time forward, the academic discipline of political science resumed in the country.

Since the rebirth of political science in China, the discipline has rapidly developed into one of the main social sciences in the Chinese academy, and the efforts of researchers in this field have yielded many outstanding achievements. In recent years, scholars of political science have discussed and written a great deal on the achievements and problems of the field and made numerous suggestions for its future development. Generally speaking, the achievements of this period include:

—With regard to the growth of the discipline, political science has already established itself as a foundational social science. In almost all comprehensive universities, independent departments of political science or public administration have been set up.

—In terms of institutional design, from the central to the local levels, comprehensive or professional research institutes focused on political science have been established.

—With respect to the cultivating and training of talented students in the specialized skills of political science research, starting in 1981 universities began offering undergraduate programs with majors in political science; in 1983 master's degrees in political science were offered for the first time; and from 1985 onward doctoral programs in political science were established. Thus, an integrated system of training in political science, composed of three levels of BA, MA, and PhD, was founded.

—In terms of the study of politics as a science, the discipline of political science has a clear research subject and a unique conceptual and methodological system. The quality of the scientific research produced by political scientists has continuously improved throughout this period.

—With respect to applied research, scholars of political science in China have been actively involved in policy research at various levels of government, have undertaken more and more research projects entrusted to them by party and government organizations, and have become important members of policy consultation circles.

—In terms of international exchanges, the discipline of political science has basically transformed from a politically sensitive discipline to a normal academic discipline and has opened itself up for foreign academic exchanges. The academic exchange activities vary. For example, domestic scholars or institutes invite foreign political scientists to China for guest speeches or lectures; domestic scholars go overseas to attend international conferences or to have academic visits; foreign scholars and Chinese scholars conduct joint research programs to study Chinese politics; and Chinese political scientists introduce and translate foreign political science works, among other activities.[4]

A review of the historical evolution and rocky development of the field of political science in the PRC allows one to make some basic conclusions. Political science is one of the oldest fields of study in human society. Its basic research subject is the state and the political system. Since political science is extremely important to understanding the development of human society, it

has attracted the attention of politicians and thinkers. As an independent discipline, political science is a product of modern times; it developed nearly
simultaneously with modern democracy. The development of political science requires a democratic and liberal academic environment. In this regard,
political science is very similar to medical science. For a long period of time,
people only knew about medical knowledge without knowing about medical
science. Independent medical science is a product of modern times. A society
can have medical knowledge without medical science; however, in a society
without medical science, the level of medical treatment will necessarily be
very backward. The practice of modern democratic politics requires political
science as an independent discipline. From the perspective of democratic politics, we can also say that political life without the guidance of political science will be backward.

Political Science as a Science

Since its beginnings as an academic discipline, there have been endless arguments on whether political science is an independent science in strict terms.
To meet the minimum standard necessary to be considered an independent
science, political science must have its own conceptual system and research
methodology, its own research question areas, and a series of axioms and
principles; to meet the maximum standard, it requires, in addition to the
requirements of the minimum standard, the application of methods that
have been used in the natural sciences to empirically test hypotheses, and
even the use of mathematical models that have the ability to make reasonably accurate predictions. Under the minimum standards, there is no doubt
that political science is an independent science. Judged by the maximum
standards, however, political science can hardly be proclaimed as an independent science.

The argument about whether political science is an independent science is
in fact an argument about what standard to apply in judging whether any
field of study qualifies as a science. This argument came to a peak with the
"revolution of behavioralism" in the 1950s and 1960s in the United States.
Behavioralists strongly advocated that political science research should be
"tested" and "quantified." They harshly attacked traditional political science.
Behavioralists emphasized empirical study and stood against normal reasoning and logical deduction; they believed in facts and value-free studies. However, traditional political scientists responded to behavioralists in the late
1970s by successfully pulling the discipline of political science back to the

minimum standard definition described here. Since then, although the majority of political scientists recognize political science as an independent science as defined by the minimum standard, a small group of political scientists judges the discipline using the maximum standard. This forms the core argument between scientism and realism, which constitutes the central debate within the discipline of political science today.

Political science studies in China totally differed from Western political science before the country's reform and opening to the outside world. Political science was not considered a science not because it could not be quantified but because it was regarded as being "fake." The Marxist critique argued that traditional political science covered up the nature of class struggle that lay behind all political phenomena. As such, political science was regarded as a tool for cheating the people—a "fake science for bourgeois classes" that should be abandoned. Scholars as well as party and government leaders regarded political science as a fake science. Even after the rebirth of political science in China, some people used class-struggle theory to replace all other political theories and refused to acknowledge any analytical methods in political science other than class analysis. These individuals denied the existence of "axioms in political science." Even today some individuals do not accept political science as a science even under the minimum standard, although they usually do not say so openly and directly.

Starting around the 1990s, with the introduction of Western political science and the return of many scholars who were trained overseas, doubts about the scientific nature of political science began to emerge in political science circles. These doubts were raised from the behavioralist perspective. Chinese behavioralists distrust reasoning and deductive research and deny the values of traditional political science. They argue that quantitative and empirical study should be regarded as the only research method for making political science a truly scientific undertaking. Compared with those scholars who attacked political science from the perspective of class struggle, the number of scholars who criticize political science from the perspective of behavioralism is far fewer, but they have been influential. Some young scholars call for a more "scientific" form of political science and have tried to answer the question "How can we restructure the study of political science to make it more scientific?" These scholars have put forward many suggestions for developing the discipline of political science in China.[5]

Deeper observation is needed to assess the degree of independent character of political science as an academic discipline. Because the study of political science was essentially banned after the founding of the PRC, there was a shortage of specialized personnel who could teach the discipline or conduct political science research when the study of political science resumed in 1979. As a result of the urgent need for people who could teach the discipline, people involved in the teaching and research activities of political science departments in the early reform era had primarily studied scientific socialism, the history of the international communist movement, or the history of the Chinese Communist Party. Most of these academics were not professionally trained in the discipline of political science, and most probably were not qualified to conduct high-quality political science research. Their research methods, analytical frameworks, and paradigms were confined to those once used in their previous research areas in philosophy and social science, such as class-struggle analysis methods, economic analysis, historical analysis, and normal documentary or field research and investigation methods. Such circumstances made it difficult for political science to resume its position as an independent science after 1979. Thus, throughout the 1980s, the degree of independence and specialization in the field of political science was quite low. Studies of political science were hardly discernible from those focused on scientific socialism or the history of international communism. Even if one were to judge political science by the minimum standard definition, it would have been difficult to claim that political science existed as an independent science during this period.

Fortunately, however, a group of scholars with a strong sense of intellectual and professional responsibility recognized this problem and started to organize the training of specialized personnel in political science. They accomplished this by translating classical Western political science texts and inviting foreign political scientists to China to give speeches and guest lectures. Their efforts achieved great effects. Beginning in the 1980s, and especially during the 1990s, a great number of middle-aged and younger scholars came to the fore. In time, their research achievements became the mainstream of political science in China. It was only in the late 1990s that political science truly became a science with comparatively independent academic standing in China, as it was at this point that a generally accepted series of theories, concepts, paradigms, methods, and research questions came to prevail among Chinese political scientists.

A word is in order about both quantitative and qualitative research methods prevalent among political scientists, as well as about normative and empirical research. A major distinction between natural science and social science is that the former is based primarily on quantitative research while the latter is mainly based on qualitative research. Additionally, natural sciences focus primarily on empirical studies, while social sciences largely involve normative studies. However, as a science, the discipline of political science should maintain a certain ratio between quantitative and qualitative research. This was the basic outcome of the argument between behavioralist political scientists and postbehavioralist political scientists in the second half of the twentieth century.

It is not surprising that the development of political science in the West led to an emphasis on normative and qualitative research. Among political scientists in China today, however, empirical and quantitative research is receiving increasing attention. For the discipline as a whole, quantitative and empirical studies are increasingly common, especially among younger scholars. However, there are still outstanding problems in that many empirical studies based on scientific methods have not received adequate attention, and in many empirical studies, scientific methods have not been applied widely or appropriately. A recent study of political science literature over the past ten years confirmed this point. This study conducted a statistical analysis of 768 journal articles published between 1994 and 2002 and collected in a volume on "political science" compiled by Renmin University. The study found that among the 768 articles the percentage of empirical studies was roughly 41 percent. Among these empirical studies, however, the traditional qualitative method of documentary analysis was dominant, with as many as 56 percent of the articles employing this methodology. The use of scientific sampling and survey questionnaires remained at a fairly low level.[6]

As a science, political science cannot avoid the question of universality and particularity. To natural science, admitting the universality of axioms, concepts, and methods is the obvious premise. In America, 1 plus 1 equals 2, in China this is also true. It is unimaginable that water would flow from a higher place to a lower place in China, but then flow from a lower place to a higher place in the United States. However, in the social sciences the situation is quite different. The kinds of universality one finds in the natural sciences are less widely accepted in the social sciences, especially since a discipline such as political science is often directly related to the practical interests of actors in a given political setting, making universal axioms of political science especially hard to come by. On the one hand, any science must be somewhat universal in order to claim status as a "science"—without universality, science as such does not really exist. From this perspective, if political science is accepted as a discipline in China, then it must be admitted that it has a set of common concepts, methods, and axioms that are shared with political scientists in other countries. For example, power must be balanced, democracy has certain common elements and forms, and so on. On the other hand, inasmuch as political science is a social science, it will exhibit its own unique features in every different environment. Its main research focus is the political reality in various countries. However, political realities obviously differ among different countries. Everyone might agree that power must be balanced and politics should be democratic, but the way for balancing power and realizing democracy is nonetheless still going to be different in different countries. Just like the political science in any other country, the discipline of political science in China is a combination of universal and unique factors stemming from the blending of the international and the national.

To observe the status of political science from this perspective is to see that most Chinese scholars view the discipline of political science as a science from the perspective of the unity of universality and uniqueness, while only a very small number of people deny the universality or uniqueness from two extreme aspects. People who deny the universality of political science generally overemphasize the uniquely Chinese characteristics of political science in China and do not admit the common concepts, methods, and axioms that exist in Western political science. Such scholars also generally deny, in whole or in part, the values of Western political science. Those scholars who deny the uniqueness of political science in China generally overemphasize the general axioms, especially the normative values that reside in Western political science, while ignoring the uniquely Chinese characteristics of political science in China. They usually completely accept the concepts, methodologies, and axioms found in Western political science. These scholars tend to regard Chinese political science as being in need of "Westernization," a viewpoint that is strongly resisted by many in the discipline of political science in the PRC. At the same time, however, the emphasis on uniqueness also contains within it certain risks. If there is a threat of Westernization in the discipline of political science in China, there is also a threat of "localization without universality."

Political Science as Knowledge

In the broadest sense, political science is the systematic accumulation of knowledge about political phenomena, political life, and political principles in human society. Indeed, it is just as Aristotle said—humans are, by nature, political animals, and therefore merely to live is to live a political life (humans beings, by nature, are rational animals; they nonetheless can only realize their rationality by entering into political life in society). As long as political phenomena exist, there is a need for political knowledge. For the common people, an immediate need for political science may not be apparent, but so long as these individuals live in a political society, knowledge about political life is necessary. The ruling class needs political knowledge to maintain the established political order, to strengthen its political rule, and to protect its own political interests. The ruled also need political knowledge to better protect their own interests under the established political framework or to look for other social and political frameworks that might be more beneficial to them. A political system involves the allocation and reallocation of the critical interests and material assets of a society, and therefore, no matter whether for the ruling class or the ruled class, political knowledge is an indispensable tool for better maintaining and advancing its own interests. Thus, it is not hard to understand why even great thinkers such as Aristotle have paid special attention to political knowledge. In fact, Aristotle regarded political science as "the principal science." Indeed, political scientists often undertake two tasks when they engage in the dissemination of knowledge about politics. The first task is to disseminate special political knowledge among professional political scientists so as to maintain and push forward the existence and development of political science as a discipline; the second is to disseminate daily political knowledge to the ruling class and the masses so as to serve interests within the particular political reality.

Based on the two different target population groups for knowledge dissemination—the ruling class and the masses—the discipline of political science in any given period of time fulfills the function of disseminating two different kinds of political knowledge. For the ruling class, the main knowledge collected and analyzed for dissemination has included information about the political structures and institutional arrangements that are compatible with the prevailing social, economic, and cultural conditions; understandings of the national political culture or traditions and the sociopolitical psychology of the masses; analyses about how best to ascertain, reflect, and satisfy the political needs of the masses; strategies and methods for preventing breakdowns in national unity and the emergence of chaos; principles for the recruitment of political elites; ideas about mechanisms for checking the arbitrariness of power and preventing corruption; experience and lessons on how political rulers in both China and abroad have managed their countries from ancient times to the present; and knowledge about the rules and norms governing international relations. For the masses, the knowledge that political science needs to disseminate includes information about a state's basic political system and the basic norms for social and political life; about the government structure and political process, especially the policymaking and policy implementation processes; about the political rights and duties of citizens; and about the legal tools and methods available to check the government's inappropriate intrusion on citizens' rights. In modern democratic polities, political science assumes the tasks of disseminating basic knowledge about democracy to both the rulers and the citizens, including information about the significance of democracy and its main elements, information about the most appropriate institutional arrangements for guaranteeing the democratic rights of citizens, data about the main channels for the public to increase participation in political life, information about effective measures for balancing government power, and historical knowledge stemming from the experiences and lessons of practicing democratic politics.

In a country like China that emphasizes political education and embraces the view that intellectuals should pursue an interest in officialdom, the government and political scientists have paid great attention to disseminating political knowledge to officials and citizens. This historical tradition was central to the reconstruction of the discipline of political science in China. From the perspective of the party and the government, the important target population for disseminating political knowledge in China included students as well as party and government cadres at various levels. For example, students from junior high school to the postgraduate level must take courses on politics. In various training and educational institutes such as the various party schools and the institutes for public administration found at various government levels, the main training consists of disseminating mainstream political ideology. The political knowledge that is disseminated through official channels consists essentially of the ideology of the ruling Communist Party. Currently, this ideological indoctrination consists of instruction in basic knowledge of the principles of Marxism, a brief introduction to Mao Zedong thought, Deng Xiaoping theory, and the important notion of the "three represents," as well as the scientific theory of development.[7] From the perspective of political scientists, the target population for disseminating political knowledge is fairly small in number and consists mostly of political and intellectual elites. The political knowledge thus disseminated is basic knowledge about political science and Chinese politics, interpretations of mainstream political ideologies and government policies, as well as the experience, lessons, and wisdom necessary for managing the government. In the aforementioned statistical analysis of political science journal articles, the distribution of topics was also analyzed. Among the 768 articles, political theory articles accounted for 53.2 percent; international politics and international relations were the subjects of 11.8 percent of the articles; Chinese politics was the focus of 11.6 percent; public administration, 11.3 percent; comparative politics, 4 percent; party and public policy, 2.3 percent; political interest groups, 2.2 percent; political science methodologies, 1.7 percent; grassroots democracy, 1.4 percent; and studies on the law, 0.3 percent.[8]

Even though both government officials and political scientists pay great attention to disseminating political knowledge, the actual effects of dissemination have not been as successful as either group might have hoped. For the Chinese government, generally speaking, there is a fairly large gap between the aspirations for disseminating political knowledge to students and the actual effects of said dissemination. A survey of students from primary school to the undergraduate level conducted in the 1990s revealed that students' recognition of mainstream political ideologies and values did not increase with their age and their increased exposure to knowledge. For some age brackets, the correlation was even negative. Other investigations have shown that middle school and college students rate the mandatory course in public politics as one of the least enjoyable courses. In some universities, teachers of the mandatory course on public policies have to take roll call just to ensure that enough students show up in class.[9] Many observers have noted that dissemination of political knowledge to government officials has also failed to achieve the desired effect. For example, a common lament uttered by officials who were convicted and jailed on charges of corruption is that they regret that they did not master the party constitution and laws and did not realize their behaviors were illegal or in violation of party codes. In political science circles in China, there is no shortage of intellectuals who enthusiastically introduce and disseminate basic political knowledge, especially knowledge about democracy. However, the actual effect of all their labors usually falls far behind the desired goal. Compared with the disciplines of law, economics, and other relevant social sciences, the influence of political science is quite weak, and the influence political scientists exert on government officials and the masses is very small indeed. For example, among the most popular social science books for sale in China, it is hard to find works by political scientists.

Several factors explain the ineffectiveness of government and scholarly efforts to disseminate political knowledge. One explanation is that the political knowledge they try to disseminate is often empty, outdated, and irrelevant to current realities. Some political knowledge cannot withstand empirical testing, lacks convincing facts and evidence, and is regarded by recipients as "fake knowledge." A second reason is that the political knowledge they disseminate tends to be repetitive and similar, lacking in newness. For example, for the content of political science courses from middle school to college and even at the graduate study level, there has been an enormous emphasis on repetition, which leads to "knowledge fatigue" among students. A third reason is that the political knowledge being disseminated lacks practical usefulness. If political knowledge is not useful for helping people solve problems in their everyday lives, people have no reason to consciously seek it out or accept it. A fourth reason lies in the qualities and teaching methods of disseminators as educators. The ancients once said: "repent yourself before criticizing others," emphasizing that one should first "cultivate one's own ethics and talents," as only then can one "rule and govern a state." The quality of instruction in political science is directly related to the effects of dissemination on recipients. If teachers do not have adequate political integrity and knowledge, it is nearly impossible to achieve good effects. Since political knowledge is sometimes boring, the use of innovative dissemination methods is important. The practical political environment, the needs of government officials and the masses for political knowledge, and the channels available for disseminating knowledge about politics also affect the success in spreading knowledge about politics.

Political Science as a Profession

Given that political science is an independent discipline, there must be a certain number of specialized people involved in this profession. There must be teachers in the departments of political science in institutions of higher education, and research institutes must have professional researchers. For those people who undertake research and teaching in these institutions, political science is a profession. In China today, the professionals in the field of political science come mainly from:

—Departments of political science in colleges, or research institutes for political science in higher education institutions; some of these institutions share the same teaching and research unit in association with institutions of public administration, international relations, or law.

—The political science research institutions in the Chinese Academy of Social Sciences (CASS) and its branches at the provincial level (which covers provinces, cities, autonomous regions, and province-level municipalities).

—The teaching and research institutions of the party schools at various levels.

—The research institutions belonging to party and government agencies, especially research institutes.

—A very small number of nonprofit research institutes that have emerged in recent years, most of which are policy research institutes.

Among these research institutes, how many of the employees are political science professionals? Up to now there have been no reliable data on this. Feng Zhifeng has conducted a statistical analysis of the backgrounds of authors of 279 top political science textbooks, and his findings indicate that 182 of the authors (65 percent) are from institutes of higher education, 31 authors (11 percent) were from the CASS, 19 authors (7 percent) came from research institutes, 16 authors (6 percent) hailed from party schools at various levels, and three authors (1 percent) came from the Central Compilation and Translation Bureau, with the remaining 28 authors (10 percent) coming from other institutions.[10] Another statistical analysis, this one performed by Xiao Tangbiao and Zheng Chuangui on the distribution of authors found that the distribution of the authors in journal articles collected in the "political science" volume produced by Renmin University was 56.9 percent from institutes of higher education; 7.1 percent from the CASS system at various levels; 3.5 percent from party schools of various levels; 2.7 percent from government research institutions; 0.1 percent from nonprofit research institutes; and 29.6 percent from other institutions.[11]

The significance of the professionalization of political science is obvious—it pushes forward discipline construction and the development of political science in four important respects. First of all, it provides political science researchers with basic material guarantees, including salary and welfare that are needed for living, and it also provides them research time, offices, and access to library facilities. Second, the professionalization of political science makes it possible to allocate and coordinate the sources of research and make comprehensive research plans, thereby better integrating and coordinating research efforts. Third, it provides a professional platform for political scientists to exchange ideas and study each other's work through formal and informal institutions, associations, groups, forums, conferences, networks, and other venues. Finally, professionalization will gradually lead to the emergence of a set of professional norms and ethics that are necessary for serious political science research, as well as subtly swaying political scientists to comply with these norms and ethics, thus ensuring the healthy development of political science as a discipline.

As political science becomes more professionalized, however, some inherent problems may also emerge. As political science is a profession, it is logically a tool for people to earn a living. Political science research offers people a comparatively stable job and an opportunity to gain promotions in professional title and official rank as well as increases in salary and welfare benefits, social prestige, and even influence in the sociopolitical process. For most people who choose political science as a profession, considerations of benefits such as social prestige and occupational development are important—there is nothing wrong with this. However, if political scientists pursue their research for largely utilitarian purposes, the professionalization of the discipline may hinder the progress of political science. For example, to gain promotion and win research funds and achievement rewards, many scholars publish repetitive or similar journal articles or works, and the phenomenon of plagiarism occurs from time to time. Some political scientists even take advantage of the "political tricks" that they have studied in their research to gain positions of greater authority or higher professional titles. Thus departments or institutions of political science can be plagued by frequent instances of "academic scandal."

Political science is an academic profession, and its practitioners should take seriously issues of academic integrity and academic ethics; they should comply with academic norms and should have the courage to investigate affairs that may touch on powerful political and economic interests. Political scientists should be encouraged to think independently and seek truth, since they belong to the group of intellectuals, and should have academic consciousness as well as social and professional obligations to the public. In addition, compared with scholars in other disciplines such as liberal arts, political scientists have an even closer relationship with political reality. As such, they should have a strong sense of political responsibility and the spirit to serve the public interest. Of course, when such standards are used to judge political scientists, political science is in fact being regarded as a noble cause.

Political Science as a Cause

Political science is a cause. I say this for the following two reasons. First, political science is an important tool for human beings to understand themselves. Political science tries to study and explore the nature of political phenomenon in human society, find principles of political change and political development, analyze the dynamics behind human political behavior, and thus gain political knowledge. Second, political science is the most important tool for pushing forward social progress. The political activities of human beings are the greatest dynamic for pushing social progress, and progress in the politics of society is the deepest progress in human society. Political science can provide ideal institutional choices for political development in human society. Political science can also be used to breed in citizens a spirit of democracy and the rule of law, cultivate the political rights and responsibilities of citizens, strengthen officials' senses of political responsibility and ethics, and motivate the public's participation in politics and political entrepreneurship. As a cause, political science has already transcended the boundaries of disciplines; it has become an essential factor for pushing forward human civilization and human progress.

At the same time, as a cause, the political science in the new era of China plays an indispensable role in promoting the development of social science, enriching the knowledge bank of the Chinese nation, and advancing the progress of sociopolitical reality. Five areas of development are particularly worth noting. First of all, the exploration of principles of Chinese political development and the summary of experiences and lessons of Chinese politics by political scientists represents a direct contribution to human knowledge and social science in China. Second, political science played an important role in liberating thinking in China after the launch of reform and opening to the outside world. Many important concepts put forward by political scientists directly or indirectly affected the progress of political reform in China and strengthened the bases of legitimacy of democratic governance. Chinese political scientists have made special contributions to the development of Chinese democratic politics. Third, an increasing number of political scientists began to cooperate with the government, undertaking policy research projects that were entrusted to them by the party and by government agencies. Many suggestions put forward by Chinese political scientists have been accepted by the government and have been incorporated into national institutions or policies. Political science has become an important tool for pushing forward the institutionalization and democratization of policymaking. Fourth, political science has become an important channel for reflecting and collecting public opinion and expressing the needs of the public. More and more Chinese political scientists have begun to conduct research through field investigations at the grassroots level; the research reports these studies have produced not only advanced the development of Chinese political science itself, but also became a special channel for expressing the political needs of the public to the government policymaking agencies, thus pushing the government to satisfy the public's needs in a timely manner. Fifth, many political scientists have directly participated in practical political life and have become a force for advancing the progress of practical politics. This contribution cannot be overlooked. For example, some political scientists serve as members of think tanks or as policy consultants for governments at various levels and contribute wisdom and suggestions to the government, while other political scientists train government officials, giving them practical political science knowledge. Still other political scientists initiate various activities and commit themselves to advancing democratic governance in China. For example, the Excellence Award Program for Innovations in Local Governance in China was initiated and organized mainly by political scientists, and it is playing an increasingly influential role in China's practical political life.

Since China launched its reform policy and opened to the outside world, comprehensive changes have taken place in Chinese society and great progress has been achieved in the area of politics. For example, the protection of human rights has been written into the PRC constitution, "constructing a socialist state under the rule of law" has been set as a national political development goal, and "constructing socialist political civilization" has come to be regarded as one of the overall national goals. Other changes include the practice of opening administrative affairs to the public, the reform of the administrative approval system, and the goal of constructing a "services-oriented government." For pushing forward progress in these and similar areas, the contributions of Chinese political scientists cannot be overstated. A recently completed research study has found that many of the great reforms and changes that occurred in areas of politics and law during the reform era were directly attributable to changes in political ideology. The growing trend toward freedom of thought, together with a number of important conceptual innovations, has been essential for forcefully advancing political progress. The new ideological notions that exert deep influences on practical politics include human rights, the rule of law, our common humanity, the privatization of property, civil society, harmonious society, political civilization, globalization, good governance, constitutionalism, legitimacy, global governance, government innovation, social management, incremental democracy, transparency, responsible government, services-oriented government, and governmental efficiency.[12] Some of these ideologies were first offered by Chinese political scientists, and some were jointly advocated by political scientists and scholars from other disciplines.

Political science as a cause requires that professionals in this discipline have a sense of responsibility and make it their mission to commit themselves to society's academic development and political progress. Political scientists should regard their academic research not only as a profession but also as a platform for contributing to social science development and the creation of democratic politics. Owing to the sensitivity of political events, the risks associated with seeking truth in the discipline of political science are much higher than those in other social science fields. Therefore, intellectuals who regard political science as a cause should also be brave enough to generate new theories and embrace a spirit of sacrifice. Political scientists should develop a strong spirit of entrepreneurship, actively participating in society's public debate and political life, and should serve the government and the citizens with their professional knowledge. More specifically, to truly treat political science as a cause that pushes forward China's modernization and democratic politics, political scientists should pay attention to "three guidelines for development" pointed out by older generations of Chinese political scientists. The first guideline is to become more scientific, that is, to approach political science research with a scientific attitude. The second guideline is to be more realistic, that is, to go deep into practical politics, and to understand deeply the problems of practical politics in China so as to provide wisdom and knowledge for solving these problems. The third guideline is to "go global," absorbing the most profound lessons that come from political knowledge of other human societies. Chinese political scientists should promote Chinese political science in international academic circles and international society and thereby make Chinese political science an important part of world political civilization.[13]

Development of the Discipline of Public Administration

The field of public administration has been one of the fastest-developing social science disciplines in China since the reforms began in 1978. Before then, only a small number of polytechnical institutions taught the discipline of management, whereas today no fewer than 584 universities and institutions have departments or colleges of management; among these at least 83 universities have been authorized to develop graduate programs offering students the degree of master of public administration (MPA). Many more universities have undergraduate programs in public administration. A large number of Chinese universities have developed an integrated three-level talent training system that provides education for students at the undergraduate, master's, and doctoral levels. Many leading Western academic theories have been introduced into management lecture courses in China, and many classic textbooks of Western management theory and practice have been translated and published in Chinese. Every year numerous Western scholars in the field of public administration are invited to China for academic exchanges and lectures. In addition, Chinese scholars have published numerous books and papers on public management, covering topics such as public policy, public administration, public finance, public health, public safety, public affairs, personnel management, crisis management, and environmental management.

These developments in the discipline of public administration have reflected the depth of the changes occurring in China over the past three decades. Since 1978 the Chinese economy has gradually been changing from a system based on central planning to a more market-oriented system. In politics, with the evolution of the Chinese Communist Party from a revolutionary party into a governing party, the focus of the political process has gradually changed from government to governance. The process of globalization has greatly accelerated the steps of transformation in China toward a market-oriented economy and a democratic form of politics. These important social and political changes have led directly to changes in the discipline of public administration, moving China from a revolutionary period toward a more management-oriented period in which public administration is playing an increasingly important role. The public sector in China consists of government and party bureaucracies, state-owned nonprofit units, and government-led social associations. With more than 105 million employees altogether, China has the largest public administration sector in the world in terms of total personnel employed. The public sector has been expanding even though governments at all levels are being urged to streamline the number of employees in the public sectors. The public sector, comprising social and cultural elites, represents the most powerful political and economic forces in society. Because of the special importance of the public sector in sociopolitical life in China, research on public administration has grown rapidly in recent years. Originally derived from the disciplines of political science, economics, and sociology, public administration has already developed into a largely independent discipline. With a rapidly increasing importance in status, public administration has become an influential and popular discipline in the social sciences.

In little more than a decade, many inspiring and exciting reform practices and positive trends have occurred in the field. First, the academic study of public administration has become increasingly professional, and people working in the public sector have in fact become quite professional. Government has instituted specific professional requirements for managerial staff in the public sector, establishing standards governing human resource recruitment, performance evaluation, promotion, and other aspects of professional employment. For example, all people who want to work in the government sector must take state-organized qualification examinations for civil servants. Second, public administration has embarked on the track of managing government according to the law. Governing by law has become an important goal of the Chinese government. In recent years, China has passed a series of important laws to manage the public sector, including laws regulating administrative permission, administrative litigation, state compensation, and civil servants. A legal system for public administration has been gradually taking shape. Third, areas of public service delivery have been expanded, and the quality of public service has been upgraded. In recent years the Chinese government has set forth the goal of building a service-oriented government and has adopted a series of measures to improve the quality of public service. These steps have included simplifying administrative approval procedures, engaging in administrative decentralization, and creating one-stop service centers for the convenience of the public. Fourth, the accountability of the public sector has been enhanced. For example, the practices of the "chief executive accountability system," the "service delivery promise system," and the "accountability investigation system" at various levels of government are specific indicators of the buildup of an ever-more accountable government. Fifth, the efficiency of public administration has been greatly enhanced. Some local governments have described the reforms as an "efficiency revolution." Sixth, transparency of public administration has been increased. The Chinese government regards transparency as an important task of political reform and is promoting it through the establishment of a "national leadership task force for opening administrative affairs to the public." Some practices in recent years such as "opening up the public policy system," the "information opening system," and the use of government spokespersons (who regularly answer questions from reporters) are important steps for enhancing transparency in public administration. All these reforms reflect the three trends of democratization, institutionalization, and decentralization in public administration in China.

Problems and Prospects for the Field of Public Administration

Despite the positive changes in public administration in China, many serious problems still exist. Corruption in the public sector is extremely common, the quality of public service is comparatively poor, the costs of public administration remain terribly high, the efficiency of public administration is usually quite low, the functions of public administration are inappropriately divided, and the absence of a clear demarcation line between duty and responsibility is very severe. Conditions such as redundant administration and absence of administration coexist.

In tandem with these problems in the practice of public administration, scholarship on public administration is generally quite weak, with little focus on empirical academic research. The research methodologies used are either old or simplistically borrowed from Western analytical methods and used to analyze Chinese society without appropriate consideration for whether they are suitable. In terms of building theoretical capacity, too many ideas are introduced from Western theories about public administration, and too few theoretical propositions grow out of the Chinese experience of public administration. In the area of applied research, many policy suggestions are overly idealized without practical plausibility. Many research subjects, including patterns and models of public administration and problems and lessons of China's administrative experience, deserve greater scholarly research.

CHAPTER THREE

The Seventeenth Party Congress and the Agenda for China's Political Reforms

There is widely believed to be a mutually reinforcing relationship between economic progress and political development.[1] With the construction and development of a socialist market economy, China has been actively, if also cautiously, pushing forward political reforms—and has made great advances. Political reforms are a matter of *must,* not *should.* This is evident from President Hu Jintao's report to the Seventeenth National Congress of the Chinese Communist Party (CCP) in 2007, in which the president said: "As an important part of the overall reform, political reform must be constantly deepened along with economic and social development to adapt to the growing enthusiasm of the people for participation in political affairs."[2]

Political reform must achieve multiple goals. These include transforming government functions, promoting economic development, enhancing administrative efficiency, improving provision of public services, maintaining social stability, and containing government corruption, among others. However, just as the president indicated in his report, the fundamental goal of political reform is "to expand the people's democracy and ensure that the people are masters of the country." With a focus on political reform, part six of the report, entitled "Unswervingly Developing Socialist Democracy," highlights "developing socialist democracy [as] a continuous goal for the party to pursue." Whereas the report of the Sixteenth Party Congress in 2002 regarded "intraparty democracy" as "the life of the party," the 2007 report regards "people's democracy" as "the life of socialism."[3] These developments indicate that the CCP not only pays great attention to developing democracy but is also determined to push forward democracy.

Similar to economic development, political reforms in China are likely to be incremental reform—in other words, incremental democratization. It is impossible for an overall breakthrough reform to occur immediately. However, occasional breakthroughs may occur in some areas. In my view, the following areas will receive special attention in the foreseeable future.

Improving Democracy at the Grassroots Level

For the first time in the history of the People's Republic of China, the report of the Seventeenth Party Congress explicitly identified developing grassroots democracy as "a fundamental project for developing socialist democracy" and put this project at the top of the political reform agenda to be "pushed forward emphatically."[4] The discussion in section two of part six indicates that grassroots-level democracy will be one of the most important arenas for constructing Chinese democracy. Grassroots democracy, which directly relates to the political interests of the public masses, is the foundation of democracy more generally, and its significance is obvious. Moreover, it is conducive to sociopolitical stabilization and the accumulation of experience in constructing democracy in a bottom-up manner, that is, developing grassroots democracy first and then developing democracy at higher levels.

Developing grassroots democracy calls for properly handling the following relationships: between the party and the government at the grassroots level; between government management and the self-governance of the masses; between civil organizations and the local government; and between citizens' rights and citizens' obligations. Currently political reforms at the grassroots level need to deal urgently with a number of issues including how to effectively curb the negative phenomenon of bribery in grassroots-level democratic elections, how to delimit the influence of family clans, and how to enhance citizens' awareness of democracy and the rule of law. Political reforms at the grassroots level will focus mainly on reform of township institutions; improvement of institutions for self-governance through neighborhood community and professional self-governance systems; expansion of the scope for direct recommendation and direct election of township party and government leaders; and transformation of the governance structure and governing methods for the city and rural areas.

Improving Intraparty Democracy

The Sixteenth Party Congress identified the strategy of first developing intraparty democracy and then moving on to build social democracy as the model for developing overall Chinese democracy. The Seventeenth Party Congress reaffirmed this strategy. Intraparty democracy is paired with grassroots democracy as a means for pushing forward democratic politics. If grassroots democracy means implementing democracy from the bottom up, intraparty democracy entails doing so from the inside out. The CCP is the only ruling party in China whose legitimacy is established by the constitution. This is one of the core tenets of constitutional rule. In China the CCP is at the core of political power, dominating the legislative, administrative, and judicial branches.

With over 70 million members, the CCP represents most of the political, economic, and cultural elites in China. As such, without intraparty democracy, there would be no democracy at the center of power. Judging from objective realities rather than subjective imaginings, without intraparty democracy it would be difficult to attain democracy in China. Thus advancing intraparty democratic reforms is the most realistic way to advance democracy in China. The central focus of improving intraparty democracy lies in the reform of intraparty election, decisionmaking, and in revamping oversight systems.

Improving Legislative and Judicial Institutions

Legislative and judicial institutions are fundamental components of the political system in any state; they are also important indicators of a country's level of political development. The reform of the legislative and judicial systems was discussed in the report of the Sixteenth Party Congress, and the points made in that document were reiterated in section three of part six of the report of the Seventeenth Party Congress. Currently several problems face the legislative and judicial systems: the legal system is incomplete; extralegal intervention in judicial practices is still widespread; public awareness of the law is comparatively weak; injustices in judicial practices as well as local protectionism are common enough to warrant serious concern; the qualifications of many legal professionals need to be enhanced; and the phenomenon of "legitimate" sector interests has begun to emerge, among other challenges.

To solve these problems—and to safeguard citizens' human rights, social equity, and justice—it is necessary to deepen the reforms of the legislative and judicial systems, uphold the supreme authority of the constitution and the law; improve and perfect the legal system; and push forward the democratization and institutionalization of the legislative and judicial systems. Among these measures, it is especially important to draft, debate, and pass laws in a more rational and democratic way; perfect the judicial system through national integration, greater independence, and freedom from extrainstitutional intervention in legislative and judicial processes; and make sure that party organizations at various levels and party members at all levels take the leading role in safeguarding constitutional and legal authority.

Improving the Policymaking System and Rational Decisionmaking

The policymaking system is concerned with the distribution and adjustment of important public interests and is thus a basic component of politics in any society. Whether the policymaking process is democratic and reasonable affects every dimension of a society. It also affects the administrative efficiency and costs of government and is concerned with the citizens' critical interests as well as with the stability and order of society. Currently many problems exist in China's policymaking system: arbitrary decisions too often cause policy failures; policies are changed too frequently and as a result often lack much-needed continuity; policy overlap, conflicts, and bureaucratic infighting often occur; and bureaucratic departmental interests too often override national interests. All these phenomena severely weaken the credibility of the party and the government.

The causes of these phenomena not only lie in the qualifications of policymakers but also stem from six specific institutional deficiencies in the policymaking process. These are the lack of a comprehensive system for public participation in the policymaking process, the absence of a policy consultation system, the lack of a public hearing system, the failure to put in place a policy evaluation system, the lack of a policy accountability system, and the absence of an effective institution for policy coordination. The Seventeenth Party Congress report states: "To ensure scientific and democratic policymaking, we will improve the information and intellectual support for [policymaking], increase its transparency and expand public participation in it. In principle, public hearings must be held for the formulation of laws, regulations and policies that bear closely on the interests of the public."[5] This statement indicates that reform of policymaking will be carried out in the above-mentioned six areas.

Improving the System of Public Oversight to Serve the People's Interests

The Seventeenth Party Congress report calls for

improving the mechanism of restraint and oversight and ensuring that power entrusted [to the government] by the people is always exercised in their interests. Power must be exercised in [an open and transparent manner] to ensure that it is exercised correctly. We must have institutions to govern power, work and personnel, and establish a sound structure of power and a mechanism for its operation in which policymaking, enforcement and oversight powers check each other and function in coordination.[6]

This description exemplifies the effort to produce a system of checks and balances with Chinese characteristics. All power must be effectively balanced; otherwise it inevitably leads to arbitrary rule and corruption. The existing problems of corruption among cadres and overcentralization of power in the hands of major party and government officials result in large part from the absence of a sound system of checks and balances.

The Western, developed countries practice a system of checks and balances predicated on institutions of representative, multiparty democracy, and divisions of power among the legislative, the administrative, and the judicial branches of government. The CCP has, to date, refused to adopt such a system. However, no matter whether in China or the West, power must be balanced and checked in some way if democracy is to be advanced and official corruption curbed. China is trying to find an innovative way to balance power not only among personnel, administrative, and financial authorities but also among policymaking, policy implementation, and policy oversight, which will leverage the interests and capabilities of the people, the party, and the media.

Making Governmental Affairs More Open and Transparent to the Public

The report of the Seventeenth Party Congress points out at several places that it is necessary to "improve institutions through opening government and village affairs to the public," to "push ahead with transparency in party affairs," to "enhance transparency of decisionmaking," to "improve the processing of various government affairs," and to "enhance transparency in government administration." The report also stresses that "power must be exercised under conditions of sunshine [transparency]."[7] All these statements indicate that the party and government pay great attention to opening up governmental affairs to public scrutiny. Political transparency is indeed the precondition not only for popular democracy and intraparty democracy but also for scientific and democratic policymaking. Furthermore, it is also the precondition for the integrity of politics and for ensuring the continuing honesty of officials. Only when power is exercised transparently and government officials do their job under the monitoring of the public eye can corruption be eradicated.

Currently the following problems still exist in terms of political transparency: some cadres are more comfortable with operating in a black-box environment, and so they consciously or unconsciously resist opening up government affairs to public scrutiny; many of the basic institutions necessary for opening government affairs up to public oversight have not been set up yet; a number of laws and regulations compatible with these institutions are still under development; the already established institutions for opening government affairs up for public oversight lack practical feasibility and are, to a certain extent, institutions in name only. Reform of governmental affairs must focus on improving the institutions for public oversight of government affairs; making realistic and practical rules and regulations for implementing public oversight; and forcefully implementing the laws and regulations necessary to push forward the establishment of institutions for public oversight of government affairs.

Improving the Social Management System and Promoting a More Harmonious Society

Along with the establishment and development of a market economy came many new kinds of social affairs, organizations, and phenomena. These put increasing demands on the government to perform new social management functions. Beginning in 1998 the central government formally set social management as a basic government function. Since the Sixteenth Party Congress, the central government has been engaged in planning the systematic reform of social policies and has gradually established "a management framework with party committee leadership, government responsibility, social coordination, and public participation." The report of the Seventeenth Party Congress identifies social system reform as a basic goal.

The report discusses the importance of "perfecting social management and maintaining social stability and unity."[8] It prescribes the focus and direction of social policy reform in the near future. With respect to social management, outstanding problems include institutional deficiencies, lack of management talent, lack of management mechanisms or bad management, high costs of management, and a focus on maintaining control rather than on providing services. The critical reforms in this area would address problems in the current social management, public aid, social security, social work, and neighborhood and community management systems, among other steps. In addition, solving these problems requires mobilizing civil society organizations and allowing them to play appropriate roles in social management, expanding self-governance by the masses at the grassroots level, and realizing cooperative management between government and citizens in social affairs.

Improving Governance and Constructing a More Service-Oriented Government

Governance is an important component of political reform today. Many important measures have been undertaken in this field. Examples include performing government administration in accordance with the law, constructing accountable government within the rule of law, simplifying the procedures of administrative approval, improving governmental efficiency, promoting government and governmental officials' accountability, strengthening the function of public service, and reconceptualizing government as a service provider. The report of the Seventeenth Party Congress devotes a whole section (section four in part six) to a discussion about the reform of the administrative system. It points out that "administrative reform is an important part of the effort to deepen China's overall reform."[9] With respect to the administrative system, the following problems still exist: overlapping and duplicative organizations, functions, and obligations; conflicting policies from different governmental organs; a distinction between administrative affairs and routine affairs; and high costs of administration.

To counter these problems, the Party Congress report draws up a plan for administrative reform. According to this plan, administrative reforms in the near future will focus on establishing an overall framework for the reform; improving the public service system; standardizing administrative practices; strengthening institutional restructuring; reducing administrative costs; streamlining the set-up of party committees and governmental organs as well as that of people's congresses and the Chinese People's Political Consultative Congress. The general trend in government administrative reforms will be to move gradually from regulatory oversight to the provision of services, from the rule of man to the rule of law, from centralization of power to decentralization of power, and from government to governance.

PART II

SOCIAL TRANSFORMATION
AND CIVIL SOCIETY

CHINA'S CIVIL SOCIETY
Conceptual Definitions, Types, and Background

Although civil society was very lively in China in the early twentieth century, the Chinese government and academic communities view its reemergence during the reform era as essentially a new phenomenon.[1] China's civil society is still in a formative, immature stage, and as a result its basic characteristics and functions have not yet become clear. Meanwhile, there are numerous ambiguities in the understanding of China's civil society, manifested most dramatically in the lack of consensus about how a number of key categories and concepts are to be interpreted. Disagreements are natural, but if key concepts are too ambiguous, deep discussion will be difficult, and, more important, the formulation of reasonable policies and regulations will be hindered. Therefore, before discussing the overall development of China's civil society, it is necessary to state clearly how key concepts are to be interpreted.

Clarification of Key Concepts

The three key concepts interpreted here are civil society, civic organizations, and the institutional environment.

CIVIL SOCIETY

The English term *civil society* is translated into Chinese three different ways: *shimin shehui, minjian shehui,* and *gongmin shehui.* Although the uses of these terms overlap, their meanings are not completely identical, and there are subtle differences between them. The term *shimin shehui* is the one most widely used and is the standard translation for *civil society.* Its origin lies in

Chinese translations of the classical texts of Marxism. However, in its traditional usage, it has a somewhat negative connotation, and many Chinese observers tend to equate it with the term *bourgeois society.* Moreover, it is easily misinterpreted to mean *urban residents.*

The earliest use of *minjian shehui* as a translation of *civil society* was made by scholars in Taiwan. This usage was embraced by mainland historians and widely adopted in research on nongovernmental organizations in modern China. It has a relatively neutral connotation, although many government officials and scholars believe that this term conveys a sense of being marginalized.

The term *gongmin shehui* (literally, citizens' society) was adopted as a translation for *civil society* after the beginning of reform and opening up in 1978. It has positive connotations and emphasizes the political science aspect of the term, both in the sense of citizens' participation in public affairs and citizens' restraints on state power. More and more young scholars in today's China prefer using this term.

Definitions of *civil society* by Chinese scholars can be divided into those that emphasize its political science aspects and those that stress its sociological angle. Both definitions identify nongovernmental civic organizations as members of civil society, but they stress different aspects of these organizations. Political scientists tend to emphasize their role in safeguarding citizens' rights and participating in some way in the government decisionmaking process; sociologists tend to emphasize the intermediary nature of these civic organizations, focusing on the fact that civil society exists in a realm between the state and business enterprises.

I define *civil society* as a public sphere outside the spheres of government and the market economy that comprises all kinds of civic organizations not affiliated with the government or businesses. Such groups include organizations for safeguarding citizens' rights, all kinds of trade associations, public interest associations, community organizations, interest groups, academic associations, mutual assistance organizations, recreational groups, voluntary organizations, and associations spontaneously created by citizens. These groups can be viewed as constituting an intermediary sector between the government and the business sector.

Civic Organizations

Civil society is a public sphere that is relatively independent from the state. However, the current understanding of civic organizations among Chinese academic circles is even more confused than the understanding of civil society. Both scholarly articles and government documents use a variety of names to refer to civil society organizations (CSOs). These terms include nongovernmental organizations (NGOs), nonprofit organizations (NPOs), civic organizations, civic groups, intermediary organizations, mass associations, people's associations, social associations, third-sector organizations, and voluntary organizations. No substantive differences between the organizations are denoted by these various names. However, based on a strict interpretation of their meanings, these concepts should be distinguishable because they stress different aspects of civil society.

The term *NGO* has been widely used lately, and it expresses an important concept. By indicating that they are clearly not part of the system of government organizations, the term emphasizes the unofficial nature of civil society organizations. In the Chinese context, however, this concept can engender two opposite ambiguities. The first suggests that only important and formally constituted civil society organizations fall within the category of civil society because the earliest use of the term *NGO* in China was to apply it to international NGOs recognized in the UN charter. International NGOs have a more formal standing and have been formally approved by governments, so a large number of informal organizations in society would probably not count as NGOs in many people's eyes. The second ambiguity suggests that because NGOs are clearly unaffiliated with the government, some might draw the wrong conclusion and assume that they are opposed to the government. Indeed, what is intriguing about Chinese NGOs is that most of them actually have rather intimate relations with the government, and many of them could accurately be described as government-organized nongovernmental organizations, or GONGOs.

The term *nonprofit organization* highlights the difference between civil society organizations and market organizations such as private for-profit enterprises and corporations. However, this term can be criticized for its tendency to blur the frequent need for civil society organizations to charge for the services they provide and to engage in for-profit activities if they are to survive and fulfill their mission. CSOs should be free of the profit motive, but because many civil organizations do not receive financial assistance, they are often forced to generate income from their activities in order to survive and develop. Thus, the services they provide are not free in China. It is very difficult to draw a line on fees charged for services and say that charges below a certain line make the services not-for-profit and charges above it make them for-profit. Therefore, using non-profit as the standard to define CSOs raises new, definitional problems.

Intermediary organization is one of the most widely used terms, most frequently in administrative regulations. The term makes it clear from the start that civil society organizations have an intermediary position between the government and enterprises. However, this term glosses over other important features of such organizations, especially their not-for-profit nature. In actuality, most organizations having an intermediary nature are for-profit bodies, and they are much more closely associated with the market than with civil society. As China's market economy develops, the number of service industries has increased and, with this, many organizations that could fairly be called intermediary organizations. They are indeed viewed as such by government administrative agencies, but they are not at all part of civil society. Examples include law offices, accounting offices, marriage agencies, public notary offices, human resources centers, real estate assessment offices, quality and technical oversight bodies, household services agencies, business advisory bodies, and commercial agent bodies. They are all intermediary organizations, but they operate on a purely for-profit basis.

Mass organization and *people's organization* are specific political terms in China's current political system. Such organizations are directly led by the Chinese Communist Party (CCP) and include trade unions, the Chinese Communist Youth League (CCYL), and the China Women's Federation, as well as a small number of specialized organizations such as the China Disabled Persons' Federation, the China Federation of Writers and Artists, and the China Association for Science and Technology. The salient feature of these organizations is that they have a strong political and administrative flavor. They have national and local bodies parallel to government administrative divisions. Their leading bodies also parallel those of government bodies, and the government formally apportions them staff since they perform certain administrative functions. In terms of their functions and nature, these organizations are more like government organizations than like nongovernmental organizations. Although the two terms are sometimes used in a general sense to pertain to all nongovernmental social organizations, their special significance is already deeply implanted in people's minds through established usage. In addition, in the Chinese political environment, the terms *the masses* and *the people* are commonly used in a political sense that signifies the recognition of a majority of citizens by the party or the government. Obviously, this connotation makes it difficult for these terms to stand in for civil society organizations.

The limitations of the terms *third-sector organization* and *voluntary organization* are relatively clear. The first is a technical term introduced from abroad only in recent years. Many people do not understand the term because they do not know what the third sector is. In the economic sphere, it is easy to confuse this term with the concept of the tertiary sector, or service industries.

The term *voluntary organization* emphasizes the voluntary nature of civil society organizations, but these are not the only kinds of organizations characterized by voluntary participation; many political party organizations emphasize that members' participation in them is voluntary. Obviously, using these terms for civil society organizations is not altogether satisfactory.

The CSOs are also frequently called social associations, citizens' groups, citizens' organizations, or civic organizations. To a certain extent, these terms indicate their civic nature and distinguish them from government agencies and commercial organizations. The term *social association* emphasizes the social nature of civil society organizations. The terms *citizens' group* and *citizens' organization* emphasize the political nature of civil society organizations because the term *citizen* is a political concept defined by a country's constitution. The term *civic organization* (*minjian zuzhi*) emphasizes the societal basis of civil society organizations, and its connotation can be extended to cover the important content of all of the aforementioned terms, so it is a relatively satisfactory concept for characterizing CSOs. As such, many Chinese scholars have proposed that when discussing CSOs, the term *civic organization* be used wherever possible to avoid the unnecessary disputes and confusions caused by the use of the other terms discussed above.

Then, what are the bodies that this chapter calls civil society organizations? Civil society organizations are nonprofit groups that are composed of citizen volunteers who seek to pursue common interests. They have four important characteristics. First, they are unofficial; that is, they take a civic form and do not represent the position of the government or the state. Second, they are not-for-profit; that is, they do not take making a profit to be the main purpose of their existence and usually focus instead on providing public benefits and services. Third, they have their own organizational and management mechanisms and independent sources of funding and are relatively independent from the government politically, administratively, and financially. And fourth, they are voluntary. These characteristics of CSOs clearly make them different from government bodies and business groups. In addition, they are nonpolitical and nonreligious; that is, they do not take obtaining political power as an important objective and do not engage in religious activities. Therefore, political and religious organizations cannot be classified as civil organizations.[2]

THE INSTITUTIONAL ENVIRONMENT

An institution is a series of regulations or norms that influence human activity. Douglass C. North, an important representative of the "institutional economics" school of political and economic analysis, states that "institutions provide the framework within which human beings interact. . . . Institutions are a set of rules, compliance procedures, and moral and ethical behavioral norms designed to constrain the behavior of individuals."[3] Institutional regulations are ready-made norms of behavior that are relatively stable and long lasting. The behavioral regulations that constitute institutions include written norms—statutory regulations that authoritative bodies endorse and enforce—as well as unwritten norms—informal rules that have not been promulgated by any authoritative body yet implicitly restrict people's actions. A political system is composed of a series of regulations that govern people's political activities and a set of rules of conduct for political life. In general, a political system is established by the state and embodies the basic interests and value orientations of the political authorities that use it to control the political activities of the citizens. A political system is more basic, restrictive, and coercive than other systems, and when in conflict with other social systems, the others usually yield.

According to North, "these rules of organizing human activity are at the very heart of economic history. Not only do these rules spell out the system of incentives and disincentives that guide and shape economic activity, they also determine the underlying distribution of wealth and income of society."[4] The activities of civic associations are commonly thought of as typical political activities that must be restricted by relevant state institutions. Hence, all formal and informal rules the state uses to regulate and control the activities of civil society organizations can be defined as the institutional environment of civil society. This environment has five aspects: the constitution, which provides the fundamental legal framework and source of legitimacy for civil society; ordinary laws, that is, the comprehensive and special laws concerning civil society organizations; administrative regulations, decrees, and rules with which the central and local governments manage civil society organizations; party policy regulations, policies, principles, and rules of political parties in power that are concerned with civil society organizations; and informal institutions that include all kinds of implicit regulations diffused throughout society and the government that influence the activities and functions of civic organizations, including the attitudes of party and government leaders at all levels toward civil society organizations.

Because civil society exists in an institutional environment, every step of its development is directly or indirectly influenced by this environment. All kinds of formal and informal regulations have effects on the civic organizations that make up civil society. By differentiating and analyzing the influences on civil society into a number of institutional factors, one can discover the overall impact that China's current institutional environment has on its civil society. Important factors of the institutional environment include the determinants of the nature and orientation of civic organizations; rules for establishing and registering these groups; classifications of civil society organizations and measures for supervising them; oversight, control, and guidance of them; financial policies for them, including subsidy, tax, and auditing policies; ways and means to intervene in their affairs; measures to support them; policies to encourage them; and restrictions on and penalties against them, including licensing, qualifications, franchising, and revocation.

Types of Civil Society Organizations

There is no standard way of classifying civil society organizations. Three different classifications are typically used in China: the official classifications used by the Ministry of Civil Affairs; the classifications used by the United Nations or foreign research bodies; and the various classification schemes proposed by Chinese scholars.

The Ministry of Civil Affairs, the government body responsible for civic organizations, classifies civil society groups that fall under its jurisdiction into three types. The first type is composed of social associations—"nonprofit social organizations voluntarily organized by Chinese citizens to achieve the common objectives of their members by engaging in activities in accordance with their charters."[5] The second type is made up of "social organizations without government funding organized by enterprises, institutions, social associations, other social forces, and individual citizens for the purpose of engaging in not-for-profit social service activities." The third type is composed of foundations dedicated to the public good—"nonprofit legal persons that use funds contributed by natural or legal persons or other organizations to carry out undertakings for the public good."[6] The Ministry of Civil Affairs classifies social associations into four types: academic groups, such as associations in the various natural and social sciences and in interdisciplinary fields; trade organizations, whose members are enterprises in the same field; professional organizations, whose members have similar skills and special funds and are all engaged in the same line of work; and federations, such as trade unions, which are associations of groups of people.[7]

Some scholars point out that although the way government regulatory agencies categorize social organizations is easy to implement, it is overly simplistic and not conducive to thorough analysis. They advocate using international standards until a comprehensive and mature standard for classifying Chinese social organizations is developed. One choice would be to use the United Nations' International Standard Industrial Classification, which divides NPOs into three major categories and fifteen subcategories. The category of education has primary education, secondary education, higher education, and adult and other education as subcategories; the category for health and social work has human health activities, veterinary activities, and social work activities as subcategories; and the category of other community, social, and personal service activities has sewage and refuse disposal, sanitation and similar activities; activities of membership organizations; recreational, cultural, and sporting activities; and other service activities as subcategories. Another choice would be to use the classification standards of research institutes in Western countries. The School of Public Policy and Management of Tsinghua University basically uses the International Classification of Nonprofit Organizations developed at the Johns Hopkins University Comparative Nonprofit Sector Project. The School of Public Policy divides China's civil organizations into twelve major categories and twenty-seven subcategories. The major categories are culture and recreation; education and research; health; social services; environment; development and housing; law, advocacy, and politics; philanthropic intermediaries and volunteerism promotion; international; religion; business and professional associations; and not elsewhere classified.[8]

In recent years, as research on civil society organizations has deepened, Chinese scholars have developed a number of classification schemes. For example, social associations have been classified based on their statutory purpose (organizations that mutually benefit their members, operational organizations, and organizations whose members work for the public good); on the kind of relation they have to the government (organizations that are government-backed, privately run, or have aspects of both); on their form of management (organizations that are managed by professionals, those that are not, and those for which management responsibility is not clear); on whether they have members or not; and on whether their organizational structure is hierarchical or flat.

In order to universalize the classification system, some scholars classify civic organizations functionally and divide all of China's nationwide social associations into seventeen functional categories: the industrial sector (trade and management associations); social services and social welfare (foundations and charitable organizations); public affairs (associations of mayors and exchange associations); information and technical services (consulting organizations and consumer groups); health (medical service organizations); sports (athletic associations); education (all kinds of educational service organizations); culture and arts (film and music associations); press and publishing (radio and television associations); science and technology (scientific research associations and organizations that popularize science); humanities and social sciences (scholarly associations in the various fields); environment and energy resources (environmental associations); special kinds of commercial or industrial associations (trade organizations of enterprises under different forms of ownership); professional organizations (associations of professionals in the same field); community organizations (local associations); fellowships of individuals (fraternities and groups based on common interests); and other groups.[9]

There are many kinds of civil society organizations, and they all have distinctive characteristics. People can classify them on the basis of various characteristics, and the choice of these characteristics will generate different criteria of classification. For example, on the basis of their legal status, civic organizations can be classified as legal or illegal; from the nature of their objectives, they can be classified as dedicated to the public welfare or not; from the nature of their activities, they can be classified as professional or general organizations; from the scope of their activities, they can be classified as national or local organizations; and from sources of their operating expenses, they can be classified as being subsidized by government funds, by social contributions, or as self-supporting. Therefore, it is not surprising that there are numerous typologies and methods for classifying them. However, the method of classification is not the main objective; its purpose is to enable us to better understand and supervise the various kinds of civic organizations. Research and supervision of civil society organizations are closely connected, but they are distinct and have important differences, including differences in the typologies they use. Accordingly, I propose methods of classification for academic research and government administration respectively.

The following two aspects are particularly important in the categorization of civil organizations. First, from the perspective of academic research, the most important criteria for classifying civil society organizations are their basic characteristics, which can be divided into the following types:

—*Trade organizations,* including trade, professional, and management associations, such as those associated with the various industries

—*Charitable organizations,* including organizations whose main functions are to provide disaster relief and aid the poor; these groups include the Red Cross, charities, disabled persons' federations, and the Soong Ching Ling Foundation

—*Academic groups,* including organizations of scholars in the same field, such as the Chinese Physical Society, Chinese Chemical Society, Chinese Association of Political Science, and Chinese Atheistic Research Society

—*Political groups,* including all kinds of citizens' organizations that safeguard the political rights of citizens, such as the CCYL, the China Women's Federation, villagers' committees, and neighborhood committees

—*Community organizations,* including groups that are engaged in neighborhood supervision and service, such as homeowners' committees, community welfare centers, community retirees' associations, community legal assistance centers, and neighborhood public security committees

—*Social service organizations,* including civic organizations that provide social welfare services and public welfare services, such as organizations engaged in environmental protection and in culture, education, sports, and health activities

—*Citizens' mutual assistance organizations,* including organizations voluntarily entered into by citizens to protect their interests, such as urban and rural mutual assistance associations, relief centers, rural agricultural associations, and rural cooperative organizations

—*Common interest organizations,* including citizens' organizations based on the common good, leisure interests, and career interests, such as sports clubs, countrymen associations, alumni associations, poetry groups, and so on

—*Nonprofit consulting service organizations,* including most privately operated noncommercial bodies.

Second, from the perspective of government supervision, the classification of civil society organizations should focus on two factors: historical developments and current situations of Chinese civil organizations; and what is needed or convenient for differentiated supervision.

On the basis of these two factors, I propose the following classification:

—*Mass organizations:* mass groups unique to China's political situation and directly under the leadership of the Chinese Communist Party, such as trade unions, the Communist Youth League, women's federations, writers' associations, science and technology associations, literary federations, and disabled persons' federations

—*Self-governing groups:* self-governing citizens' political organizations, such as villagers' committees and neighborhood committees

—*Business and professional groups:* all kinds of organizations and associations in a particular industry or profession, including organizations having regulatory functions, and self-policing organizations, such as the China National Council of Light Industry and China Consumers' Association

—*Academic groups:* all kinds of associations in the fields of natural and social sciences and interdisciplinary studies

—*Community groups:* organizations of community residents that provide community supervision and services

—*Social associations:* all other kinds of social organizations not described above

—*Public welfare and charities foundations:* organizations that finance public welfare and charities undertakings.

China's Civil Society Past and Present

Civil society, in the current sense of the term, arose in China at the end of the Qing dynasty and the beginning of the Republic of China. The development of civil society in China had many setbacks in its first decades, and it was only after the 1980s that normal progress occurred.

CSOs in the Republic of China (1912–49)

In traditional Chinese society, unofficial and nongovernmental organizations were severely restricted; political organizations came under especially frequent attack. Notable incidents involving considerable loss of life are recorded in the history of every dynasty from the Eastern Han down through the Tang and Song to the Ming. This reality is reflected in the Confucian saying "The superior man avoids partisan associations," and indeed during these centuries this idea took on the force of a political maxim. However, a number of civil society organizations were still present in traditional Chinese society, including guilds (whose purpose was to promote their trade by standardizing practices and limiting competition), associations of people from the same locality who had taken up residency in other parts of the country, associations of clan members in the same village, and various kinds of mutual assistance associations. The upper classes had recreational and cultural associations for enjoying poetry or music or for sharing learning; these associations played an important role in transmitting knowledge and culture and had a roundabout effect on the court. Of course, these kinds of groups were very different from civil society organizations as they are currently understood. The vast majority of these groups had no connections with the government.

In Chinese history, civil society was always overshadowed by the political state, and a relatively independent civil society was born only with the introduction of a market economy and the experiments with democracy that began in the reform era in the early twentieth century. Two factors contributed to the rise of civil society organizations. One was the differentiation of professions and diversification of interests, and the other was the importation of Western scholarship, particularly the discipline of sociology, the theory of evolution, and the ideology of democracy. When China was extremely poor and weak, associations gave powerful expression to aspirations for the survival and salvation of the nation. Thomas Huxley's maxim that "the natural course of evolution is for those that congregate to procreate and those that do not to perish, and for those who congregate well to survive and those that do not to perish" emphasized the significance of forming mass organizations for the survival of the nation.

Reformists like Kang Youwei and Liang Qichao particularly stressed the importance of forming scholarly associations and establishing relationships with strong countries with enlightened populations. They believed that the cause of China's weakness was its strict prohibition on forming associations, which they said sapped the spirit of the people; they argued that it was impossible to free people's thinking and acquire knowledge without relying on group activities. These scholars asserted that if the masses are ruled by the wisdom of the many, they will thrive, but if they are ruled by the wisdom of the few, they will perish. At the beginning of the twentieth century, under pressure from within and without, the Qing government began to institute political reforms. In 1908 it promulgated the "constitutional program," which for the first time in history stipulated that "within the scope prescribed by law, the emperor's subjects have freedom of speech, press, and association." This gave civil associations legal recognition. It is estimated that before the Revolution of 1911, there were more than 2,000 business, educational, and agricultural societies. In addition, there were quite a few self-governing groups and groups formed to promote the adoption of a constitution.[10]

In the Republic of China, the number of civil society organizations grew considerably. According to statistics from the Ministry of Social Affairs in 1946, there were more than 46,000 registered people's organizations, including more than 40,000 business organizations (peasants' associations, trade unions, fishermen's associations, groups of industrialists and businessmen, and groups of free-lance professionals) and more than 5,000 social associations (cultural, religious, charitable, public service, sports, health, and women's groups). This count included only groups registered with the government. The actual number of civil society groups was surely much greater, and estimates of their number vary widely. For example, some publications report that there were about 1,000 civil organizations in China in the first half of the twentieth century, but other research puts the number at over

80,000. During this period, civil society gradually became more mature and began to play an important role in social and political life.

Accordingly, the institutional environment in which civil society existed underwent a number of substantive changes. This was most evident in the government's attention to institution building. During this period, a relatively complete body of laws and regulations concerning civil society organizations was adopted that put them on a firm legal basis. Particularly when the national government was located in Nanjing between 1927 and 1937, legislative work was unusually intense. Laws concerning important kinds of civil society groups like trade unions, peasants' associations, and women's federations were revised several times. Every kind of professional organization had laws and regulations to follow, such as the trade union law, the peasants' associations law, the chambers of commerce law, the lawyers law, the news reporters law, the law on the oversight of charitable organizations, and the midwives law. In addition, a number of general laws governing all people's organizations were promulgated, including the law for mass organizations in extraordinary times, the general rules for the selection of staff members of mass organizations, and the ways for guiding organizational reform of mass organizations. For a number of influential and important civil society organizations, the government also promulgated detailed regulations concerning approval, registration, enrollment, elections, leadership, internal management, and collection and disbursement of funds.[11]

CSOs before Reform and Opening Up

After the Chinese Communist Party came to power in 1949, it implemented socialist public ownership of property and a mandatory planned economy as well as a highly centralized system of political power under the monolithic leadership of the CCP in the political sphere. The CCP abolished nearly all of the civil society organizations that had been established before 1949, including all the long-existing civic organizations that peasants had established in their villages, such as temple and clan associations, ancestral temples, village sage associations, and mass organizations. Only a small number of special groups, such as the China Democratic League and the "September 3 Society," groups that had assisted the CCP during the civil war, were allowed to continue to exist. The CCP created a number of mass organizations, such as trade unions, the CCYL, and women's federations, but their types and numbers were extremely limited. In the 1950s there were only forty-four national mass organizations; by 1965 their number had still not reached a hundred, and there were only about six thousand local mass organizations. Mass organizations were basically limited to nine types, including trade unions, the CCYL, women's federations, scientific societies, and industrial and commercial associations. This situation persisted without substantive change until the launching of reform and opening up in the late 1970s.[12]

CIVIL SOCIETY IN CHINA TODAY

After 1978 the reform and opening up policies instituted under the leadership of Deng Xiaoping brought fundamental changes to Chinese society, including fundamental changes in the economic, political, legal, and cultural environments that civil society depended on for its existence and development. This was the first time in China's history that social organizations were promoted on a large scale. At the end of the 1980s, China began reforms to reorient the economic system toward a greater use of market signals. It gradually abandoned the former planned economy and introduced a socialist market economy. It also transformed the monolithic system of ownership by collectives and the state into a diverse system that complemented ownership by the state and collectives with ownership by various forms of private ownership such as single proprietorship, joint venture, and foreign investment. These reforms greatly increased productive forces and raised people's standards of living. These conditions were the basic source of the surge in the growth of civil society organizations since 1978. In the 1980s China's political system underwent great reforms, many of which either directly or indirectly stimulated the development of civil society. For example, the government placed increased emphasis on the legal system and the rule of law; citizens' freedom of assembly began to take on more substantive meaning; and the government divested itself of considerable power and began to transform the functions it performed in the economy and society. The government stopped exercising direct supervision over most spheres of production, business, civil affairs, culture, the arts, and academic life, transferring many of its regulatory functions to civil society organizations, such as nongovernmental trade associations, professional organizations, and volunteer groups.

These changes in the economic and political environments set off a rapid expansion in civil society organizations beginning in the late 1980s. By 1989 there were 1,600 national mass organizations and more than 200,000 local ones. After the political turbulence in Beijing in 1989, the Chinese government required all mass organizations to undergo a process of reregistration and reapproval. As a result, the number of civic groups temporarily declined; by 1992 there were only 1,200 national mass organizations and 180,000 local ones. However, the number soon began climbing again. By 1997 the number of social associations at the county level or higher reached 180,000, of which 21,404 were at the provincial level and 1,848 were at the national level. By 1998 there were more than 700,000 civilian non-enterprise bodies.[13] It is difficult to get an accurate count of civil society organizations because the number of registrations of such groups has fluctuated widely. According to the most recent statistics, as of March 21, 2005, there were a total of 147,937 social associations of all kinds, 131,322 of which were civilian non-enterprise bodies and 714 of which were foundations.[14]

No official data on civil organizations below the county level are available at this time. Several scholars have made general estimates of the number of such organizations based on their own research. According to one estimate, more than 3 million civil society organizations currently exist in China. Some scholars have noted that at the end of 2003, China had 142,000 registered social associations, 124,000 registered civilian non-enterprise bodies, 40,000 unregistered social associations, and 250,000 unregistered civilian non-enterprise bodies. (The numbers for unregistered bodies are estimates made by officials of the Bureau for Supervising Civic Organizations of the Ministry of Civil Affairs.) At that time, there were an estimated 5,378,424 primary-level organizations of the eight major types of mass organizations (including trade unions, the Chinese Communist Youth League, women's federations, students' federations, peasants' associations, literary federations, friendship associations, and associations of industry and commerce); 1,338,220 quasi-governmental, primary-level social associations such as disabled persons' federations, family planning associations, and art and literature federations; and 758,700 grassroots organizations, such as students' groups, community recreational groups, homeowners' committees, and Internet groups. Thus, the total number of social associations is estimated to be 8,031,344.[15]

Perhaps more important than their numbers, the new civil society organizations were very different in nature from the social associations that existed before reform and opening up. By the early 1990s, civil society organizations had become much more citizen-oriented, self-determining, organized, voluntary, and legitimate.

CHAPTER FIVE

THE CHARACTERISTICS OF CHINESE CIVIL SOCIETY

Administrative Regulations and Institutional Environment

China's emerging civil society has several distinctive characteristics.[1] These are particularly evident in administrative regulations and the institutional environment, both of which have significantly shaped the formation and growth of Chinese civil society organizations (CSOs) in the reform era. To a great extent, administrative regulations and the institutional environment are closely intertwined. Administrative regulations concerning civil society organizations reflect the essence of the institutional environment in which these organizations operate. With its own distinct features, which largely reflect historical, cultural, and political factors, the institutional environment regulates and constrains the growth of China's civil society.

Administrative Regulations

Five main elements constitute the core of China's administrative regulations governing CSOs, namely, the constitution, ordinary laws, administrative statutes, party policies, and other informal regulations. These five elements complement each other and form a relatively comprehensive network that decisively influences the development of China's civil society. A discussion of these five elements is necessary to understand the institutional environment of Chinese civil society.

THE CONSTITUTION

The constitution is the basic law of the country. It determines the country's political nature, the organizational form of society, and the basic rights of citizens. It also provides the main legal framework for civil society. An important difference between traditional and modern political systems, or between dictatorial and democratic political systems, lies in whether a relatively independent civil society is permitted to exist.

At the end of the Qing dynasty, with the Manchu regime under pressure both internally and externally to undertake thorough-going political reforms, the government tried to transform the empire into a constitutional monarchy. In 1908 the Qing court promulgated the "imperial constitutional program," which stipulated that "within the scope prescribed by law, the emperor's subjects have freedom of speech, press, and association."[2] This gave civic associations legal recognition for the first time in Chinese history. After the Republic of China supplanted the Qing dynasty in 1912, the government promulgated a "provisional constitution," which clearly stated that "the people have the freedom to speak, write, publish, assemble, and form associations."[3] Although the constitution was revised several times thereafter, the right of the people to form civic associations was an inviolable principle in the Republic of China.[4]

After the founding of the People's Republic of China (PRC) in 1949, the right of citizens to form civic associations was affirmed in the constitution. "The Common Program of the Chinese People's Political Consultative Conference," which was promulgated as an interim constitution in 1949, stipulated that "the people of the PRC shall have freedom of thought, speech, publication, assembly, association, correspondence, person, domicile, change of domicile, religious belief, and the freedom of holding processions and demonstrations." The first constitution of the People's Republic, passed into law in 1954, reaffirmed the people's right of association. Major revisions were made to the constitution in 1975, 1978, and 1983, but the right of association, which guarantees the legality of civil society, was never deleted. Therefore, it can be said that, at least in principle, from China's first constitution until the present day, the right of civil society to exist has always received constitutional protection and has enjoyed basic legal status.

ORDINARY LAWS

The constitutional promise of the freedom to form civil associations is a prerequisite for the establishment of civil society, but an article in the constitution is far from enough to ensure its normal growth. This promise must be embodied in specific laws to have real meaning. In principle, these laws not only should clearly define the nature, position, and role of CSOs in the political and social life of the country but should also specify the scope of their activities as well as their legal responsibilities and social obligations. Because civic organizations play an important role in society and because many of them are legal entities that can become parties to civil disputes, two kinds of laws should apply to them—general laws pertaining to all civic organizations and special laws pertaining to particular kinds of civic associations.

In the Republic of China, the national government tried to create a relatively complete legal environment for civil society, promulgating a series of general and special laws concerning all kinds of civic organizations, such as the conventional law for associations; specific laws applying to cooperatives and the oversight of charitable organizations; and separate laws for fishermen's associations, chambers of commerce, education associations, trade associations, peasants' associations, and central academic societies. In addition, other laws dealt with matters concerning CSOs and had clauses in them concerning the regulation of the activities or functions of civic organizations. For example, the clauses of the General Principles of Civil Law concerning legal entities clearly specified the legal standing and responsibilities of civil society groups.[5]

China's current legal system, however, still does not have general laws concerning CSOs. The laws that do exist are of two kinds: ordinary laws that have clauses dealing with civic organizations and special laws that concentrate on a number of important CSOs. The first type includes the General Principles of Civil Law; the Civil Procedure Law; the Law of the PRC for Contributions to Public Service Institutions; laws promoting private education and scientific and technological progress; laws safeguarding the rights and interests of women, children, disabled persons, and returned overseas Chinese and their families; and individual laws applying to teachers, lawyers, sports, registered public accountants, and practicing doctors. These laws are not concerned solely with CSOs, but some of their clauses contain provisions concerning such groups in general and some address specific kinds of social organizations. For example, the Civil Law and the Civil Procedure Law specify the legal standing of CSOs and their legal responsibilities, and other laws deal with the rights and interests of particular kinds of CSOs in their work and the responsibilities they must fulfill.

The second kind of law includes the Organic Law of Villagers' Committees, the Organic Law of Neighborhood Committees, the Trade Union Law, and the Red Cross Law. They provide institutional safeguards for social organizations that the government considers important.

ADMINISTRATIVE STATUTES

Administrative statutes and government regulations refer to decrees, directives, and ordinances issued by government administrative bodies. Their main function is to put in place practical measures to implement the provisions of the constitution and other laws. Generally, government regulations usually state specific measures, rules, and instructions for implementing the state's ordinary laws. China currently does not have any general laws concerning civil organizations, and therefore most of the government regulations regarding civil organizations (except for specific measures for implementing ordinary laws) are concerned with civil organizations' nature, status, responsibilities, rights, and functions. Most of the government regulations concerning civil society originate from the central government, including its administrative bodies, or from local governments. Indeed, during both the Republic of China and the People's Republic, government regulations have constituted the largest part of the institutional environment of civil society.

CENTRAL GOVERNMENT REGULATIONS. Currently, the most important central government regulations regarding civil organizations are those governing the registration and supervision of social associations, civilian non-enterprise bodies, foundations, and foreign business associations. These regulations specify the position of CSOs in China's political life, their relation to government organizations, application procedures for their establishment and dissolution, their basic rights and legal obligations, the administrative system for government supervision, methods for financial oversight and auditing of these entities, the scope of activities of various kinds of civic organizations at various levels, and other matters. The regulations provide a basic institutional framework for the existence and development of civil society. The most important of the above-mentioned regulations are the Regulations Concerning the Registration and Supervision of Social Associations. The administrative system established by this body of law serves as the core of the system China currently uses to supervise CSOs.

Shortly after the founding of the PRC, the Government Administrative Council adopted interim measures for registering social associations in September 1950, and the Ministry of Internal Affairs adopted regulations to implement the interim registration measures in March 1951. These measures established a central principle for registering social associations at different levels, namely, that national associations should register with the Ministry of Internal Affairs and local associations at all levels should register with the appropriate government department at their level. Some scholars believe that the main reason for promulgating these statutes at the time was to deal with social associations remaining from the old society by getting them to reorganize and reregister. According to these scholars, "after completing this task, these two regulations gradually fell into disuse principally because various government departments took charge of approving and supervising bodies in their field, so the unified system of registration was no longer used."[6] Other scholars believe that the main reason these two regulations fell into disuse was the outbreak of the Cultural Revolution. According to one, "after the Cultural Revolution began in 1966, all kinds of rebel factional organizations were established in large numbers and started vying for power, but all kinds of legally registered social associations stopped functioning. Consequently, the institutional environment conducive to the growth of social associations was completely destroyed. This situation persisted until the end of the Cultural Revolution in 1976."[7]

After reform and opening up began in 1978, all kinds of CSOs proliferated, and the regulations promulgated in the 1950s were no longer suitable for the new situation. In order to strengthen supervision of all kinds of rapidly emerging civic organizations, the Central Committee of the Chinese Communist Party (CCP) and the State Council in 1984 jointly issued the Notice on Strictly Limiting the Establishment of National Organizations. The Commission for Restructuring the Economy, which was then responsible for supervising social associations, revised its policies in keeping with the spirit of this notice and subjected national social associations to strict approval procedures and supervision. However, these interim policy regulations could not meet the development needs of CSOs. Therefore, in 1987 the Ministry of Civil Affairs, under the auspices of the State Council, drafted the Regulations Concerning the Registration and Supervision of Social Associations. This set of regulations was then promulgated and implemented by the State Council in October 1989, and since that time these regulations have played a very important role in encouraging and standardizing all kinds of CSOs.

As the market economy grew and democratic demands expanded, CSOs constantly exhibited new characteristics, and the new regulations quickly became incompatible with the development needs of China's civil society. The Ministry of Civil Affairs therefore again undertook a substantial revision of these rules, and a new set of regulations was promulgated in the form of State Council Decree 250 in 1998. Although the regulations were revised several times since the middle of the twentieth century, the institutional framework for CSOs, involving dual supervision and registration at various levels of government, still has not changed substantially since it was established in the 1950s.

REGULATIONS BY ADMINISTRATIVE DEPARTMENTS OF THE STATE COUNCIL. Regulations promulgated by various administrative departments of the State Council include all kinds of specific directives, including rules and regulations for implementation, supplementary provisions, departmental policies, and concrete measures formulated by the ministries and commissions of the State Council in accordance with their administrative responsibilities. The most important characteristic of departmental regulations is that they are operational and targeted—they are the means by which the central government's decrees can be effectively implemented. In terms of numbers, it takes far more departmental regulations than central government regulations to standardize all kinds of CSOs. These regulations are generally of three kinds: regulations of the Ministry of Civil Affairs—the ministry of the State Council with primary responsibility for supervising civic organizations; regulations of the various ministries and commissions tasked with supervising CSOs whose activities involve matters under their jurisdiction; and laws and regulations jointly promulgated by the Ministry of Civil Affairs and other ministries and commissions of the State Council. The Ministry of Civil Affairs has published on its website more than fifty decrees and regulations concerning the supervision of civil organizations.[8]

LOCAL GOVERNMENT REGULATIONS. Local supervision of CSOs takes place at three levels: the provincial level (including municipalities directly under the central government and autonomous regions); the regional level (including prefectural cities and municipal districts); and the county level (including county-level cities). Most local ordinances are specific measures to implement central authorities' documents and state regulations. Zhejiang Province, for example, in recent years passed ordinances for supervising civilian non-enterprise bodies (2000, 2004), regulating the activities and professional registration of social associations (2002), and requiring annual inspections of civilian non-enterprise bodies (2002).

The regulations promulgated by local governments at every level have local characteristics grounded in the specific conditions of the localities. Some economically developed cities pay particular attention to cultivating and regulating industry associations. For example, the Shanghai municipality promulgated three regulations concerning industry associations in 2002 alone, including one to promote the development of trade associations. Some provinces where agriculture is important pay particular attention to farmers' economic cooperative organizations. For example, in 2004 Jiangxi Province issued an Opinion Concerning the Trial Implementation of Professional Village Economic Associations in Jiangxi Province and a Notice of the Jiangxi Provincial Civil Affairs Office on Doing a Good Job of Promoting the Development and Supervising the Registration of Professional Village Economic Associations throughout Jiangxi Province.

PARTY POLICY REGULATIONS

In China's unique political circumstances, the party forms the government and guides the people in formulating laws, and therefore state laws embody the will of the ruling party to a considerable extent. The policy regulations of the ruling party have authority and validity equal to legal regulations of the state, and in some sense play an even more decisive role. The formal documents and policies of the CCP Central Committee and its leading departments, including directives, notices, announcements, regulations, measures, opinions, ordinances, standards, and decisions, as well as the instructions, writings, and formal speeches of the highest leader of the party, have the same authority as the documents of the Central Committee and constitute the policies and regulations of the party.

During the period of the Republic of China, it was normal for regulations of the ruling party to replace state laws in the supervision of CSOs. Some scholarly research has discovered that during the Republic, most of the important laws and regulations for supervising CSOs were not state laws but were issued by of the Central Executive Committee of the Nationalist Party, or Kuomintang (KMT). For example, in the 1930s the KMT Central Executive Committee promulgated many important regulations that constituted the basic institutional framework for the supervision of civic organizations by the government authorities at that time. These included the Revised Plan for Guiding Mass Activities, Revised Plan of Mass Organizations, Guiding Principles for Organizations, Measures for Putting Mass Organizations in Order, Measures for a General Review of National Mass Organizations, Regulations Concerning Reporting about Mass Movements, Revised Measures for Restructuring Mass Organizations, Brief Rules for Registering Membership of Mass Organizations, Revised General Rules for Issuing Permits to Mass Organizations, Revised Rules for Granting Operating Subsidies to Mass Organizations, Revised General Rules for Electing Officers of Mass Organizations, and Revised Measures for Reporting Disputes in Mass Organizations. In effect, the policies and regulations of the KMT were the most significant component of the institutional environment of civil society during the era of the Republic.[9]

Since the advent of reform and opening up in 1978, the CCP has particularly stressed the goal of ruling the country by law, and its basic way of exercising power has been to use the state's laws and regulations to supervise social affairs, including the activities of CSOs. As the party's governing capacity has improved, its direct intervention in, and supervision of, CSOs has consistently declined. As a result, contrary to the situation in the Republic of China, where the KMT supplanted the government by directly supervising CSOs, in the current period PRC state laws and regulations serve as the principal means by which the party and government carry out the normal supervision of CSOs. At the same time, it is undeniable that the CCP sets the direction in which civil society develops, and party policies are essentially the compass that directs the state's legislative work. It is also true that the party's policies and stipulations are still the most important components of the institutional environment of civil society. The party guides and regulates the development of civil society in the following three ways.

First, the party carries out macropolitical and macroeconomic restructuring, creating the institutional spaces in which civil society can develop. Since the beginning of reform and opening up, and especially since the early 1990s, the CCP Central Committee has constantly promoted the socialist market economy and the transformation of government functions. The central authorities have transferred selected government functions to intermediary social organizations and industrial associations. At the same time, the party has vigorously promoted the development of socialist democracy and stressed the role of primary-level self-governing organizations. These policies created the basic political conditions for the creation and development of CSOs. For example, the Fifteenth National Congress of the CCP made the important decision to put great effort into developing the so-called intermediary social organizations (institutions linking the government and social groups or individuals), thus vigorously promoting their development. The Fourth Plenary Session of the Sixteenth CCP Central Committee passed the Decision of the CCP Central Committee Concerning Strengthening the Party's Governing Capacity, which emphasized the important role social associations, intermediary organizations, and industrial associations play in supervising society. This document called for "expanding the role of urban and rural primary-level self-governing organizations in harmonizing interests, resolving conflicts, and mediating disputes; expanding the role of social associations, industry organizations, and social intermediary organizations in providing services, reporting grievances and requests, and standardizing behavior; and making concerted efforts to provide social supervision and social services."[10]

Second, on the basis of real needs, the party guides the government in passing legislation or formulating policies and regulations to directly stimulate the development of certain kinds of civic organizations or to carry out overall regulation of the development of civic organizations. For example, to solve more quickly the problems facing agriculture, rural areas, and farmers, the CCP Central Committee issued several "Annual No. 1 Documents" in various years, vigorously promoting the growth of rural development cooperative organizations. These documents urged party committees at every level to promulgate a series of policies to encourage rural mutual assistance cooperatives in professional, technical, and economic fields. The Ministry of Civil Affairs quickly formulated corresponding measures and promulgated the Guiding Opinions Concerning Strengthening the Cultivation and Development of Rural Professional and Economic Associations and their Registration and Supervision (2003), which simplified the registration procedures for rural cooperative organizations. In addition, because the growth of social associations seemed to be too fast, in the mid-1980s the CCP Central Committee and the State Council together issued the Notice Concerning Strictly Controlling the Establishment of National Organizations. The State Commission for Restructuring the Economy, which at that time was responsible for supervising social associations, revised its policies to conform with this notice and subjected national social associations to a strict examination and approval process, after which the Ministry of Civil Affairs was commissioned by the State Council to draft the Regulations Concerning the Registration and Supervision of Social Associations. Further, in July 1996 the general offices of the CCP Central Committee and the State Council jointly issued the Notice Concerning Intensifying Supervision of Social Associations and Civilian Non-enterprise Bodies, which made a series of legislative proposals, including revising the regulations for registering and supervising social associations and drafting interim measures for registering and supervising privately run economic entities. In August 1998 the general office of the CCP Central Committee issued a Notice Concerning Further Strengthening Supervision of Social Associations and Civilian Non-enterprise Bodies, which implemented the requirements embodied in the spirit of the 1996 notice. On this basis, the State Council in October 1998 issued revisions to its regulations on registration and supervision of social associations and privately run economic entities. In 1999 the general offices of the CCP Central Committee and the State Council issued a Notice Concerning Further Strengthening Supervision of Civil Organizations, after which the Ministry of Civil Affairs issued the Opinions Concerning Reexamining and Registering Civilian Non-enterprise Bodies.

Third, to strengthen and improve the party's leadership of mass organizations, the party established clear rules concerning founding party organizations in CSOs and the positions of leading party cadres in them. For example, the Organization Department of the CCP Central Committee and the Ministry of Civil Affairs jointly issued a Notice Concerning Issues Pertaining to Establishing Party Organizations in Social Associations in 1998. In the same year, the general offices of the CCP Central Committee and the State Council issued a Notice Forbidding Leading Cadres of the Party and Government from Simultaneously Holding Leading Positions in Social Associations, after which the Ministry of Civil Affairs issued an explanation of the notice. In 2000 the Organization Department of the CCP Central Committee separately issued Opinions Concerning Strengthening Party-Building in Social Associations, after which the General Office of the Ministry of Civil Affairs issued a Notice Concerning Transmission of the Opinions Concerning Strengthening Party-Building in Social Associations.

INFORMAL INSTITUTIONS

Informal institutions refer to informal rules that have not been promulgated in official documents but that nevertheless continue to influence the development of civil society. Implicit rules are a kind of informal institution. Officials' attitudes and the customary orientation of political culture and political traditions toward civil society are the most important informal rules affecting China's civil society. Informal rules are difficult to study because they are diffused throughout daily life and ordinary ways of speaking. However, detailed observation and analysis reveal some very interesting discoveries regarding these informal rules.

Recent research has shown that party and government officials at all levels have a complex and contradictory attitude toward civil organizations. On the one hand, they saw that China's implementation of a socialist market economy was followed by a transformation of government functions and that some government functions were given to civil organizations. Therefore, the rise of civil society was not only inevitable but also had its benefits. Officials generally had an affirmative, supportive, and encouraging attitude toward social organizations that help the poor or work for their members' mutual benefit or the public good because they enrich people's personal lives and promote community harmony, so these leaders adopted a series of measures to support such groups and make full use of their positive contributions. For example, local party and government leaders tacitly gave a green light to grassroots civil organizations and their activities so long as these posed no threat to the government, approving of events such as flower fairs, temple fairs, lantern festivals, retirees' fairs, and folk-dancing fairs, even if they were not registered with the civil affairs authorities.

On the other hand, many officials harbor a dread of civil society organizations. They are afraid such organizations will grow to the point where they become uncontrollable and the tail starts to wag the dog. In addition, they fear that after CSOs mature, they will become adversaries of the party and government. Therefore, these officials are wary of such organizations and are constantly on guard. The leaders of some party and government departments are particularly concerned about CSOs whose work pertains to politics, ethnic groups, religion, human rights, and ideology, as well as about foreign nongovernmental organizations and foundations and the domestic civil organizations they work with. Officials often keep these civil organizations under surveillance, frequently stop their activities, and limit their development. A typical example occurred during the SARS (severe acute respiratory syndrome) outbreak in 2003. The government used the pretext of standardizing the donations market to designate two official nonprofit organizations as recipients of SARS donations and prohibit all other nonprofits from accepting donations. This indirectly reveals the thorough-going distrust that some government officials have of nonprofits.[11]

Ordinary citizens also lack faith in civil society. One of the basic orientations of China's traditional political culture is to overvalue government and undervalue the unofficial organizations, which in this case means that faith in government bodies greatly exceeds faith in CSOs. When people encounter institutions or organizations whose nature is unclear, the first thing they will ask is, "What kind of establishment is this? Does it belong to the government or not?" In the minds of many people, a body can be trusted only if it belongs to the government. According to a report by the Women's Law Research and Assistance Center, a civil organization affiliated with Peking University School of Law, many people are accustomed to considering "unofficial" as "nongovernmental," which they think of as unorganized and anarchistic. They think civil organizations are watched by the government and are frequently suspected of improperly involving themselves in sensitive matters. The primary limitation to the development of civil organizations is thus perceptual. This way of thinking leaves many people unprepared to accept CSOs.[12] This distrust and scorn for civic organizations in China's traditional political culture greatly inhibits the healthy maturation of China's civil society.

The Institutional Environment of China's Civil Society

The characteristics of China's civil society discussed here are intimately related to the institutional environment in which it exists. A comprehensive analysis of the formal and informal institutional environment constraining China's civil society reveals the following general characteristics.

Macro Encouragement and Micro Restrictions

Overall, China's institutional environment has been beneficial to the rapid growth of civil society during the reform period. First of all, the constitution and the CCP's principal policies basically take a positive attitude toward CSOs, laying a legal foundation for the existence of Chinese civil society. The constitution promulgated in 1982 confirmed freedom of association as one of the basic rights of Chinese citizens. Since the initiation of the reform and opening-up policy in 1978, a whole series of important steps and policies formulated by the CCP have created legal and institutional space for the development of civil organizations. These steps include promoting the socialist market economy, carrying out rural and urban structural reform, promoting villagers' self-governance and other primary-level democracy, establishing socialist rule of law and political civilization, encouraging the separation of party and government, promoting the separation of government and business, and raising the party's governing capacity. In addition, economic restructuring focused on the rural land contract responsibility system and on the market economy created realistic conditions for fostering civil organizations. After the 1980s China began to institute market-oriented economic restructuring, gradually abandoning the former planned economy in favor of the socialist market economy, and it changed the original unitary system of ownership by collectives and the state to a diverse system of state, collective, and private ownership by single owners, partnerships, and foreign owners. These changes greatly expanded productive forces, raised people's standards of living, and established an economic basis for the vigorous development of civil organizations. Further, since the 1980s numerous important changes have occurred in China's political system that have directly or indirectly facilitated the development of civil society. For example, the government has continually paid greater attention to the legal system and the rule of law, and citizens' freedom of assembly has begun to take on more substantive meaning. The government has delegated many of its operational, decisionmaking, and human resources powers to enterprises and most of its economic responsibilities to society. It has also gradually relaxed its supervision over citizens, giving rise to an unprecedented increase in citizens' freedom of action. Finally, the government has begun to transform its functions. In most areas of production, business, civil affairs, culture, arts, and academic affairs, the government no longer exercises direct supervisory functions but has transferred those functions to civil organizations such as nongovernmental industry associations, professional associations, and volunteer groups.[13]

While it can be said that China's macro-institutional environment is generally favorable for the development of civil society, its micro-institutional environment is generally negative for five reasons. First, the laws and regulations of government departments that directly affect civil organizations are oriented toward controlling and restricting these organizations. For example, most of the laws and regulations promulgated by civil affairs departments from the central to local levels are supervisory in nature, and very few of them have encouraging clauses. Second, government regulatory departments focus on issues of entry and erect obstacles to the establishment and registration of civil organizations. For example, there are strict regulations concerning the names, structure, location, staff size, spending, charter, and regulatory affairs. Third, CSOs are subject to duplicate supervision. The law stipulates that all civic organizations must submit not only to the oversight of government civil affairs departments but also to the leadership of agencies responsible for their area of professional activities, and that these agencies generally have the primary responsibility for supervision. Fourth, the spending, scope, and content of CSOs' activities are strictly limited. For example, laws and regulations concerning supervision stipulate that civic organizations can operate only within designated localities and can engage only in the activities approved when they register; any other activities are considered illegal. Fifth, the government exercises overall control over CSOs similar to its overall control of the economy. When civic organizations expand quickly in a short period of time or when an unusual domestic political development occurs, the CCP Central Committee, the State Council, and various government departments issue documents or policies requiring that civic organizations be investigated and put in order. For example, in 1984, 1989, 1996, 1998, 1999, and 2004 the CCP Central Committee and the State Council published important documents exercising control over the development of CSOs.[14]

HIERARCHICAL REGISTRATION AND DUAL SUPERVISION

China has not yet passed a formal law concerning CSOs; currently the Regulations Concerning the Registration and Supervision of Social Associations and the Regulations Concerning the Supervision of Civilian Non-enterprise Bodies are the most important laws affecting social associations. These two regulations establish the basic framework for government supervision of CSOs, namely, the model of hierarchical registration and dual supervision.

The basic content of this kind of supervisory system is that all CSOs must simultaneously accept dual leadership from the civil affairs department at their level and the government department responsible for their area of activity. The civil affairs department is responsible for approving and registering them, and the other department is responsible for regular supervision.

Hierarchical registration means that, at the county level or above, civil affairs departments of the people's government are responsible for approval, registration, annual inspections, modification, dissolution, and oversight of civil organizations. According to this system, civic organizations that operate nationwide are approved and registered by the Ministry of Civil Affairs; organizations that operate locally are approved by local government's civil affairs departments at all levels from the county level or above. Civic organizations that operate across administrative boundaries are approved by the civil affairs departments of the next higher level of government. Specifically, civil affairs departments at all levels that are the statutory bodies for approving and registering civil organizations are responsible for examining and approving CSOs that have been accepted by the responsible professional agency; carrying out statutory procedures of registration, annual inspection, modification, and dissolution for CSOs in their locality that have received approval; formulating supervisory principles, policies, regulations, and oversight procedures for social associations and civilian non-enterprise bodies; conducting the registration and annual inspection of domestic CSOs (including civilian non-enterprise bodies and social associations of Hong Kong and Taiwan people in the Chinese mainland), social associations of foreigners in China, and agencies of international social associations in China; guiding the activities of CSOs, and studying and proposing plans for the development of civic organizations, including standards for membership dues and measures for financial management; and overseeing the activities of civil organizations and investigating any of these groups' activities that appear illegal as well as any organizations that have not registered and are operating illegally under the guise of social associations.[15]

The regulations stipulate that the responsible professional agencies for industry, academic, and professional social associations are the relevant departments of the State Council and the local people's governments from the county level or above, as well as organizations empowered by the State Council and local governments. According to the current model of dual supervision, the main regulatory functions of departments that supervise civil organizations are to approve and appoint the main leaders, including the president, vice president, members of the executive council, and secretary general of the CSOs under their supervision; to approve their major activities; to oversee their daily work; to provide professional guidance for their activities; and to audit their finances. In addition to the principle of hierarchical approval and registration, the professional departments also implement hierarchical principles. In other words, according to differences in the areas of jurisdiction or administrative levels of departments responsible for supervising civic organizations, the administrative level of a supervising body and the bodies it registers and supervises will in principle be the same. For example, the supervising body for national civil organizations must be a ministry or commission at the central level, and CSOs that operate throughout a province must be supervised by a provincial-level party or government body. Therefore, the practice of dual supervision in the current supervision model of CSOs and the system of hierarchical registration and supervision are mutually complementary.

Dual Supervision Leading to Multiple Supervision

The system of dual supervision leads inevitably to multiple supervision. Dual supervision requires that every civil society organization must accept dual leadership from a government supervising body and a professional regulatory body of the relevant civil affairs department, the latter providing leadership of its regular professional activities. The regulations provide only general rules. Party and government bodies at and above the county level and bodies appointed by governments at and above the county level may all become functioning regulatory bodies of civic organizations. The inevitable consequence of this is the proliferation of such regulatory bodies. It is evident that different functional departments of the party and government frequently become regulatory bodies of civil organizations under their jurisdiction. For example, the organization departments of party committees at all levels are generally the regulatory bodies of party research institutions at the same level; the united front departments are regulatory bodies for united front research centers at the same level; government cultural offices and bureaus are regulatory bodies for all kinds of unofficial cultural groups; sports bureaus or sports commissions are regulatory bodies for all kinds of unofficial sports groups; and science and technology commissions, offices, and bureaus are regulatory bodies for all kinds of mass science and technology groups.

Not only do the functional departments of the party and government become mothers-in-law to all kinds of civil groups within the scope of their authority, but in fact for various reasons many CSOs have to look elsewhere for an appropriate mother-in-law, and many mothers-in-law have little relationship with the fields in which the civil organizations they supervise operate. For example, a government cultural bureau might supervise a people's fitness association while a government sports committee might supervise a people's arts association, and a government science commission might supervise a training center while an education commission supervises a civil science and technology service center. Civil society organizations with relatively abundant resources, especially well-funded industry supervision organizations, have to accept leadership not only from the regulatory bodies for their industry, but also, directly or indirectly, from other important party and government bodies.

STATE LAWS AND PARTY POLICIES

Government laws and regulations and party policies are mutually complementary, and both are authoritative standards for the supervision of civil organizations. Together they constitute the basic institutional environment of China's civil society. Every leading party body and government organ of power from the central to the local level has responsibilities for supervising civil organizations. The basic purpose of government supervision of civic organizations is to improve and strengthen party leadership of civic organizations. Government regulation of civic organizations relies principally on state law and administrative regulations, and party regulation relies mainly on party policies. These policies take two forms: formal documents, directives, notices, regulations, measures, opinions, rules, standards, and decisions of the CCP Central Committee and local party committees at every level; and informal instructions, directives, speeches, and writings of party leaders at every level. Party policies concerning the supervision of CSOs are similar to government laws and regulations. Vertically, party committees from the CCP Central Committee to local committees all have a series of policy documents concerning the regulation and supervision of CSOs; horizontally, party committee departments, such as the general office, organization department, publicity department, and united front department, all have the power to formulate supervisory policies within the scope of their responsibilities. In recent years, these leading party committee departments have issued a stream of policy documents in the spirit of the CCP Central Committee's documents and have become an important component of the supervision of civic organizations.

The coexistence of government laws and regulations and party policies concerning the supervision of civic organizations reflects to a certain extent the unique relationship in the current Chinese political situation between the party and the government, between law and policy, and between the rule of leaders and the rule of law. On the one hand, establishing the rule of law in China is both an objective of the CCP constitution and a goal of the PRC constitution. Party organizations and leaders at all levels must operate within the scope of the constitution and the law. The rule of leaders is gradually being supplanted by the rule of law, and party policies are daily yielding precedence to laws, while in the country's political life party decisions are becoming supervisory tools subordinate to the law. China still has a long way to go to achieve the objective of ruling the country by law. The rule of leaders still plays a very important role in the social and political life of the country, and policy plays a more important role than law in many circumstances.

Institutional Excesses and Deficiencies

The coexistence of institutional excesses and deficiencies is a hallmark of the institutional environment of China's civil society. On the one hand, many regulations concerning civil organizations are redundant, overlapping, or trifling. For example, the regulations include not only the State Council's regulations on social associations and the Ministry of Civil Affairs' rules and regulations for implementation, but also supervisory rules promulgated jointly by the Ministry of Civil Affairs and other ministries and commissions, as well as those put forth independently by such ministries and commissions. Some local governments also formulate numerous implementation measures for supervising civil organizations. Not only do provincial-level governments or regulatory bodies have their own provisions, rules, and regulations for implementation, but regional, municipal, and county governments also have their own measures and official opinions. Not only do government civil affairs and professional regulatory departments formulate numerous laws, regulations and rules, but party committees and governments at all levels also occasionally issue important regulatory documents and policy measures as circumstances require. There are too many of these rules and regulations, and they create an institutional excess in the process of supervising civil society.

Institutional excess is most obvious in the overlapping functions of government civil affairs regulatory bodies and functional regulatory bodies in the supervision of the same civil organization. The regulations currently in effect stipulate that bodies that register and supervise CSOs have three oversight responsibilities. They are responsible for registering the formation, modification, and dissolution of social associations and civilian non-enterprise bodies; conducting annual inspections of social associations, civilian non-enterprise bodies, foundations, and representative bodies of foreign foundations; and investigating allegations of violations of regulations by social associations and privately run enterprises and administering penalties for such violations. Likewise, functional bodies responsible for supervising civil organizations have five responsibilities. They are responsible for approving the establishment, modification, and dissolution of social associations and civilian non-enterprise bodies and for overseeing and guiding these entities, ensuring that these groups observe the state's Constitution, laws, regulations and policies, and engage in activities in accordance with their charters. They make preliminary investigations of associations and civilian non-enterprise bodies ahead of these bodies' annual inspections, and they assist the registered regulatory body and other agencies in investigating illegal activities of social associations and civilian non-enterprise bodies. Finally, they guide, together with other agencies, social associations and civilian non-enterprise bodies in their liquidation. It is easy to see that the functions of the two kinds of regulators overlap. This is a great waste of institutional and government resources. In addition, institutional duplication does not necessarily make government guidance of civil organizations more effective; on the contrary, it generally weakens it. The original intent in setting up the system was to make it doubly safe by duplicating approval and responsibility, but in practice overlapping and duplicate responsibilities readily lead to both agencies shirking their responsibilities, leaving gaps in oversight. In addition, the oversight tasks and responsibilities of the functional supervising body are invariably greater than those of the registering body, but they do not receive any payment for their efforts, so they lack incentives to carry out their oversight functions. Yet once they receive supervisory fees paid by the civic organizations they oversee, they usually let the organizations do whatever they please. The supervising bodies that register civil organizations readily ignore routine oversight because the functional supervising bodies have primary responsibility for it. In the end, the duplicate supervision system degenerates into a mere formality.[16]

Alongside the institutional duplication, there are also large gaps in the supervision of civil organizations, which are evident in three ways. First, there is no comprehensive law for the supervision of CSOs. Currently supervision rests mainly on several regulations of the State Council, which are not formal state laws. Only a few formal laws, such as the Trade Union Law, touch on the supervision of civic organizations, and most of these are special laws. China still does not have a mother law for supervising civic organizations. Second, there is a lack of directed and operational regulations. For example, no regulations are directed specifically at various categories of civil organizations, such as industry associations, professional groups, academic groups, federations of social associations, or volunteer work. Some scholars point out that China's current system of supervision lacks general laws and regulations concerning what entities constitute CSOs and regulating their qualifications, activities, property, responsibilities, and oversight. Third, many existing regulations are already relatively unsuitable to the current circumstances. Some scholars believe that a considerable portion of regulations concerning civic organizations are "too complex, opaque, and difficult to understand" and that their "technical details are crude, their content is general and vague, and they are difficult to apply."[17]

These institutional deficiencies invariably leave many CSOs at a loss as to what to do; even some that have been set up under the auspices of the central government are confused. For example, in recent years, the central authorities have especially encouraged farmers' occupational and cooperative organizations, but in many places throughout the country these organizations have encountered institutional difficulties. For instance, the Fourteenth Session of the Standing Committee of the Tenth Zhejiang Provincial People's Congress passed China's first regulations concerning farmers' professional cooperative organizations on November 11, 2004. According to the third article of these regulations, the bodies that this regulation calls farmers' professional cooperative organizations are defined using the family contract responsibility system. Such organizations operate under the principles of voluntary participation, with freedom to withdraw, democratic supervision, and profits returned to the members. According to their charter, they are mutual assistance economic organizations that engage in common production, business, and service activities. However, this definition does not give farmers' professional cooperative organizations clear legal standing because "mutual assistance economic entities" can be either enterprise or non-enterprise economic organizations. Because their legal standing is not clear, their development is constrained by a series of legal, institutional, and tax factors. Whether cooperatives are economic, social association, or cooperative legal entities is not given clear legal specification. The farmers' professional cooperative organizations in Wenling in Zhejiang Province registered as stock cooperative enterprises and are treated as such by tax agencies and financial institutions for the purposes of assessing taxes and making loans. At the same time, however, the nineteenth article of the Regulations of Zhejiang Province Concerning Farmers' Professional Cooperative Organizations stipulates that the sale by cooperatives of agricultural goods produced by members of the cooperatives should be treated the same as goods produced and sold by households. Primary-level agricultural goods produced and sold by farmers are not subject to tax, but if the goods are turned over to a cooperative for sale, then they are subject to tax. This greatly undermines farmers' enthusiasm for establishing and joining cooperatives. In addition, seeds, fertilizers, and pesticides are sold exclusively by agricultural supplies agencies, and the slaughter and sale of pigs is under the unified control of food companies. This kind of business system greatly confines possible cooperatives' scope of operations and places them at a competitive disadvantage in the market relative to other players that specialize in this area. Another problem is the difficulty of getting financing. Farmers' cooperative organizations register with administrations for industry and commerce as legal persons, but banks do not recognize their status as legal entities and do not grant them loans. They can get loans only in the names of their individual members, who must pledge their property as collateral. This is not beneficial for expanding the scale of rural professional cooperative organizations.[18]

ACTUAL AND INSTITUTIONAL SPACE

The institutional space for CSOs is much smaller than their actual space, a fact that is another important characteristic of China's institutional environment. Institutional space is here interpreted as the space allotted to civil organizations by China's regulatory laws and regulations, whereas actual space is interpreted as the physical space civic organizations have. A typical example of how civil society's actual space exceeds its institutional space is the fact that the number of existing civil organizations greatly exceeds the number formally registered with government departments. The Chinese government published data in March 2005 showing that about 149,000 social associations, 132,000 civilian non-enterprise bodies, and almost 1,000 foundations—a total of 282,000—were registered with civil affairs agencies at the four levels of government. However, scholars estimate that numerous nongovernmental organizations have not registered with civil affairs agencies. It is impossible to determine their exact numbers because there are no reliable statistics, but a conservative estimate puts the number between 2 million and 2.7 million.[19] The National Conference on Developing Village Occupational Economic Associations held by the Ministry of Civil Affairs revealed that at the end of 2004 there were already 100,000 village occupational economic associations throughout the country, but just slightly more than 10,000 had registered with civil affairs departments.[20] A research study done by Tsinghua University shows that in addition to legally registered civic organizations, China currently has at least ten kinds of extralegal civil organizations: nonprofits registered with administrations for industry and commerce, primary-level urban community organizations, social associations affiliated with various kinds of bodies, village community development organizations, farmers' cooperative organizations, village community public welfare or mutual assistance organizations, foreign financial aid organizations, foreign project organizations in China, foreign chambers of commerce and industry associations in China, and religious groups.[21]

An interesting phenomenon is that the institutional space within China's civil society varies considerably depending on variations in the standards for attaining legal standing. Relatively speaking, the institutional space for civic organizations required to register with civil affairs agencies is the smallest. Civic organizations that are not required to register with civil affairs agencies but that the government views as legally constituted have more institutional space. These organizations tend to be of two kinds. The first are the civic organizations that the CCP Central Committee, the State Council, or the Ministry of Civil Affairs have specially designated as not needing to register. For example, the Ministry of Civil Affairs has issued a notice clearly exempting three kinds of social associations from having to register: people's organizations that belong to the Chinese People's Political Consultative Conference (CPPCC); social associations approved by regulatory agencies under the State Council and exempted from registration by the State Council; and groups that are established by institutions, agencies, and enterprises and that operate within them. The notice enumerates rules and regulations for these organizations, pointing out that the following people's organizations belong to the CPPCC: the All-China Federation of Trade Unions, the Chinese Communist Youth League, All-China Women's Federation, the China Science and Technology Association, the All-China Federation of Returned Overseas Chinese, the All-China Federation of Taiwan Compatriots, the All-China Youth Federation, and the All-China Federation of Industry and Commerce. It points out that the following social associations have been exempted from registration by the State Council: the All-China Federation of Literary and Art Circles, the Chinese Writers Association, the All-China Journalists Association, the Chinese People's Association for Friendship with Foreign Countries, the Chinese People's Institute of Foreign Affairs, the China Council for the Promotion of International Trade, the China Disabled Persons' Federation, the Soong Ching Ling Foundation, the China Law Society, the Red Cross Society of China, the Chinese Workers' Ideological and Political Work and Study Association, the Western-Returned Students' Association, the Whampoa Military Academy Alumni Association, and the Chinese Professional Education Association.[22]

The second are CSOs established with the encouragement of party committees and governments at all levels under the instructions of higher-level committees and governments to meet work needs, such as the widespread and numerous farmer cooperative organizations. There are no formal regulations stipulating that organizations like these are exempt from approval and registration, but because they are established at the urging of the party and government, they are always considered to be legal even though they have not been approved or registered by a civil affairs department. A survey of civic organizations in one city revealed that the municipal civil affairs department had formally registered 163 civic organizations, but the civil affairs department had records of more than 1,200 civic organizations that had not undergone formal approval and registration. The latter number is seven times more than the former. A spokesman for that municipal civil affairs department added that there were even more civil organizations for which the civil affairs department had no records.[23]

Concluding Thoughts

The growth of the market economy has brought with it the gradual rise of China's civil society, which is exerting an ever-increasing influence on China's social and political life. CSOs, which are the constituent elements of civil society, must be nongovernmental, not-for-profit, and independent; and membership in them must be voluntary. The existence and development of such organizations in Chinese society since the inauguration of the reform and opening-up policy differs profoundly from those in the preceding period. CSOs in China are also very different from those in the West.

The vast majority of China's CSOs were established by the government and are led by the government; this is especially true of the most influential civil organizations, which are legally registered groups such as industry organizations, professional organizations, academic associations, and interest groups. Although the CCP and the Chinese government have tried to increase the independence of CSOs and have repeatedly issued documents stating that officials in party and government departments may not hold leading positions in civic organizations and civilian non-enterprise bodies, government dominance of civic organizations remains a prominent feature of China's civil society.

Compared with their counterparts in Western countries, China's civic organizations are still very immature, are not entirely independent nor voluntary, and are not always nongovernmental, which are typical characteristics of their Western counterparts. The vast majority of China's civic organizations began to come to the fore after the mid-1980s, and thus have had less than twenty years in which to mature. They are currently in the process of change and growth, and neither their structure nor their functions have yet taken on a set form. For example, the latest government regulations require all civic organizations to separate themselves from the government, yet the government bodies the organizations are attached to guide their important activities. In addition, a number of civic organizations are directly guided and controlled by the government and are not as independent, voluntary, and nongovernmental as civic organizations need to be. Additionally, some civic organizations are at the other extreme—they have been formed by the spontaneous initiatives of the people, they are not registered with government departments, and they receive no guidance from the government. The transitional nature of CSOs is just one aspect of similar changes taking place throughout the whole of Chinese society.

CHAPTER SIX

CIVIL SOCIETY ORGANIZATIONS
Challenges and Responses

Despite the multitude of differing views on China's civil society, there is at least a consensus in the country that Chinese civil society is rapidly growing along with the development of the market economy and political development.[1] It has been widely noted that civil society organizations (CSOs) are playing an important role in the political, economic, and social life of the country. However, China's civil society must solve many problems and overcome a lot of difficulties, the most pressing of which arise from its institutional environment.

This assessment has been verified by several public opinion surveys. The Peking University Social Groups Research Center recently did a massive investigation of civil organizations in Zhejiang Province and Beijing using questionnaires administered over the course of two years. To the question "What factors are the most detrimental to the development of civil organizations?" 38.7 percent of the Beijing respondents (40.8 percent of those from Zhejiang) said the organizations lacked funds or an operating site, or both; 33.4 percent (22.7 percent in Zhejiang) said the supervisory system was too strict or chaotic and there were too many restrictions; 22.8 percent (20.5 percent in Zhejiang) said their position and legal status were not sufficiently clear and relevant laws were inadequate; and 22.0 percent (19.9 percent in Zhejiang) said the government did not attach sufficient importance to them.[2] A nationwide sample survey of social associations by Tsinghua University's NGO [nongovernmental organization] Research Center in 2000 revealed that the main problems facing civil organizations are lack of funds, lack of availability of sites to hold activities, shortage of operating equipment, insufficient government support, lack of personnel, lack of information exchanges and training opportunities, inadequate laws and regulations, inadequately standardized internal supervision, and excessive government interference.[3]

Some scholars enumerate eight institutional predicaments that beleaguer China's civil society:

—The registration predicament. Registration itself is difficult, required annual inspections are complicated, finding a sponsor is difficult, and start-up costs are high. As a result, many CSOs are unwilling or unable to register and end up operating in a legal limbo.

—The function predicament. The administrative functions of some academic societies and similar associations have become so prominent that the groups have become quasi-governmental institutions. Some civilian non-enterprise bodies have become very much like business enterprises, and their objective is to make a profit while avoiding paying taxes.

—The personnel predicament. In many civic organizations, employees receive low pay and poor benefits, working conditions are poor, and career prospects are uncertain. This makes it difficult to recruit highly qualified people, which in turn undermines the overall quality and strength of civic organizations.

—The funding predicament. Civic organizations receive very little funding from the government, enterprises, or international foundations, and their funds are woefully inadequate. Government purchasing still does not benefit CSOs; regulations concerning enterprises' tax-deductible contributions are not clear; and there are many obstacles to the establishment and operation of private foundations.

—The knowledge predicament. Civic organizations provide inadequate training to their employees, information does not flow freely, and organizations lack operating experience and professional knowledge. Also, the government does not provide sufficient support for staff training.

—The confidence predicament. There is a widespread lack of confidence in CSOs both within the government and among the general public. Some civic organizations lack self-discipline mechanisms. Their operations often lack transparency, and incidents of corruption and embezzlement have occurred, which fuel public mistrust. Some officials have an entrenched view of civic organizations as competitors whose success comes at their expense, so the officials are suspicious of such groups and try to restrict them.

CIVIL SOCIETY ORGANIZATIONS 77

—The participation predicament. Chinese civic organizations and their members very much want to participate in politics, but the principal way the current institutional framework allows their participation is by making suggestions, recommendations, and requests to their professional supervising bodies. Because civic organizations are heavily dependent on these bodies, however, what they say has very little influence and often does not get the attention it deserves.

—The oversight predicament. Supervising bodies focus the majority of their attention on issues of registration, neglecting supervision of CSOs' activities. Many professional supervising bodies busy themselves with interfering in the internal management of civil organizations and duplicating the oversight work of civil affairs departments, so they are unable to carry out their proper oversight functions. Meanwhile, taxation authorities rarely carry out their oversight functions, nor do judicial departments generally perform their oversight duties.[4]

This chapter elaborates on the challenges in the development of China's civil society from six different aspects. This critical discussion may help formulate better policies that are conducive for improving the current institutional environment and promoting the healthy development of CSOs.

Judgment and Attitude

The understanding, judgment, and attitude of the party and the government concerning CSOs have a direct bearing on the kind of policies and regulations they formulate. Many party and government officials still lack a correct understanding of these groups. Some officials are largely cut off from the social developments that have occurred since reform and opening up and still do not acknowledge that a relatively independent civil society is rapidly rising in China; others think of civil society as an import from the West. Some view civic organizations as a dissident force that resists or opposes the government, while others are terrified of these groups because of the antigovernment role they played in the drastic changes in the former Soviet Union and Eastern European countries and more recently in the "color revolutions" in Eastern Europe. Still others misunderstand CSOs, believing them to be nothing more than appendages of government departments.

Not only are these views wrong and one-sided, but they also do considerable harm to the healthy development of China's civil society. In fact, civil society is an inevitable product of the market economy and political democratization.

China's implementation of a socialist market economy and democracy will inevitably bring into being civil society. Since reform and opening up began in 1978, a relatively independent civil society has risen rapidly in China, where it has played an increasingly important role in improving the market economy, transforming government functions, expanding citizen participation, implementing grassroots democracy, making government administration more transparent, improving supervision of society, and promoting public welfare undertakings. Furthermore, the cooperative supervision of public and political affairs by government departments and civil society is the key to achieving democratic governance. A healthy civil society is an important basis for the long-term, stable governance of the country, for social unity and harmony, and for democracy.

It can be said that the level of maturity of a modern country is equal to the level of development of its civil society. At the same time one should note that the market economy has just taken hold in China and is not at all standardized or mature. Civil society is still in its infancy and far from its ultimate mature form. Civil society can make both positive and negative contributions to the transformation of governance. Therefore, one should neither overlook nor exaggerate its role—nor conclude that civil society makes government unimportant. No matter how strong civil society becomes, government will always be the engine that drives social development. This is especially true in China.

Contrary to the views of some scholars who exaggerate the positive role of civil society, the greatest mistake some officials make is to exaggerate the negative effect civil society has on China's socialist modernization and democratization and especially on strengthening the governing capacity of the Chinese Communist Party (CCP). They believe that the growth of civic organizations is sure to weaken the party's ability to lead society and the government's ability to supervise society. For them, many problems are related to the growth of civil society and the antigovernment role civic organizations have played in the recent color revolutions in Eastern Europe. Without question, there are many problems in China's civil society. For example, it is hard to distinguish the good civil organizations from the bad. Some CSOs' management is haphazard, and their orientations are sometimes unclear. Legal and illegal civic organizations coexist; so too do civic organizations that cooperate with the government and those that resist it. Civic organizations within and outside the state system coexist; for-profit and not-for-profit civic organizations coexist; and tangible and intangible civic organizations coexist.

It is an incontrovertible fact, however, that even though civic organizations are plagued with a variety of problems, most of them make a healthy and positive contribution to modernization and democratization, and they are very willing to cooperate with the party and government. At the same time, these groups are like a double-edged sword in their relation to the government. When government policies and actions are appropriate, groups in civil society readily cooperate with the government, which is beneficial for social harmony and stability, but when policies are ill advised, cooperation between CSOs and the government is difficult, sometimes to the extent that civic organizations oppose the government, which is harmful to unity and stability.

Owing to misunderstandings and wrong judgments, four kinds of unfriendly or inappropriate attitudes toward these groups have developed among some party and government cadres. First, some officials underestimate and ignore civil organizations and think that they play an insignificant role in China's social and political life. Second, some do not trust civil organizations and think they are unreliable because they are not formal institutions. Third, some are fearful of civil society and think that once it becomes strong, it will seek to throw off government supervision, thereby undermining the government's ability to govern society. Finally, some officials are hostile to civic organizations because they think these organizations do not cooperate with the government and that they are rivals and troublemakers that need to be firmly curbed.

The first thing that needs to be done to overcome the challenges facing China's civil society is for government officials to correct their attitude toward this phenomenon. If the government is going to deal correctly with all kinds of CSOs, it cannot antagonize or neglect them, it cannot fear or pamper them, and it cannot indulge or stifle them. Far-sighted party and government cadres should establish relationships, trust, and friendship with all kinds of legal civil organizations, actively supporting all kinds of civic organizations that cooperate with the government. This is beneficial for the country since civic organizations promote the public good, grassroots democracy, and citizen self governance, and play important roles in supervising society, expanding citizen participation, and making society harmonious.

Regulations and Policies

It has been widely noted that legislation for civil society in China has three obvious inadequacies. First, there is no mother law for supervision of civil organizations, only a random assortment of laws and regulations. Second, the guiding thought underlying legislation is distorted. It emphasizes government supervision at the expense of safeguarding rights and interests and focuses on preapproval examination and administrative measures while ignoring postapproval oversight economic constraints. Third, the level of legislation is rather low. Currently, the main laws and regulations concerning CSOs are three administrative regulations promulgated by the State Council, which have not been made into general state laws.[5]

This kind of situation is completely inconsistent with the objective of creating a law-based socialist state and developing a socialist political civilization. In addition, China has already signed the International Treaty on Civil and Political Rights, which requires signatories to ensure that "everyone has the right to enjoy freedom of association with other people, including organizing and joining trade unions and safeguarding their rights and interests." Only a law can place any necessary restrictions on citizens' right of free association. Moreover, such restrictions must be grounded in legitimate reasons and pressing needs, such as safeguarding national security, social stability, and the rights of others.[6] In light of these domestic and international conditions, legislative bodies should intensify the work of writing a unified law for the supervision of civic associations that accords with the constitution's intent to safeguard citizens' right of free association and the actual developmental conditions of China's civil organizations. Such a law should clearly specify the legal status, subject qualifications, registration procedures, principles of operation, sources of spending, taxation treatment, oversight and regulation, and internal discipline of civil society groups. Such a unified law can provide a basic legal foundation for formulating regulations and policies for the supervision of civic organizations.

As already noted, departmental laws, regulations, and rules concerning the supervision of civic organizations are repetitious in some places and lacking in others; taken as a whole they lack unity. This makes it difficult for government regulatory bodies to properly exert their supervision functions and leads to three kinds of negative effects. First, it impedes the healthy development of civil society by imposing high hurdles on the establishment of civic organizations while controlling too strictly the activities of already existing groups. Second, it leads to the disorderly development of some civic organizations by not properly supervising them. Third, it duplicates supervision of civil organizations, which lowers administrative efficiency and raises administrative costs. An official in a local civil affairs department who has experienced these problems made the following five-point observation:

—Administrative laws and regulations lack unity and are frequently contradictory. Industry-based administrative laws and regulations are often at odds with regulations concerning the supervision of civilian non-enterprise bodies.

—There is no clear specification what organizations are to be supervised. For example, all the civic organizations in the system of scientific associations, such as those of the various science and industry associations, use financial documents from the system of scientific associations, and they do not receive financial auditing or oversight from the appropriate regulatory body and appear unwilling to subject themselves to annual inspections.

—Supervisory requirements lack consistency. The scope of the annual inspection of civilian non-enterprise bodies that were established before the regulations were promulgated is much simpler than that for newly established bodies, making supervision more difficult.

—There is poor coordination between the departments responsible for civic organizations. On the one hand, certain professional supervising bodies were solely responsible for registration and supervision in the past, and after the regulations were passed, they were not willing to relinquish this power. On the other hand, some such bodies want to turn over supervision of difficult cases to civil affairs departments.

—Law enforcement measures are too weak, undermining law enforcement.[7]

Therefore, a complete review of all existing laws and regulations concerning the supervision of civic organizations should be undertaken to revise and improve them. Redundant rules and regulations should be eliminated, the number of supervisory links decreased, departments prevented from working at cross purposes, and the efficiency of supervision increased.

In addition to state laws and government regulations concerning the supervision of civil organizations, there are a large number of party and government policy documents on the issue. These policy initiatives, together with the laws and regulations, constitute the regulatory system for the supervision of civil organizations. From the perspective of the actual political conditions prevailing in China, not only is there an objective need for these documents, but they also play a very positive role in stimulating the healthy growth of China's civil society. However, one must also take note of two kinds of problems. First, policy documents impose too many restrictions on CSOs and contain relatively few policies that encourage and support them. Second, some policies are inconsistent with, and sometimes directly contradict, the laws and regulations currently in force. For example, some CCP Central Committee documents promote farmers' cooperative organizations, but there are no corresponding laws concerning them. As someone complained, "The greatest problem facing the development of rural cooperative organizations is that there are no laws safeguarding them. The General Principles of Civil Law stipulate that the category of legal persons [entities] does not include cooperative organizations. Further, the registration of cooperative organizations is not effectively standardized, so that there are rural cooperative organizations registered with industry and commerce, civil affairs, or agricultural authorities, and 60 percent of them are not registered at all."[8] The CCP and the Chinese government have already set establishing a socialist state based on the rule of law as the objective of the country's political development, but the current situation is clearly not in accord with that objective. A simultaneous revision and adjustment of policy documents, laws, and regulations concerning supervision of CSOs needs to be carried out. On the one hand, party and government policy documents that are conducive to social development should be made into state laws and government regulations. On the other hand, both the party and the government need to operate within the scope of the constitution and laws, so if their policy documents are in conflict with current state laws, precedence should be given to state law.

Approval and Registration

A point that scholars and government officials agree on is that the current laws and regulations make it too difficult for civil organizations to register. According to the Regulations Concerning the Registration and Supervision of Social Associations, in order for a social association's application to a civil affairs department to be accepted, not only does it need to have such basic qualifications as a standard name, meet certain organizational requirements, and have a fixed location, full-time staff, a minimum number of members, financial assets and capacity, it also has to accept the exclusive noncompete principle and agree to limits on the number of branches it opens nationwide. Most important, it must affiliate itself with a department that can assume responsibility for it. Such departments must be formal institutions with fixed functions, structure, and staffing that have been approved by the CCP Central Committee, the State Council, or a local party committee or local government at or above the county level.

All these restrictions naturally lead to several consequences. First, many civil organizations that could make a positive contribution to civil society die before they are even born. This phenomenon is not beneficial to the healthy growth of civil society. Second, many civil organizations give up trying to register with civil affairs departments and instead register as enterprise organizations with the industry and commerce authorities, distorting the normal form of civic organizations. Third, many civic organizations do not register with any government body and simply go their own way without any oversight of their social activities, which results in a certain loss of control over the development of China's civil society.

To deal with this situation, many scholars have proposed measures for reforming the registration and approval system. A point of common agreement is that China should draw on the experiences of foreign civil society to establish a three-tiered system of registering civic organizations. The system proposed here, which integrates a number of related and similar suggestions, has three main objectives. First, a platform should be established that enables all civil society organizations to register, and all CSOs should be encouraged to register with civil affairs departments. This will give basic rights and privileges to all registered civil organizations (those that are clearly engaged in illegal activities would not be registered). Second, important CSOs that have considerable influence and extensive activities and that are involved in citizens' democratic participation in government, social, or political life should be issued permits and accorded legal person status if they meet the following basic qualifications: a standard name, necessary organization, a fixed site, a full-time staff, sufficiently large membership, adequate financing, and civil capacity. Finally, civic organizations engaged in public welfare undertakings, in addition to getting a government permit, should undergo more rigorous procedures to register as public interest legal persons, after which they should receive special treatment in the areas of finances and taxation and be subject to more rigorous administrative and social oversight.[9]

Overall, establishing a three-tiered system of recording CSOs and registering them as legal persons or public interest legal persons would be a very positive step that could be implemented gradually. Given current circumstances, implementation of this system should take the following points into consideration. First, pilot projects should be undertaken in some provinces and municipalities where civil society is relatively more active, and then implementation should gradually be expanded based on experiences there. Second, the system of examining qualifications and registration should treat the different types of CSOs differently, from relative leniency to strictness, according them different policy treatment and giving them different rights and responsibilities. Third, the government should take advantage of the opportunity afforded by the registration of all CSOs to carry out a comprehensive census of civic organizations of all kinds, including social groups that are not currently registered at all or not registered with civil affairs departments, in order to obtain basic information about China's civil organizations. Fourth, only CSOs such as interest groups, coworkers' groups, and community groups that are relatively small, engage in limited activities, and do not concern themselves with important political issues should be registered. Fifth, people's organizations that have been exempted from registration in the past by the CCP Central Committee or the State Council, such as trade unions, the Communist Youth League, and women's federations, should continue to be exempted.

Responsibility and Oversight

I have already pointed out that the current system of dual regulation of CSOs by government civil affairs departments and professional supervisory bodies inevitably results not only in conflicting policies and duplicate supervision but also in some civil organizations going unsupervised and having nowhere to turn for help. Many scholars think that this system of dual regulation should be reformed to eliminate regulation of civil organizations by professional supervisory bodies. Some scholars go further and suggest that the administrative level of agencies that regulate civil associations should be raised and their regulatory functions strengthened. They propose establishing a China Civil Organizations Regulatory Commission similar to the China Securities Regulatory Commission and the China Banking Regulatory Commission. I firmly believe that in the long run, this is the correct direction that reform should take. What needs to be done first, however, is to establish a basic principle for classifying degrees of regulation. For highly specialized civic organizations and those that are staffed by state employees, the system of dual supervision should be continued, and the organizations should be regulated jointly by civil affairs departments and professional regulatory bodies; however, regulatory responsibilities should be divided between them reasonably to avoid duplicate regulation in some areas and regulatory gaps in others. Trials of unitary supervision by civil affairs departments can gradually be carried out for ordinary civic organizations.

One widespread criticism of the current regulatory system for civic organizations is that it emphasizes scrutiny before approval while neglecting oversight afterward; scrutiny is strict, but oversight is lacking. Without a doubt, this kind of criticism is reasonable. This kind of phenomenon exists at all stages from the formulation of laws and regulations to the actual practices of regulatory bodies, and it occurs for several reasons. First, the laws and regulations lack provisions specifying effective oversight measures for regulating the daily activities of civic associations. Second, the system of dual regulation itself has weaknesses. Although professional regulatory bodies have oversight responsibility, in many cases CSOs are merely affiliated with professional regulatory bodies, which do not conscientiously carry out any regulatory functions. Third, people are not accustomed to overseeing civic organizations through public opinion, so there is too little oversight of civic organizations by society.

To deal with these issues, oversight of CSOs should be strengthened in the following three ways. First, regulatory laws should be improved by writing provisions that specify measures for managing finances, internal self-discipline, oversight by society, dissolution and auditing, as well as punishments for violations of regulations. Second, the government needs to redirect the focus of state regulatory bodies away from scrutiny of CSOs before registration toward oversight of them once they are registered. At the same time, the regulatory responsibilities of civil affairs departments should be expanded to include both the scrutiny and registration of civic organizations and regulation of their normal functioning. Third, society's responsibility for overseeing CSOs should be strengthened at the institutional level to guide public opinion to pay more attention to the functions and activities of civil society; gradually a system of oversight and regulation would be established in which administrative regulation, financial auditing, and social oversight are well coordinated.

Objectively speaking, the various shortcomings in China's civil society result in part from both the external and internal environments in which it developed. On the one hand, China's laws lack detailed rules concerning internal management of CSOs, and on the other hand, many CSOs have practically no internal mechanisms of self-discipline. As a result, in some CSOs the employees are of poor quality, the organizations lack effective internal rules, and their internal management is completely chaotic. Some CSOs claim to be not-for-profit, but they move heaven and earth to earn profits and avoid paying taxes. Some civic organizations pursue every avenue to acquire administrative functions and to be able to seek economic rents. Therefore, improving the institutional environment of China's civil society requires improving their mechanisms of self-discipline, establishing internal rules for civic organizations, raising the quality of their employees, using institutional means to dispel the profit-seeking inclination of civil organizations, and compelling CSOs to bear greater social responsibility.

Funds and Taxes

Funding shortfalls are a common problem for many CSOs, many of whom turn to foreign foundations for assistance. A sample survey of civic organizations reveals that on average, they have only 20,000 yuan to spend every year.[10] Those organizations that are fortunate enough to receive funding from foreign foundations still face both financial and political difficulties. From the financial perspective, reliance on foreign foundations for funding is not a good strategy for long-term development; in the long term, CSOs in China should depend mainly on domestic companies and foundations and the local and national governments for their funding grants. From the political perspective, financial assistance from foreign sources brings with it a kind of intangible political pressure, particularly under China's political conditions. These kinds of funding issues significantly affect the institutional environment of civil society because government policies and laws directly or indirectly cause funding difficulties for civil organizations in two ways—by providing too little assistance to them and by failing to provide tax policies that would encourage more contributions from society.

To attain good governance, the government and civil society need to cooperate closely. CSOs not only perform important functions in social and political life that the government cannot, but they also share the burden of regulating society and providing public services. To establish a civil society with which the state can cooperate, the government first needs to actively support civil society. Besides political trust, the most needed support for CSOs is financial assistance. In Western countries, where contributions to CSOs from society are commonplace, government subsidies still constitute a significant portion of such organizations' financing. The Chinese government should increase financial subsidies to CSOs by directly allocating funds to them when they are engaged in public welfare undertakings, especially those involving environmental protection, public health, compulsory education, and poverty alleviation. Second, the government should adopt the method of open bidding to contract out some public services to capable CSOs to ensure that organizations that assist the government in providing public services receive the financial support they need.

Since the inauguration of reform and opening up in 1978, more and more foreign CSOs have entered China. According to statistics, approximately 1,000 foreign foundations and social organizations are operating in Beijing alone.[11] Foreign funds have already become an important source of funding for China's CSOs. This is an extraordinary situation. Government regulation of foreign foundations and civil organizations lags considerably. There are no specific laws regulating them and no effective regulatory measures, which means that foreign CSOs escape even such basic oversight as registration. It should be acknowledged that the majority of foreign CSOs in China are philanthropic organizations without any political motives. However, it cannot be denied that some of them are not welcome by the Chinese government. The government must scrutinize them carefully, encourage and protect those that are engaged in legitimate activities, and strictly guard against and ban those that engage in illegal activities.

Currently three main problems with tax policies affect civil organizations. There is no suitable unified policy or complete taxation system applicable to CSOs and their public service activities; the tax breaks for contributions from society to organizations engaged in public service are too low; and taxation policies accord different treatment to different kinds of CSOs engaged in similar public service activities. For example, CSOs that are registered with civil affairs departments are taxed differently from those registered with administrations for industry and commerce, even if they share more or less the same nature and activities. Taxation policies, laws, and regulations are an important tool for controlling civil society, and the government must give the appropriate use of these policy tools a great deal of consideration. The government should give more tax breaks to CSOs that provide public services. It should formulate rules and regulations for implementing the Welfare Donations Law of the PRC to make it applicable to all public service activities of civic organizations. It should standardize the registration procedures for all CSOs so that all groups of the same kind and with similar functions receive the same taxation treatment. Civic organizations that have been hiding their for-profit activities under not-for-profit status should be punished in accordance with the law.

The issue of regulation of civil society groups' property is another problem that has recently emerged. Because the basic nature and legal standing of CSOs is relatively vague, the issue of their property is extremely complex. It is often not clear who the actual owners of the property are, management is often poor, and oversight is frequently weak. In a discussion of the regulation of civic organizations, a government official responsible for auditing CSOs listed five problems concerning the regulation of their property: CSO property is not always distinguishable from that of the government department it is affiliated with; leaders of social associations sometimes treat their association's property as their own; property management is poor, and creditors' rights and liabilities are not clear; examination and assessment of CSOs' property is not standardized; and funds belonging to civil organizations are sometimes used in for-profit activities.[12] Decisionmaking bodies should formulate better laws and regulations concerning the management of CSOs' property that clearly define property rights for such groups, strengthen auditing and oversight, and increase professional training for bookkeepers and accountants of these groups. At the same time, CSOs themselves must strengthen internal financial management, improve their systems of verification, and standardize their property management according to the law to keep members and leaders from treating the organization's property as their own and from using the organization's property in for-profit activities.

Leadership and Staffing

It is widely believed that the way leaders of CSOs are chosen should be more democratic than the way leaders of party and government departments are. In fact, however, the current ways of selecting leaders of such groups are far from democratic. Leaders of social associations that have administrative rank and staffing quotas similar to party and government departments are often appointed by the higher-level departments to which they report. Leaders in nationwide professional associations are oftentimes people who also hold positions in the institution with which the association is affiliated. The leaders of important industry associations are usually former leaders of the government department responsible for that industry. Those heading up civilian non-enterprise bodies are frequently appointed or recommended by whoever provides the bulk of their financial assistance. By and large, it is only the leaders of CSOs that are relatively independent but not very influential who are elected under the procedures set out in their charters. The number of party and government leaders who concurrently hold leadership positions in civic associations decreased sharply after the CCP Central Committee issued a document forbidding the practice. But large numbers of former party and government officials still lead these groups, in part because retired officials can generally obtain government and social resources for their CSO that others cannot so easily come by. In fact, there is little cause for objecting to retired officials heading civil organizations in general; what is crucial is that they be selected democratically in accordance with the organizations' charters and that responsible departments and major donors do not interfere in nondemocratic ways. The effective functioning of CSOs is directly related to the abilities and social influence of their leaders. The government should establish a system for training leaders of CSOs and should work to constantly improve the quality of civic groups' leaders and professional administrators.

Currently, there are four kinds of administrators in civil organizations. First are civil servants, principally making up cadres in a few people's organizations such as trade unions, the Chinese Communist Youth League, and the women's federations. Second are employees of institutions, principally administrators in professional and industry associations, such as the Chinese Public Administration Society and the China Association for Science and Technology, who carry out administrative functions specific to their associations' professions and industries. Third are social association administrators, who are approved by professional regulatory bodies in accordance with policies of civil affairs departments. And fourth are administrators hired under contract. These four different kinds of administrators are in some sense reflections of different social positions. The positions and remuneration of the first two types of administrator are basically the same as those of government employees. Research reveals that administrators in many civic organizations clearly expressed the wish that they could receive this kind of treatment. However, the direction that reforms of the government administrative system are taking is not one that will continue to treat the staff of CSOs like those of government institutions and give staff members civil service status. The need to adapt to the market economy and the new system for regulating society should be met by gradually improving staffing of civil organizations and the system of contractual hiring. In short, China should establish a human resources management system for employees of civil organizations.

The existence of different kinds of staffing is an indication not only of different social positions but also of different levels of remuneration and social security benefits. Staffing issues have direct relevance to a whole series of issues of vital interest to the employees of CSOs, including household registration, pay scales, housing, professional title, fringe benefits, children's education, medical insurance, unemployment insurance, and retirement benefits. Until these issues are solved at the institutional level, CSOs cannot attract exceptional workers, and this will affect the stability of civil society's administrative workforce and its overall quality. Since it is impossible to return to the days of the iron rice bowl, the government and all sectors of society, including CSOs, have a responsibility to work together to establish a reasonable system of salaries, benefits, retirement, insurance, unemployment programs, and professional titles for employees of civil organizations. There is also a need to coordinate this system with policies pertaining to other sectors of society in order to dispel people's hesitation to work for civil organizations. Assurances of basic human resources are needed for the healthy growth of China's civil society.

Concluding Thoughts

After more than twenty years of development, China's civil society has reached a new stage in which many aspects of the current institutional environment are no longer conducive to the further growth of CSOs. Some institutional factors have already become a hindrance to growth, making it necessary to undertake reforms. Reform should be based on a thorough understanding of the logic of the development of civil society. It should further transform the understanding of civil society, correctly define civil society, and classify CSOs rationally. It should revise and improve laws, regulations, and policies concerning civic organizations as soon as possible. It should energetically support, enthusiastically assist, correctly guide, and rationally standardize the approval, registration, regulation, funding, and taxation rules that apply to CSOs. It should prevent CSOs from becoming adversaries of the government and promote cooperation between CSOs and the government, so that they work together toward a society with democratic governance and a high degree of harmony.

III

CULTURE, MODERNITY, AND SUSTAINABILITY

CHAPTER SEVEN

CULTURE AND MODERNITY IN CHINESE INTELLECTUAL DISCOURSE
A Historical Perspective

Debates over the nature and direction of modernity have accompanied the process of economic modernization in China ever since the late nineteenth century. Major periods within this overall time frame have included the reform movement at the end of the Qing dynasty, the May Fourth movement that began in 1919, the Kuomintang modernization efforts of the 1930s, and the socialist transformation during its various incarnations after the founding of the People's Republic of China in October 1949.[1] Throughout these modernization drives, a fundamental issue of concern to most Chinese observers and participants has been the fate of Chinese culture. Different attitudes toward this issue have shaped Chinese intellectual discourses about the desirability of modernization and about the pathway that China should follow to modernity. To a great extent, these debates reflect a continuing preoccupation with China's subjectivity in the modern world. As China embarks on a new stage of modernization today, the issue is once again at the forefront of Chinese thinking.

The issue of the relationship between Chinese culture and modernity appears repeatedly in the debates over the past century both on the legitimacy of the end goal (that is, whether to modernize) and on the means for achieving it (how to modernize). While certain general attitudes toward these questions have appeared consistently in all the debates, the parameters of the questions have changed over time in accordance with historical experience, as well as with the national and global circumstances of the debates. Indeed, the very idea of Chinese culture itself underwent changes, as successive generations of intellectuals brought different understandings of the concept of culture to their discussions, with some even seeing it as a source of China's problems.

This chapter focuses on the debates concerning modernity and culture in the 1930s, a period that has received relatively little attention from historians. Two reasons make this study particularly valuable. First, the debates of the 1930s, in their efforts to overcome the limitations of earlier debates, produced a sophisticated appreciation of the problem of modernity, which was reflected in a more comprehensive and critical understanding of the problem of culture than had been the case in the debates of either the late Qing or May Fourth periods. Second, these debates were the immediate precursors to post-1949 debates. The generation of Chinese intellectuals who were the main participants in the debates about Chinese culture in the early decades of the People's Republic came of age during the debates of the 1930s. The May Fourth movement as a turning point in modern Chinese history has received much attention and, because of its dramatic consideration of the problem of culture, has served as a frame of reference for all subsequent discussions of culture's relationship to modernity. I believe that the debates of the 1930s, in the scope of the questions raised, are much more pertinent for an understanding of contemporary discussions of culture and modernization than the debates in earlier periods. Students of China are largely unaware that the contemporary discussions about culture and modernity often replay the themes of the 1930s discussions.

This chapter aims to highlight two of the perspectives offered in these debates on the question of modernization: modernization as Westernization versus modernization in a particularly Chinese way. The debates, as I will endeavor to show, included a far more complex array of positions than this simplified and stark juxtaposition suggests. But this approach, in its very reduction of the alternatives to a simple China-versus-West dichotomy, has been central to all the debates on modernity that came afterward, and it enables readers to underline the differences of this debate from earlier ones by showing how the perceptions of both China and the West changed from the turn of the century to the 1930s.

Modernization as Westernization

Modernization as Westernization, a legacy of the May Fourth period, appeared in the 1930s in a number of guises, with subtle differences that produced disagreements among pro-Westernization advocates themselves. Advocates of Westernization ranged from those who were in favor of total

Westernization (*quanpan xihua*) to those who qualified the possibility of Westernization with some recognition of the difficulties of achieving that goal. The differences in these views appeared in the course of the debates, as advocates of Westernization engaged with the arguments of their opponents, and are discussed below in the evaluation of the debates. Suffice it to say that advocates of Westernization shared a common premise that modernization is the equivalent of Westernization, which should be the goal of China's social development. They defined the modern period of human history in terms of Westernization, rather than as modernization or industrialization. At the extreme, some even refused to use terms such as modernization and industrialization, which were gaining in popularity during the 1930s. One such staunch supporter of Westernization was Chen Xujing, a U.S.-educated university professor, who wrote in 1935:

> Mr. Yan Jicheng thinks that the term *Westernization* is not good and should be changed to *modernization* (*xiandaihua*). Mr. Hu Shi uses the word *globalization* (*shijiehua*). I myself also have employed these terms in my essays. But I think that, essentially and fundamentally, the so-called global culture and modern culture are little more than Western culture. The term *Westernization,* therefore, not only contains both of them, but also is more specific and easier to understand. Moreover, Mr. Hu Shi continues to use the term *maximum possible Westernization* (*chongfen de xihua*) side by side with *globalization.* As for Mr. Yan, he still uses the words *total Westernization* even though he objects to *Westernization.* Thus, I believe that there is no problem with using the term *Westernization.*[2]

Defining modernization as Westernization was a product of early modern Chinese history. It had its origins in what Chinese intellectuals, beginning in the late nineteenth century, perceived as a conflict between Chinese and Western civilizations. As Western powers "opened" China's doors with their advanced weapons and high-quality, low-priced commodities, progressive Chinese who recognized the necessity of change came to perceive a broad gap between an advanced West and a backward China. By the time of the May Fourth movement in 1919, in the eyes of progressive intellectuals, the West had come to stand for everything that was advanced, to which China must adopt if it wanted to survive. Westernization or Europeanization was in their view the ultimate goal of China's development. They understood Westernization in a total sense to include the material (modern science, technology, economy) as well as the spiritual (politics, education, culture, art, and so on) aspects of civilization. As such, there was almost no difference in their eyes between Westernization and modernization.

Before the 1930s, the terms *Westernization* and *modernization* were often used interchangeably in scholarly writings, without any distinction. Another commonly used term appearing in the writings of radical advocates of modernization such as Chen Duxiu and Hu Shi during the May Fourth era was Europeanization. Indeed, only in the 1930s was a clear distinction drawn between Westernization and modernization. One historian writes that "it is in the 1930s that the word *modernization* was used in newspaper and magazines as a term of social science. So far as we know, it first began to be used widely in *Shenbao Monthly*'s July 1933 issue, which was a special issue entitled 'Problems of China's Modernization.'"[3]

Like their May Fourth predecessors, scholars writing about Westernization in the 1930s stressed that it was "cosmopolitanism" (*shijiehua*), which was an inevitable trend of world history. Whoever rejected it, they argued, would be doomed. "Western civilization is the trend of world civilization," Chen Xujing wrote, "in fact, Western civilization is world civilization today. We have to follow the trend unless we decide not to live in the world."[4] According to the advocates of Westernization, Western civilization had transcended the boundaries of Western societies to become a global imperative and the common heritage of all human beings. Hence, total Westernization did not constitute an imitation of any one country but instead implied the assimilation of the common values of humanity: "So-called Western civilization is not a patent registered by Westerners . . . it has prevailed in the whole world . . . and so is appropriately called world civilization. We assimilate the so-called Western civilization in order to realize China's modernization and to change China into a major member of the world community."[5]

A major argument of those who opposed the notion that modernization was nothing more than Westernization was that even though Western material civilization was more advanced, China still retained superior spiritual values. Advocates of Westernization, however, refused to recognize such a distinction. To them, spiritual values were embodied in material civilization, and as Western countries surpassed China in material civilization, they did so in spiritual values as well. Lin Yutang, a pro-Westernization writer and linguist, addressed this issue specifically in an article entitled "Machine and Spirit." In Lin's view, Western countries' science, politics, scholarship, and education, all of which fall in the realm of spiritual civilization, surpassed China's. As he colorfully put it: "A person who shits in a modern bathroom does not necessarily degenerate spiritually, and a person who shits on the outdated commode made in Suzhou or Yangzhou is not necessarily more noble spiritually." [6] He concluded that "machine civilization is a manifestation of the human spirit, since machines come from science, and foreign commodities which are warmly welcomed by everyone, come from Westerners' industrial spirit, which constantly improves their products."[7]

Hu Shi, another standard-bearer of Westernization, also rejected the idea of a necessary conflict between spiritual and material civilizations and argued that Western material civilization reflected the West's spiritual civilization. He listed in detail Western scientific, moral, and religious institutions as examples of the spiritual civilization that was missing in China. Hu also asserted that Western civilizations "use the totality of human wisdom in searching for the truth in order to liberate man's mind and maximize the welfare of the greatest number of people. Such a civilization satisfies the spiritual needs of human beings; such a civilization is a spiritual civilization, an idealist civilization, and not a materialist civilization."[8]

Advocates of Westernization stressed the backwardness of Chinese civilization in both the material and the spiritual realms. Their emphasis was on the backward state of spiritual culture in China since there was little need to belabor the generally recognized backwardness of Chinese material development. They argued that the Chinese national spirit was corrupt, and that such corruption characterized all of Chinese history, not just the current period. They claimed to recognize an accelerated process of degeneration in recent years, but even in traditional morality they found little worth praising. On the contrary, they held that the Chinese nation was the most morally corrupt nation in the world. As one such critic, Wu Shichang, a literary historian, lamented:

> China is a nation that speaks of morality much more than all other nations in the world. In the present age, many people advocate on behalf of native culture, specific national conditions, the four principles and eight virtues, and native morality. But in the end, China is a very degenerate society, which is helpless morally. . . . At first, I believed that it might have been a temporary phenomenon produced by the particular political environment we find ourselves in today. However, after I thought it over, I found that indeed we have no moral heritage from our ancestor's culture, which, ironically enough, was full of the word "virtue."[9]

By comparing Chinese and Western culture systematically, Chen Xujing attempted to show that even in the area of culture China was by no means more advanced than the West, arguing that "Western culture is [in fact] better than Chinese culture, no matter whether in thought, art, science, politics, morality, philosophy, or literature."[10] When some scholars suggested that Chinese civilization was idealistic whereas Western civilization was materialistic, Hu Shi answered sarcastically that it was Chinese civilization that was so greatly confined and dominated by material conditions that it could not surpass material limitations and use the human mind and knowledge to transform and improve the existing civilization. Indeed, Hu replied, China had "the civilization of a nation that is lazy and short on initiative."[11]

The crux of the pro-Westernization argument was that material civilization is a product of a nation's spiritual civilization, which together constitute a holistic system of civilization. According to this logic, if China wanted to develop economically and become a strong and prosperous country, it would have to introduce Western material civilization; and if it wanted to introduce Western material civilization, it must also be prepared to accept Western spiritual values and thoroughly negate traditional Chinese culture at the same time. China could not effectively incorporate advanced Western technology while still holding on firmly to traditional Chinese culture. In the more extreme versions of this argument, any effort to reconcile Western material accomplishments with traditional Chinese culture was seen as little different than trying to fit a horse's jaw in an ox's mouth—China had no alternatives but complete Westernization or total conservatism. In the view of Yan Jicheng, a prominent advocate of Westernization, China was suffering from a variety of problems, and the resolution lay either in Westernization or conserving the past. To Yan, there was no third way.[12]

Since they saw as futile any effort to reconcile Chinese and Western civilizations, advocates of Westernization concluded that such efforts were obstacles to change. Concerning the long-standing *ti-yong* formula ("Chinese learning as the substance [literally, body], Western learning for the function"), Lin Yutang said: "If we insist on preserving Eastern spiritual values while utilizing Western material products, following the fantastic theory of 'Chinese substance and Western function' (after all, body and its function cannot be separated; can we say that stomach is the 'body' while liver is its 'function'?), we will learn nothing from Westerners and will have no choice but to ride in Western cars with a volume of outdated Chinese classics in hand."[13]

Some Westernizers went a step further and blamed the failure of modernization since the late Qing dynasty on efforts to combine the irreconcilable civilizations of China and the West. Instead of devoting itself wholeheartedly to modernization, China had only used Western material technology while retaining its own political and cultural traditions. For these thinkers, the use of Western technology alone could not be called modernization because the essence of modernization was the assimilation of Western culture. In their view, those who sought to blend the best of the two cultures were conceding tacitly that "China should be reformed but cannot be reformed."[14] As Hu Shi put it:

> The reason China has been unable to adjust to the modern world is the failure of its leaders to embrace an attitude of wholehearted modernization. Wholehearted devotion to modernization is the only attitude that will lead to modern civilization. The reason Chinese no longer talk about rejecting Western civilization is that conservatives have found shelter in so-called "alternative" modernization. China has made a little progress by utilizing such products of Western civilization as the telegram and telephone, railways and ships, and in military improvement, political reform, and establishing a new economic system. . . . This little progress, for the most part, was imposed by foreigners or Chinese who worry about our nation becoming extinct. All this progress is not consciously, sensibly, or knowingly introduced into China.[15]

While the idea of modernization as Westernization dominated before the 1930s, it was challenged in the 1930s by advocates of modernization in a Chinese mode. It is to their arguments that we now turn.

Modernization with Chinese Characteristics

Advocates of "Chinese-style modernization" ranged across a broad spectrum but shared a common assumption that China could not realize Westernization and would instead have to pursue a brand of modernization suited to China's own specific circumstances. These scholars believed that it was possible to combine Chinese and Western civilizations, absorbing the cream of Western culture while retaining the better parts of traditional Chinese culture. In short, they sought to achieve a Chinese mode of modernization, or modernization with Chinese characteristics. As the philosopher Zhang Shenfu wrote in an article entitled "On Chinese Characteristics":

> We believe that it is for China itself to reform China. . . . We seek to reform China from within . . . although we can borrow major measures from foreign countries. Thus, we should endow foreign things used in China with Chinese characteristics. Moreover, these foreign things must

be endowed with Chinese characteristics if they are to function in China. . . . If we are the hosts of our country, if we try to endow foreign things with Chinese characteristics and to combine them with Chinese conditions, then we can utilize all foreign things without any doubt or rejection. In this way we will be able once again to make China as powerful as it once was. We hope to build a new China in such a way.[16]

The advocates of Chinese-style modernization began by redefining the concept of modernization. They no longer defined it as Westernization but as social progress with industrialization at its core. As Hu Qiuyuan wrote, "so-called modernization means nothing more than industrialization or mechanization, a national industrialization."[17] Hu's views paralleled those of Zhou Xiawen, who argued that "as a matter of fact, so-called modernization is industrialization."[18] For scholars who favored this approach, the central meaning of modernization was economic development, the advancement of higher productive forces, and a much stronger nation. One such proponent, Yang Xinzhi, writing in *Shenbao Monthly* in 1933, argued that "the major meaning of so-called modernization, of course, lies in its emphasis on economic reform and increasing productive forces. Without question, the Chinese economy should be reformed and productive forces advanced, regardless of whether China's future is capitalism or socialism."[19]

It was critical for modernization with Chinese characteristics to distinguish modernization from Westernization, for this distinction made it possible to separate Western industrial civilization from Western politics and culture and to realize modernization without fundamentally abandoning China's political and cultural heritage. In this view, China could carry out modernization without Westernization. As Zhang Sumin, an economist writing in 1933, stated:

In terms of individuals and commodities, modernization refers to social progress. A modern person should be better than an ancient person; modern commodities should be better than ancient ones. Persons and goods are modern if they are really better than ancient ones. Otherwise they are not modern. This is the broader meaning of modernization. In terms of a nation and society, however, modernization equals industrialization. A modern country is an industrialized country. There is no necessary relationship between democratic politics, the Jesuit religion, and industrialization. Japan is a modern country, but its politics are not completely democratic and its religion is not Jesuitical.[20]

Theorists who favored a specifically Chinese mode of modernization chose the terms and concepts they used very carefully. They stressed attention to the meaning of terms, rather than quibbling over vocabulary. For example, Zhang Xiruo, a distinguished professor, warned that "if someone would like to imply *Westernization* by use of the term *modernization,* it is of course all right. But do not forget: while *modernization* can entail *Westernization, Westernization* is not limited to *modernization.* This is not to quibble over words but to adopt a different stance."[21] Similarly, the philosopher Feng Youlan corrected his friends when they talked about Westernization, arguing that " I have always corrected my friends by noting that they meant *industrialization* when they used the word *Westernization.* This is not purely a semantic distinction; indeed, it stands for two views."[22]

A basic premise of the pro-Westernizers was that Western industrialization was built on the basis of Western spiritual values, which led them to conclude that to industrialize, China would have to abandon its culture. This proposition was criticized severely by advocates of modernization with Chinese characteristics. These analysts believed that human civilizations were pluralistic; Eastern and Western civilizations, rather than being absolutely contrastable as ancient versus modern, were instead simply two different systems of civilization. Liang Shuming, a representative of the Chinese native culture position, described three different world civilizations in his book *Eastern and Western Cultures and their Philosophies: Indian, Greek and Chinese.* He argued that Eastern civilization represented the highest development of all civilizations in the world. Accordingly, he predicted that Western civilization would soon come to an end, to be replaced at the summit of human civilizations by a rejuvenated Chinese civilization. In short, the future of world culture would witness the revival of Chinese culture, as Greek culture had been revived in the modern age.[23]

Liang's view was similar to advocates of Westernization such as Hu Shi and Lin Yutang inasmuch as he insisted that Chinese and Western civilizations were incompatible; whereas Hu and Lin argued that Western civilization should replace Chinese culture, Liang prophesied the victory of Chinese values over Western cultural norms. Supporters of Chinese-style modernization, however, mostly hewed to a more pluralistic view of civilizations and their compatibility, believing, as Xiong Mengfei argued in 1935, in the possibility of "blending Chinese culture with Western culture, as mingling milk with water, so that Chinese culture comes to absorb elements of world culture and world culture comes to include elements of Chinese culture."[24]

Intellectuals who believed in the recombinatory possibilities of different cultural and civilizational value systems placed special emphasis on the complementarity that they believed existed between Chinese and Western cultures. Zhang Dongsun, a well-known scholar, writing in 1935, argued for "introducing Western culture on the one hand, [while] reviving traditional culture on the other. I do not think these two processes are in conflict; quite the contrary, I think they are mutually complementary."[25] Lu Yudao, a famous scientist, also writing in 1935, emphasized the same point: "So-called culture is the resource on which a nation survives and it is an accumulation of history as it is. There is no need for us to dispute what is Chinese and [what is] Western, or what is old and [what is] new. Every culture is available to us if it is useful to our nation's prosperity. Western countries did not become Chinese because they used a Chinese compass. That our country utilizes Western ships and trains is not Westernization either. We need not pursue total Westernization at the cost of abandoning our traditional inventions such as the compass."[26]

Advocates of combining Chinese and Western cultures argued that there was much of value worth preserving in traditional Chinese culture, and that the losses would outweigh the gains if the introduction of Western civilization were to lead to the total elimination of traditional culture. Most proponents of this position sought to adopt the best of Western culture while preserving that which was of value in traditional culture. One such advocate, Chen Shiquan, illustrated their views as follows:

> On the one side, it is foolish of some people to hold a parochial arrogance with regard to traditional culture, denying the efficacy of science; on the other side, it is wrong to fetishize Western civilization by negating all that is good in traditional culture. For example, such products of traditional culture as the invention of the compass and calendar had their own scientific bases; other aspects such as politics, philosophy, ethics, education, law, music, and art all had their own originals. As everyone knows, the Chinese notions of "loyalty, filial piety, kind-heartedness, love, honesty, justice, harmony, and equality" represent great and noble ideals.[27]

Proponents of Chinese-style modernization acknowledged some tensions between Chinese and Western civilizations while at the same time emphasizing the value of combining the two. Recognizing that China existed under specific circumstances, they warned that blind imitation of Western civilization would fail and might even bring disaster to China. They pointed out that many advanced Western products lost their progressive nature as soon as they were introduced into China because they were not suited to Chinese conditions. While Westernizers blamed the failure of China's modernization on the incompleteness of Westernization, advocates of a mixed Western and Chinese path to modernity attributed it to the neglect of the specific characteristics of Chinese society. As Xiong Mengfei observed bitterly:

> A nation's characteristics refer to what is commonly called *national conditions*. Due to the lack of a clear understanding of the country's conditions, the reforms and revolutions of the past sixty years have all failed in the end. Advocates of Westernization acted in a Procrustean manner so that Western parliamentary politics in China became "pig politics." . . . The output of American cotton was reduced when it was planted in China; and Italian bees made less honey after they came to China.[28]

What were "Chinese national conditions" and Chinese characteristics? Proponents of Chinese-style modernization diverged in their answers to these questions. Some believed that Chinese national conditions meant the "needs of the present," which included "enriching people's lives, developing the national economy, and striving for the nation's survival."[29] Others regarded Chinese national conditions as including the natural environment, the idea of population "quality" (*suzhi*), and the national culture. Xiong Mengfei offered one detailed explanation:

> Whether in the past or the present, the rise and decline of a nation is closely related to three factors that affect each other: the nation's quality, the natural environment, and its culture. National quality refers to blood heritage and its variation as a result of elimination through selection or competition; natural environment stands for the advantages or disadvantages with regard to natural material resource endowments; and culture means the lived experiences of the ancestors and the evolution of social experience, resulting from its degeneration and the invasion of foreign culture.[30]

As they pointed to valuable aspects of Chinese culture, proponents of Chinese-style modernization sought to show that Western culture embodied much that was less than desirable. For instance, Western countries could not escape economic crises even though their economies were much more advanced than China's. "As everyone knows," wrote Ye Yin, a professor of philosophy, "the United States is a very advanced capitalist country. Its technology is also very advanced. But [even] such techniques as Ford's conveyor system and Taylor's piecework system cannot resolve the [challenge of avoid-ing] economic crises."[31] Westerners were richer than Chinese, but there existed polarization between rich and poor, and workers were exploited by capitalists. As Qu Qiubai, a radical thinker and literary critic, wrote:

> On the one hand, due to overproduction, a lot of cotton and food is burned, a lot of milk is thrown into rivers, and fish are dropped back into the sea. What is the other side? Thousands of unemployed suffer hunger and cold. Modernization of production and technology alone, therefore, cannot avert the lopsided development of the world and its extreme tragedy. Is not the First World War the consequence of progress in production and technology?[32]

In the eyes of these critics, the biggest problem of Western civilization was its spiritual degeneracy. Citing high rates of crime, mental disorder, and sui-cide in Western countries, Chinese critics concluded that Western civilization was in decline. "It is true that Western capitalist culture is more advanced than our feudal culture," Chen Gaoyun opined, but nonetheless "Western culture today is full of flaws and [is] degenerating."[33]

A few extremists went further, believing that Western civilization was already in complete decline. They argued that Westerners were waiting for Chinese to save them by exporting Chinese civilization to Western countries, and it was the Chinese people's duty to save Westerners from their cultural degeneration. Liang Qichao, before his death in 1927, was a noted spokesman of this view. In 1920 he wrote:

> I remember what Simmon, a well-known American journalist, told me. He asked me: "What will you do after you go back to China? Do you want to bring some [elements] of Western civilization to China?" "Of course," I replied. He heaved a deep sigh and said: "I say, how pitiful it is! Western civilization has been destroyed." I asked him: "What will you do after you go back to your country?" He replied: "I shall close my gate and wait for you to save us by introducing Chinese civilization into our country.". . .
>
> Our population is one-fourth of the world's population. Accord-ingly, we should hold one-fourth of the responsibility for the world. If we are derelict in our duties, we do a disservice to our ancestors, to humankind, and in fact, to ourselves. To our lovely young people I say: stand up and move on! Millions of foreigners overseas are crying out "Help us!" in a melancholy tone. They are waiting for you to save

them. Our ancestors and the ancient sages alike are looking to you to complete their great cause, and are protecting you with their spirit.[34]

Grounds for Compromise

An important point stands out in the 1930s debates on China's modernization. Although the proponents of the two modes of modernization had some fundamental differences, there were very few advocates of extremist views. Most of the participants, of whichever inclination, no longer rejected absolutely those with whom they disagreed. Proponents of Chinese-style modernization did not completely deny that Western civilization had some merits, and pro-Westernizers were careful to qualify their repudiation of Chinese civilization. The moderation these intellectuals evinced was in large part a consequence of the better grasp they had than their predecessors of the intricacies of the problems of culture and cultural change that both camps had spent time wrestling with.

Hu Shi and Liang Shiqiu, acknowledged spokesmen for Westernization, nevertheless conceded that it was impossible to realize Westernization thoroughly. In the 1930s Hu Shi revised his long-standing advocacy of total Westernization in favor of "maximum possible Westernization," on the grounds that the culture of daily life resisted total transformation. Now, he explained, he was of the view that it was sufficient for Westernization to be "wholehearted" even if not "total."[35] Liang Shiqiu, who thought that very few aspects in Chinese culture were worth praising, nonetheless came to hold that "if we divide culture into several parts we can see that: 1) some parts of Chinese culture are superior to some parts of Western culture; 2) some parts of Western culture are better than some aspects of Chinese culture; 3) some parts of the two cultures are either equally good or equally flawed; and 4) parts of both cultures need to be improved."[36]

Both Liang Qichao and Liang Shuming were universally recognized as representatives of a more nativist attitude toward Chinese culture, yet even they did not reject absolutely Western culture. Liang Qichao for instance regarded Chinese and Western cultures as complementary. In his eyes, it was necessary "to use Western civilization to supplement our civilization; to use our civilization to supplement Western civilization; and finally, to blend them into a new civilization."[37] Likewise Liang Shuming, after long consideration, came to conclude that "as for Western culture, we should change our attitude toward it. At first, we should completely accept Western culture and then fundamentally transform it."[38]

The willingness to compromise suggests that by the 1930s Chinese intellectuals had begun to acknowledge trends in world history: on the one hand, the development of modern science and technology and the needs of the capitalist market economy sparked a trend toward globalization that led to increasing exchanges among nations in the fields of politics, economics, and culture; on the other hand, a trend toward nationalism expressed itself as an emphasis on national sovereignty, local conditions, national traditions, and specific characteristics. Three important arguments were made for Westernization: it was a world trend; Western civilization was irreconcilable with Chinese civilization; and traditional Chinese culture was worthless. The latter two arguments were so weak that they were easily dismissed by opponents, who argued that all civilizations were more or less mixed. There was almost never a pure civilization, at least in Chinese history. So-called Chinese civilization itself was a mixture of multiple civilizations. Moreover, the fact that Chinese civilization had been in existence for thousands of years provided strong evidence that it offered much that was worth retaining. As noted above, by the 1930s more and more advocates of Westernization themselves had come to concede this point.

The first argument, however, was rather more difficult to refute. Westernization, to many scholars, actually meant a process of adapting to a rapidly globalizing form of capitalism. The modernization of advanced Western capitalist countries entailed the expansion of markets across the globe, which to some conflicted with national barriers. Advanced Western countries needed to sell their commodities, to import natural resources, and to search for cheap raw materials and labor worldwide, which required international trade. They brought their cultures to other countries as they exported their commodities. Backward nations could hardly withstand the advanced products, or the weapons that backed them up. In this sense, Westernization was indeed globalization. As early as 1848, Karl Marx observed that

> the bourgeoisie, by the rapid improvement of all instruments of production, by the immensely improved means of communication, draws all, even the most barbarian nations into civilization. The cheap prices of its commodities are the heavy artillery with which it batters down all Chinese walls, with which it forces the barbarians' intensely obstinate hatred of foreigners to capitulate. It compels all nations, on pain of extinction, to adopt the bourgeois mode of production; it compels them to introduce what it calls civilization into their midst, i.e., to become bourgeois themselves. In one word, it creates a world after its own image.[39]

In light of the modern Chinese historical experience, Westernization or globalization as a process of the expansion of global capitalism was both a trend and a fact that even the most intense opponents of Westernization had to recognize. Liang Shuming, for example, had this to say with regard to Westernization:

The world we see is almost a completely Western world! Needless to say, European countries and the United States are the Western world. Among Eastern countries, a nation or a state is able to stand up only if it is Westernized, and a nation is [generally] occupied by Western powers if it is not Westernized. Japan is the former case. It is able to survive and stand up in the world only because it [has] completed [a process of] Westernization. India, Korea, Vietnam, and Burma are [all in] the latter [camp]; they did not undertake Westernization [and as a result] all of them are [now] occupied by Western powers. [Even] China, the source of Eastern civilization, [has] suffered oppression [at the hands] of Western powers. Westerners opened China's gate by force, and compelled Chinese to change their lifestyles and accept Westernization, even though Chinese had been accustomed to Eastern culture for thousands of years. It is indisputable that our life is full of Western culture, whether in spiritual, social, or material life."[40]

The exclusive focus of advocates of Westernization on the benefits of globalization neglected the drawbacks of the phenomenon that led to the contradictory trend of a growing nationalism that coexisted alongside globalization. Many opponents of globalization expressed their resistance to it in terms of Chinese culture. They believed that it was impossible for Chinese society to do away with its traditional culture that had persisted for thousands of years and totally accept Western culture. Hu Shi, who was himself a major representative of the pro-Westernization school, conceded the impossibility of total Westernization, which he explained in terms of "cultural inertia," arguing that "there is an 'inertia' inside culture, and the result of thorough Westernization naturally tends to a mixture."[41]

More important, besides cultural inertia, Westernization was unacceptable to many because thorough Westernization was likely to lead to dependence and a loss of identity. As many opponents of Westernization noted, the process of China's modernization did not result from spontaneous development but from foreign pressure. In the process of capitalist globalization, China, like all late-developing countries, was situated in a peripheral position to the capitalist core composed of the advanced industrialized countries. The essential ideas of dependency theory, which emerged in the post–World War II era, could already be seen in a vivid metaphor expressed by Feng Youlan, writing in 1936:

> Today, the nations of the world have been divided into two groups: 1) the economically advanced nations who are the so-called "city dwellers"; and 2) the economically backward nations who are the so-called "country folks." In other words, the economically advanced nations are the exploiters and the oppressors while the economically backward nations are the exploited and the oppressed. The former are oppressing the latter. Unfortunately, our Chinese nation belongs to the category of the backward in the present circumstances, that is, our nation is the unfortunate "country folk" and the oppressed. Knowing our nation's status in the world, we can see that the direction of all nations is to seek "freedom and equality" or to be a "city dweller"—that is, to be the equal of the economically advanced nations and free from foreign oppression. Thus, the major goal of the Chinese nation is to struggle for freedom and equality.[42]

Besides its impossibility in practice, there were some conceptual limitations to Westernization. As we have seen, Westernizers defined China's modernization as a process of Westernization, a concept entailing both geographical and cultural elements. As such, there were three limitations and weaknesses in the argument that advocates of Westernization made. First, since Westernization was conceived to be the goal of China's modernization, the logical implication was that all things in Western countries were worth imitating, whether good or bad, out of date or up to date. Obviously, this was not reasonable since every civilization clearly has some negative components. Second, by defining China's modernization as being achievable only through Westernization, such scholars risked suggesting that nothing worthwhile remained in Chinese civilization. This was unacceptable since there is almost certainly something valuable and worth preserving in any great civilization. And third, Western culture contains quite a broad and diverse array of components. Both capitalism, for which many followers of Westernization longed, and communism, which many hated, originated from Western culture. As the sociologist Wu Jingchao pointed out,

> There are a number of conflicting subcultures that fall under the broad rubric of Western culture. Autocracy is found in Western culture while democracy is also found in Western culture; capitalism is a Western

cultural value while communism is Western culture too; individualism is Western culture while collectivism is also Western culture; free trade is Western culture just like statism is Western culture. There are many things like this. Does so-called complete Westernization stand for autocracy or democracy, for capitalism or communism? The contradictions inside Western culture are fatal for the theory that China's problems will be solved through total Westernization.[43]

These political and conceptual deficiencies of the pro-Westernization school resulted in a decline in support for this approach beginning in the 1920s. By the 1930s few supported it. Chen Xujing, the extreme advocate of Westernization, wrote with a sigh in 1935: "I would say, we should not forget there are very few advocates of thorough Westernization. Most people are deeply entranced either by the idea of mixing Chinese and Western cultures, or by the conservative notion of preserving 'Chinese substance' while adopting 'Western functions.'"[44] Chen hoped that the number of those supporting Westernization would grow in time, but the number of his supporters decreased as time passed.

Advocates of Chinese-style modernization built their arguments on three major grounds. First, they argued, it is possible to combine Chinese with Western civilization. Second, they noted, there are some valuable things in Chinese civilization and some worthless things in Western civilization, just as there are some valuable things in Western civilization and some worthless things in Chinese civilization. Third, China has its own specific conditions or characteristics that need to be considered in the process of modernization. Abstractly or theoretically, it seems hard to refute these arguments since all of them were verified by later developments and experience. For example, there was a popular opinion during the 1920s and 1930s that Chinese written characters were ill-suited to modern civilization and were one of the major obstacles to China's modernization. As Chen Xujing said, "I think that one of the major barriers to Chinese development is the Chinese written language. It would be an important step to abolish Chinese characters if we really want to speed up our development."[45] Followers of Westernization in general agreed with this opinion. Even Lu Xun, one of the towering thinkers of modern Chinese history, held the same view. There was a common feeling that "China would wither away if Chinese characters were not abolished." This view was revived again in the beginning of the 1980s when computer technology became popular in China. Since almost all the software was designed in English, many people believed that Chinese characters could not be computerized. In a few years, however, many types of software were designed in Chinese, and competitions revealed that the speed of inputting Chinese into computers could even surpass the speed of inputting English.

Nevertheless, there was also a very dangerous implication behind the advocacy of modernization with Chinese characteristics: conservatives could use it to defend their rejection of modern civilization and social progress and to protect authoritarian and despotic forms of politics. Everyone could explain so-called "Chinese conditions" and "Chinese characteristics" in terms of their own preferences and then oppose those elements of modernization, especially in the political realm, that were unfavorable to their own interests. As the prominent pro-communist philosopher Ai Siqi stated in his 1939 article "On China's Special Characteristics":

> All reactionaries in modern China have had a particular affection for what might be called "closed-doorism" in thought. . . . It [deliberately] overemphasizes "Chinese conditions" and "Chinese characteristics" and negates the universal laws of human history, thinking that China's development can only follow its own specific laws and particular way. China's own way seems to be outside of the general laws of human historical development. Thus, whenever Chinese revolutionaries devoted themselves to China's progress, to catching up with the advanced countries, to learning from revolutionary theory and practice and the best of science and technology so as to complete more quickly the Chinese revolution, these "closed-door" advocates always opposed them, arguing that China's conditions differed too greatly from foreign ones to make revolutionary solutions relevant. Foreign science, culture, and revolutionary theory and experience could not be applied to China, and should not be accepted but opposed, they argued. Even if they conceded that they needed to accept some things from foreign countries, they always said that we should accept them under the precondition that Chinese traditions were preserved and not changed, that is, under the condition of "taking the Chinese essence as the base and Western learning solely for use."[46]

One example of such politically opportunistic notions of Chinese-style modernization was the influential idea of Chinese nativism developed in the 1930s by Sa Mengwu and Tao Xisheng, two important theoreticians of the Nationalist Party. Ten professors, including Sa and Tao, published a "Declaration of Chinese Native Cultural Construction" on January 10, 1935, demanding that the Nationalist authorities promote "Economic Reconstruction under the Three Principles of the People." The essence of the declaration was to focus on Chinese native politics rather than on Chinese native culture. "Chinese political forms, social organization, and thought have been losing their [distinctive] Chinese characteristics. People experiencing these politics, society, and thought without Chinese characteristics are becoming non-Chinese," the declaration read.[47] The authors attempted to convince people that since the Nationalist authorities had completed the great political revolution, "although there were a variety of difficulties, China has gained a great deal of success in politics through years of effort." As such, the biggest task in the future was not political reform but cultural construction; cultural construction was much more vital than political reform.[48]

The Politics of Intellectual Discourse on Culture

In fact, by negating the need for political reform in China, these scholars tended to promote resistance to democracy and helped sustain authoritarian politics. When asked what *Chinese nativeness* meant, these scholars answered that it centered on "the needs of the present," that is, on the need "to enrich people's lives," "to develop the national economy," and "to sustain national survival."[49] Democracy and political reform were not included in these "needs of the present." As Zhang Xiruo argued as soon as the declaration was published: "The essence of [the notion of] Chinese native culture is to deny [the need for] democracy; indeed, democracy is thought by these scholars to be 'the higher stage of development of the Three People's Principles.' Plainly speaking, to advocate on behalf of Chinese native culture is to advocate the construction of despotism."[50]

The underlying logic of the "Chinese substance–Western function" formula from the late Qing dynasty was to use advanced Western products, science, technology, and machines without adopting political reform or Western democracy. The theory of Chinese nativism in the 1930s was essentially little more than an updated version of the earlier formula, although the advocates of this position were critical of the *ti-yong* formula. Hu Shi, however, argued that the similarities between "Chinese nativism" and the *ti-yong* formula outweighed any minor differences:

> The ten professors say in their Declaration that they disagree with the "Chinese substance–Western function" formula. It is surprising, for their "Chinese native cultural construction" is [nothing but a] new disguise for "Chinese substance and Western function." The same spirit

pervades the two, even if the words are different. "Chinese nativism" is "Chinese substance," is it not? "Absorb what should be absorbed critically" is "Western function," is it not?[51]

In a fundamental sense, both approaches to China's modernization remained superficial because they both ignored the crucial problem of politics. Proponents of each position blamed the other for the failure of competing modes of modernization, while ignoring the importance of Chinese characteristics or of being insufficiently whole-hearted about Westernization. Regardless of the mode of modernization pursued, the process of modernization in China has encountered great resistance in the attitudes and behaviors of the political elites. As soon as modernization has appeared to run counter to the interests of the elites, they have been quick to suspend modernization, especially political reforms. The question of culture is a crucial question for modernity and modernization, and it cannot be separated out from the prior question of politics. This may be the lesson of the 1930s debates for the present.

CHAPTER EIGHT

THE TRANSFORMATION OF CHINESE CULTURE SINCE THE LAUNCHING OF REFORM

A Historical Perspective

Globalization, characterized by intensified economic relations across the globe, is a worldwide trend of historical significance.[1] Although the primary manifestation of globalization is economic integration, economic globalization also exerts deep influence on the totality of human social life, including its political and cultural spheres. Economic globalization not only has greatly changed production, consumption, and commercial exchange patterns; it has also altered modes of thinking and behavior. Above all, it has had a major impact on national cultures.

The influence of globalization on Chinese culture first became apparent following the New Culture movement of the early twentieth century. Since the 1980s deep, multidimensional tensions have reemerged in Chinese culture. These tensions include conflicts over tradition versus modernity, conservatism versus radicalism, nationalism versus globalization, and Sinification versus Westernization. During this period, heated debates emerged among Chinese intellectual circles; these debates came to be known as the culture fever. This chapter will briefly examine several general issues of culture in these debates, starting with the logic of Chinese culture as it unfolds against the backdrop of modernization and globalization, and ending with comments on the current situation of Chinese culture as well as its future development. The chapter argues that cultural transformations that originated during the May Fourth period of the 1910s and 1920s are now coming to an end. As a result, a new kind of Chinese culture is forming that represents neither a simple renaissance of traditional culture nor a carbon copy of one or another Western culture. Instead, it is deeply rooted in Chinese tradition but also absorbs some of the superior aspects of the cultures of other civilizations.

Cultural Modernization

From a historical perspective, the process of reform and opening since 1978 is essentially one of steady and comprehensive embrace of modernization and consequently of thorough-going social transformation. Modernization's economic dimension requires industrial civilization and a market economy; its political dimension calls for democracy; and its cultural dimension upholds such core values as freedom, equality, and the sovereignty of human subjectivity. On the whole, Chinese traditional culture is usually seen as being incompatible with the political, economic, and cultural dimensions of modernization. As such, the first response of Chinese intellectuals to the reform and opening-up project was to consider how best to revamp traditional values to better fit with the requirements of cultural modernization.

This effort at cultural modernization aims at realizing the transformation of traditional culture, importing advanced modern culture, and making Chinese culture compatible with the processes of political and economic modernization. Some scholars have pointed out that cultural modernization is a basic requirement and organic component of social modernization. As one put it, "modern social life, as well as 'modern people' will inevitably accompany modern culture. Cultural modernization means formation of a new culture, which absorbs the merits of other cultures and is compatible with modern society. The modernization of economic and social life, the modernization of 'people,' and the modernization of culture are inseparable components of modernization. They are interrelated, interactive, and irreplaceable."[2]

Chinese cultural modernization has two basic elements. On one hand, it entails revamping traditional culture, rejecting negative and outdated elements, and critically retaining its rational components. On the other hand, it means absorbing the merits of other advanced civilizations and incorporating them into a new Chinese culture. To most Chinese intellectuals, both of these elements are necessary to the modernization of Chinese culture, and they are equally indispensable. As one scholar has argued, "although it is necessary to learn from Western culture [in order] to construct a modern new culture, it is also crucial (and probably more important) to rediscover and carry forward [themes from our own] national culture [as well as] the essence of the national spirit."[3] Chinese intellectuals have differed, however, over the relative emphases of inheriting tradition or learning from the West, and as a result fierce debates have ensued.

For some intellectuals, the criticism of tradition is the first step toward modernizing culture. Although they do not necessarily deny the existence of reasonable and excellent elements in traditional culture, they nevertheless point out that traditional culture as a whole is incompatible with modernization and argue that it is the biggest obstacle to social modernization. This is particularly true, they say, of China's autocratic feudal traditions, which strangled human nature, disregarded freedom and equality, stressed agriculture, despised commercial activities, and viewed men as superior to women. Scholars who prioritize abandoning many of the central tenets of traditional culture argue that only with the elimination of such traditions can people's thinking be liberated and that in the absence of such liberation, social modernization will be impossible. As the prominent historian Li Shu wrote in a 1979 article: "In China, it is extremely difficult to launch an ideological revolution to eliminate feudal influence. It is even harder to make people identify with such a revolution."[4] Therefore, he argued, "completing the antifeudal ideological revolution that originated with the May Fourth movement is an important prerequisite to modernization, as well as [to] the victory of socialism in China."[5] This influential article was the first declaration of the ideological liberation campaign of the late 1970s.

Scholars who stressed the criticism of tradition argued that social modernization must be built on the basis of science and democracy, which were lacking in traditional culture. The May Fourth movement was the first attempt at ideological liberation in modern China and also the first attempt to modernize China's traditional cultural values. The preeminent demands of the May Fourth movement were for "Mr. Science" and "Mr. Democracy." Pioneering thinkers of the May Fourth movement, such as Lu Xun, Chen Duxiu, and Hu Shi, were unanimous in arguing that traditional cultural values were incompatible with science and democracy. Based on their analyses, they concluded that in order to replace its traditional culture, China must construct a new culture with democracy and science as its core values.

Such views reemerged after the launching of reform and opening. There were heated debates among Chinese intellectuals in the 1980s over whether Chinese traditional culture contained scientific and democratic elements. Li Shenzhi, an influential and well-known scholar, pointed out emphatically that "neither democracy nor science existed in Chinese traditional culture." Li intoned with emotion that "the year 1999 is the eightieth anniversary of the May Fourth movement. Recalling the past in the light of the present, we should feel ashamed that we have not lived up to the expectations of the pioneers of the May Fourth movement because we have made little progress in achieving either democracy or science."[6]

Since the late 1970s Chinese intellectuals criticizing traditional culture have not only raised the flags of science and democracy but have also advocated the rule of law, which distinguishes them from their predecessors in the May Fourth movement. Chinese traditional culture paid great attention to rule *by* law, but almost no attention to the rule *of* law. Although seemingly similar, the two have substantial differences. The emphasis of rule by law is on handling events in accordance with laws made by an absolute monarch, which presupposes that the emperor is above the law. The essence of the rule of law, by contrast, is that no person or group can be above the law. The principle of the rule of law did not exist in traditional Chinese culture and was actually inconsistent with the very logic of traditional culture. As such, modernizing China's traditional culture requires not only democracy and science, but also the construction of a modern state premised on the rule of law.

Cultural Renaissance

The first high tide of the culture fever in the reform era centered around cultural modernization based on a critique of traditional culture; the second tide ironically centered around the idea of a cultural renaissance. Those who advocated cultural renaissance also called for cultural modernization, but they regarded cultural renaissance, rather than the criticism of tradition, as the best way to achieve that goal. They argued that Chinese traditional culture is not incompatible with modernization. In their view, the reason China has lagged behind the West since the nineteenth century lay not in the backwardness of tradition but in the failure to carry forward the meritorious elements of traditional culture. They argued that it was extremely unreasonable to completely deny the role of traditional culture in the modernization process. In this view, fully implementing traditional culture was an important precondition to modernization. The renaissance of tradition and modernization were two sides of the same coin. These scholars found support for their arguments in empirical examples such as the "four Asian tigers" of Hong Kong, Singapore, South Korea, and Taiwan, all of which were heavily influenced by traditional Chinese culture. These societies were successful in their efforts to modernize, and yet they did not completely deny their traditions.

Instead, they made every effort to retain the basic values of traditional Chinese culture.

This wave of renaissance for traditional Chinese culture consisted of three parts: a resurgence of interest in Confucianism and the emergence of New Confucianism; a surge of cultural revivalism; and the renaissance of so-called national studies. There are similarities as well as differences among the three strains of cultural renaissance thinking. Each of these social trends takes a conservative attitude toward traditional culture, emphasizing the values of traditional culture in the present and insisting that its basic values should be revamped or reinvigorated while retaining basic core principle values. By so doing, advocates of each argued, traditional culture would become compatible with, and could contribute to, China's on-going modernization process. At the same time, however, the three parts have different emphases: New Confucianism regards Confucianism as the backbone of Chinese traditional culture and advocates the renaissance of traditional culture through the reinvigorating of Confucianism. Cultural revivalism pays greater attention to the important role Chinese culture once played in the world and hopes that Chinese culture can play a dominant role in the twenty-first century. The national studies approach emphasizes reviving ancient knowledge, which it views as the basis of traditional culture.

New Confucianism aims at reinvigorating the spirit of Confucianism. This approach originated in the 1920s with Liang Shuming, who served as its most influential advocate. New Confucianism flourished in Hong Kong, Taiwan, and the United States after 1949. Since the 1980s, New Confucianism has become increasingly influential in mainland China.[7] The New Confucianists not only have insisted on reinvigorating Confucianism but have also attempted to make New Confucianism into the dominant ideology of China's modernization process. In their view, this is the only way to revive and modernize China.

Jiang Qing, one of the most famous advocates of New Confucianism in contemporary China, argues that since the nineteenth century, China has lost both internal cohesion and international position, largely because of the degeneration of Confucianism. As Jiang argues: "In mainland China today, Marxism and Leninism, both imported alien cultures, have become the dominant ideologies with the help of state authority. However, these alien cultures cannot become the cultural foundation of the Chinese nation to express the national spirit. They mark the climax of a situation, under which the Chinese nation has been culturally rootless for centuries."[8]

In Jiang's view, the biggest obstacle to the modernization of China is nothing other than "the complete denial of Confucian tradition" as well as "the complete Westernization of China."[9] He concluded that reinvigorating Confucianism is the most urgent issue in contemporary China. Confucianism should replace Marxism and Leninism to become (as it once was) the dominant ideology of the Chinese nation. Some extreme New Confucianists have advocated developing Confucianism into a religion. One has even argued that "the government should impose a Confucianism legacy tax as well as other effective measures in order to change Confucianism into a national religion."[10]

The second approach, which focuses on cultural revivalism, has two basic theses. First, cultural revivalists assume that a direct correlation exists between the flourishing of Chinese culture and the prosperity of the Chinese nation. Cultural revivalists argue that the fate of Chinese culture is closely tied to the fate of the Chinese nation. The flourishing of Chinese culture always accompanied the prosperity of the Chinese nation. The Chinese nation once enjoyed great prosperity and glory in history, and China was among the strongest nations in ancient times. Chinese culture is one of the world's great cultures, which was once acknowledged by neighboring countries. Therefore, culture revivalists argue, from a historical perspective, the revival of Chinese culture is a precondition to China's modernization.

In addition, cultural revivalists argue that Chinese culture enjoys an "intrinsic superiority" over its Western counterparts. The failure to make full use of this intrinsic superiority is the reason why China has lagged behind the West. China has been growing ever more powerful since the implementation of the reform and opening policy. They argue, however, that to become a really great power, China must spread its own culture throughout the world. Only if China pursues this evangelizing mission on behalf of its cultural values can the intrinsic defects of Western culture be amended by the intrinsic superiority of Chinese culture. The cultural revivalists conclude that Western culture has fallen into a cul-de-sac and its dominance in the world will come to an end, while Chinese culture will be reinvigorated and become the mainstream of global civilization.

Liang Qichao and others observed in the late nineteenth century that "on the other side of the globe, there are hundreds of millions of people who are worrying about the bankruptcy of materialism and desperately calling for help! It is time to give them a hand!"[11] Similarly, in the beginning of the twenty-first century, Zhang Dainian, Ji Xianlin, and eighty-four other Chinese culture researchers together issued "A Statement of Chinese Cultural Renaissance" (the subtitle of which was "Striving for a Great Renaissance of the Chinese Nation and World Peace and Development in the 21st Century").[12] They announced passionately and proudly to the world: "The twenty-first century is a century for Chinese culture!" In addition, they argued, that

> in the contemporary world, clashes between different cultures, rampant heresy, religious extremism, environmental degradation, the degeneration of humanity as well as the side-effects of science all pose obstacles to social safety and development. Chinese culture will play an irreplaceable role in the settlement of these clashes and issues . . . . The twenty-first century is characterized by cultural confluence between the East and the West, while "dominance of Western culture" will be replaced by "dominance of Eastern culture." The renaissance of Chinese culture will not engender confrontation with Western culture. It means the creation of a new global culture with Eastern culture's absorption of its Western counterpart.[13]

The third school of thought, known as the national studies approach, focuses, generally speaking, on the knowledge system of Chinese traditional culture. In addition to such traditional ideologies as Confucianism, Buddhism, and Daoism, it also pays great attention to Chinese traditional literature, military studies, astrology, drama, painting, mathematics, and other fields. Therefore, the national studies approach actually aims at reinvigorating Chinese traditional culture in a broader sense. Compared with cultural revivalists, advocates of national studies are more practical and down to earth in their quest to reinvigorate Chinese traditional culture, which they go about by systematically sorting out, exploring, and teaching traditional forms of knowledge. One important method they have used is the creation of national studies institutes as well as training programs. A seminal event in the development of this approach was the 2005 establishment of the National Studies Academy at Renmin University, which began recruiting students for its bachelor program. Ji Baocheng, the president of Renmin University, became the first director of the National Studies Academy. Furthermore, a National Studies Club was established by the commercial circles, and Peking University established a Qianyuan National Studies Class, which was nicknamed the Bosses' Class, because it charged every student 24,000 yuan annually for tuition. Propelled by the "national studies fever" in academia, traditional private schools (*si shuyuan*) have reemerged.

The cultural renaissance movement has stirred up heated debates among Chinese intellectuals. Some support it, but a greater number have been critical.

Some moderate critics admit that traditional culture has several excellent elements that are still valuable. The modernization of China will benefit greatly from carrying forward these traditional values. Nevertheless, in their view, Chinese traditional culture as a whole is an obstacle to the modernization objective China is pursuing; the hope of reviving the Chinese nation by reviving traditional cultural values is destined to fail. As one critic of New Confucianism pointed out, "Confucianism long circumscribed the ideological freedom of Chinese people. In order to make Confucianism dominate Chinese national culture and national spirit, they [New Confucianists] have decorated Confucianism with the discourse of 'modernization.' It is totally absurd! It cannot help us accelerate the modernization process. It will become an obstacle instead."[14]

Some radical critics are more straightforward. They have labeled the cultural renaissance movement as cultural conservatism or nationalism and attacked it fiercely. Similar to the enlightenment thinkers of the May Fourth movement, they argue that traditional Chinese culture as represented by Confucianism is incompatible with modernization. The economic miracles of the "four Asian tigers" are not enough to draw the conclusion that Confucianism will propel the modernization process, they argue. The modernization of traditional culture lies neither in reinvigorating traditional culture nor in reviving Confucianism; instead, it hinges on the construction of a new culture by absorbing the meritorious elements of other cultures (particularly Western culture). Some critics argued that it is extremely ironic that cultural revivalists are still dreaming of a Chinese empire; they are "cultural nationalists." For these critics, to view the twenty-first century as a century for Chinese culture is an illusion.

Cultural Self-Consciousness

The reform and opening-up policy aims at advancing the political, economic, and social modernization of China through the transformation from traditional to modern culture. Against this background, the "modernization of traditional culture" has become a consensus goal among Chinese intellectuals for the first time since the May Fourth movement. But differences nonetheless exist over how best to handle traditional Chinese culture. What are to be the relations between traditional culture and modernization? How should the transformation process of traditional Chinese culture be accelerated? And what does cultural modernization mean in practice? These questions have triggered heated debates among Chinese intellectuals. Since the

1990s China's political, economic, and social spheres have faced ever greater pressure from globalization, which has completely changed the context of cultural debates. New questions have been raised: What kind of challenges does globalization pose to traditional culture? How does Chinese culture interact with Western culture within the context of globalization? What course will cultural development follow in the future? How should China present its culture in the world against the background of globalization?

In this context, a new cultural discourse has emerged since the 1990s, which has received wide attention and further propelled the spread of culture fever among Chinese intellectuals. The new discourse is often called cultural self-consciousness. It was initiated by the famous sociologist Fei Xiaotong, who first proposed the concept of cultural self-consciousness in 1997 at the Second Advanced Seminar on Sociology and Anthropology held at Peking University. Fei argued that cultural self-consciousness "expresses Chinese intellectuals' response to economic globalization. It also reflects the anxiety of human beings in general provoked by increased frequency of cultural contact. Social development leads people to think about such questions as the origins of national culture, its formation, essence, and future."[15] In Fei's view, the Reform movement of 1898, the May Fourth movement of 1919, and every political movement after 1949 all held high the flag of "destroying the old and establishing the new." They counterposed modernity to tradition and regarded traditional culture as the enemy of modernization. But Fei holds that cultural modernization does not mean simply destroying the old and establishing the new—it also means weeding through the old to bring forth the new as well as learning about the new by returning to a study of the old for insight. Modernization both destroys and incorporates tradition, raising the question of cultural transformation. In his lecture, Fei argued that

> the concept of "cultural self-consciousness" has profound connotations. It can be applied to every nation across the world as well as to the analysis of the common concerns of human beings. Its power lies in the fact that people know their own national culture very well. They are aware of the history, formation process, [and] characteristics, as well as tendencies of their own national culture. Self-consciousness can enhance the nation's autonomy in the process of cultural transformation, as the nation will be in a position to adapt to a new environment as well as determine its cultural orientation independently.[16]

Cultural self-consciousness aims to find a way to preserve Chinese culture against the backdrop of globalization and modernization. Chinese scholars concerned by this challenge have had to ask themselves: What is the essence of cultural self-consciousness? What is its focus? How can one achieve it? Chinese intellectuals have given different responses to these questions. Some, for example, place greater emphasis on culture's role in social development. Such scholars argue that culture plays a more and more significant role in social modernization in the era of globalization. It is not only a critical impetus to social development but also an important constituent of a nation's competitiveness. This is particularly true of today's China. Having already achieved the development of a large-scale economy and a preliminary institutional framework, the key to the successful accomplishment of a modern civilization in China lies with the modernization of culture. In this view, cultural self-consciousness means that China must be conscious of culture's significance in social development and adjust the nation's strategy of cultural development consciously based on the needs of social development. These scholars argue that "competition in the era of globalization is essentially competition between cultural forces. Countries with powerful cultural values, science and technology, production standards as well as management models export these to the whole world, which countries with poor cultural appeal have to accept. This is the cultural dilemma facing developing countries in the era of globalization."[17]

By contrast, some scholars place the emphasis of cultural self-consciousness on Chinese culture's significance for world culture. They insist that Chinese culture be looked at from the perspective of world history. Gan Yang, a prominent scholar of Chinese culture, has noted that cultural self-consciousness has at least two meanings. First, Chinese people must realize that the rise of the Chinese economy is an important event not only in the history of the world economy but also for the history of world civilization. This makes it totally different from the economic rise of the four Asian tigers. The West looks at China's rise as the determining cause of change in a world structure of Western dominance, which has lasted six hundred years. Chinese people must be conscious of China's position in the contemporary world. They must look at China and its relationship to the rest of the world from the perspective of world civilization and world history. Second, the idea of cultural self-consciousness indicates that Chinese culture does not measure up to China's current position in the world. From a parochial perspective on culture and history, China's cultural foundation is pretty narrow. Cultural self-consciousness does not mean cultural egotism. Instead, it aims to construct culture while resisting the appeals of "cultural fickleness" and "cultural showmanship."[18]

Other scholars focus on the revival of traditional culture. They argue that cultural self-consciousness means either rediscovering the merits of traditional culture and carrying traditions forward or pushing forward the transformation and innovation of traditional culture through examination of the disparity between the claims and realities of traditional culture. Some equate cultural self-consciousness with "Confucian self-consciousness" and advocate reforming and reviving Confucianism. These scholars argue that "Confucianism still has both theoretical significance and practical significance in the new historical context, and what we should do is to combine the conscience and spirit of Confucianism and modern values. As for the Chinese nation, the first step is to consciously carry forward Confucianism."[19]

Some scholars place greater emphasis on the innovation of traditional culture. They argue that cultural self-consciousness calls for looking at traditional culture rationally and for consciously pushing forward cultural innovation and development. In their view, the aim of cultural self-consciousness is not to return to traditional culture but to innovate and develop it. For example, Yue Daiyun, a researcher at Peking University, notes that "cultural self-consciousness advocates neither the return of traditional culture nor cultural capitulationism. Its essence lies in adjusting national culture according to new historical conditions."[20] In this view, the best way to preserve tradition is to develop it.

Still other scholars understand cultural self-consciousness from the perspective of methodological and theoretical concerns. In their view, cultural self-consciousness implies treating culture as a research subject and making it into an academic discipline that can be studied within a theoretical framework. Tang Yijie, a professor from Peking University, is an advocate of this perspective. He argues that researchers must be conscious of the theories and methodologies they use in their research; this is, after all, a precondition to any mature academic discipline. In Tang's view, researchers of Chinese culture must look at it as their research subject and carry out their research systematically, creatively, and practically. "Only by so doing can they find both the advantages and disadvantages of Chinese culture and then consciously discover its intrinsic values. Only in this way will it be possible for the Chinese people to absorb the excellent elements of other cultures."[21]

If cultural self-consciousness is a strategy of preserving tradition as well as innovating to meet the current demands of Chinese society as it evolves against a backdrop of modernization and globalization, as most Chinese intellectuals argue, then the two opposing forces of cultural globalization and cultural localization must be properly understood and accounted for. I turn first to cultural globalization.

Cultural Globalization

Cultural globalization is such a controversial concept that some scholars oppose its use. Some state directly that, based on economic globalization, cultural globalization is nothing but a synonym for the spread of Western culture.[22] Some believe that the notion of cultural globalization itself is a conceptual contradiction. As some scholars observe, "the concept of cultural globalization has met with resistance in the Chinese context," and many argue that cultural globalization is impossible or an illusion with no real basis.[23] Others reject it because they fear the threat it poses to Chinese culture. Whatever the reality may be, despite the aforementioned concerns, the concept of cultural globalization is finding increasing acceptance among Chinese scholars, many of whom are thinking seriously about its implications.

Analysts who adopt the framework of cultural globalization assert that with the acceleration of economic globalization, cultural globalization has become, or will become, a reality as well. What is at issue for these scholars is not a value judgment about the desirability of cultural globalization but the reality of its existence. These analysts make three general observations. First, the free and rapid flow of capital, technology, information, and labor across the globe compels nation-states to conform to "international standards," and accept "international norms" or "global rules," which has resulted in the collapse of the political and economic as well as the cultural barriers of nation-states, altering their ideologies, social values, and institutional norms. Second, apart from exporting capital, technology, and production to the developing countries, the developed countries also attempt to impose their values, ideas, literatures, arts, and even lifestyles. Under the assault of Western culture, the national cultures of developing countries are weakened, and many national traditions collapse. Finally, globalization has intensified connections among human beings. Such issues as ecological crises, environmental pollution, terrorism, resource crises, the global population explosion, the spread of communicable diseases, and nuclear proliferation are becoming "globalized." These global issues threaten the survival of human beings as a whole and call for "global action." Thus, "global consciousness" and a "global culture" are urgently needed.

Li Shenzhi, a leading advocate of "global culture," points out that "we are living in a changing world. Not only has the 'balance of power' in the world changed, but global forces and issues have emerged. These represent global demands that transcend divisions of East and West, or North and South. To cope with these issues is a challenge for all countries in the world and calls for the emergence of a 'global culture.'"[24] To most of its advocates, cultural globalization is not about the homogenization of national cultures but about the interconnections among different national cultures as well as the increasing consensus about and consciousness of global issues. As one scholar has argued, "cultural globalization is essentially a process of cultural integration. Based on economic globalization and information technology, different national cultures have been updated and integrated through intensified interactions. . . . In this sense, cultural globalization is neither an accomplished reality nor the death knell of disadvantaged nations."[25]

Although culture is an overarching concept and its boundaries are hard to define, at its core culture is about human values. Following this logic, some scholars have paid a great deal of attention to universal, or global, values in their studies of cultural globalization. In this view, globalization not only makes people realize that they share a common fate but also helps them identify with such basic values as freedom, equality, justice, security, welfare, and dignity. Pursuit of such basic values is the core principle, as well as the ultimate destination, of cultural globalization. It is incumbent upon nation-states to pursue such values. For example, Li Shenzhi has argued:

> Global values do exist, [and are enshrined,] in such documents as the Universal Declaration of Human Rights, the Declaration of Environmental Protection, the Nuclear Non-Proliferation Treaty, [and other international conventions]. But these values have not yet been observed by nations voluntarily; [indeed, at times] they could even ignite conflicts. As for nations, the biggest glory is to increase their contributions to the formation of global values. The future of globalization is the formation and dominance of global values.[26]

Cultural interactions in the era of globalization have their own characteristics that distinguish them from exchanges among nations in the past. One scholar has pointed out that cultural globalization has three basic characteristics. First, cultural and economic affairs are becoming increasingly integrated. Economic advantages bring about cultural advantages. Second, cultural exchanges are degenerating into culture exportation. Based on their economic and technical advantages, the developed countries have sought to spread Western culture to the whole world, sparing no effort to erode cultural heterogeneity. Therefore, cultural exchanges between West and East have degenerated into cultural exportation or cultural imposition. Third, the functions of culture are expanding, exerting an ever more comprehensive influence on social life. With the rise of the culture industry, culture is spreading into many new areas besides education, including consumption, aesthetics, economic affairs, and entertainment. Culture not only affects the ideology and value systems of human beings but also exerts a deep influence on their lifestyles, consumption patterns, manufacturing, and social psychology.[27]

Debates about cultural globalization in China always bring out advocates of cultural localization. These two, seemingly contradictory sides of the debate about culture have been bound together since the launching of the reform and opening-up policy in 1978.

Cultural Localization

The aim of cultural localization is to highlight the characteristics of national culture or to endow national culture with its own characteristics. Cultural localization is a natural response to globalization; they are two sides of the same coin, supplementing each other and constituting a "rational paradox" of cultural development. Cultural localization is a concept relative to cultural globalization, and it would be misleading to discuss the former without reference to the latter. The localization of Chinese culture once again became a "hot topic" among Chinese intellectuals in the 1980s and 1990s. As one scholar pointed out:

> For some countries or regions, globalization means the demise of local culture. We must realize that globalization is a process through which Western countries spread their culture to the rest of the world. . . . Modernization or globalization has brought about a sense of "homelessness," which has resulted [for many peoples] in a crisis of cultural identity. . . . [Such an] identity crisis and the sense of frustration that comes with it made people aware of the significance of local culture to national survival. [As a result,] antiglobalization campaigns erupted under the banner of "returning to local culture."[28]

Some may ask how feasible cultural localization or cultural nationalization is against the backdrop of globalization. In the views of some Chinese scholars, in the era of globalization national cultures are under pressure from both homogenization and pluralization, as well as showing tendencies toward both universalism and particularism. Cultural globalization does not erase the diversity of national culture; instead, it gives prominence to the value of local or national characteristics. Cultural pluralism develops alongside cultural globalization, which is rooted in the diversity of local or national cultures. Even globalization has a hard time erasing the cultural diversity of human societies. Cultural diversity, just like cultural universalism, is an intrinsic element in the survival and development of nations. Cultural diversity is an important precondition for cultural continuity and human development. Both integration of and conflict between different cultures push forward cultural development of human societies.[29]

Against the challenges of globalization, the localization of Chinese culture refers to efforts to sustain the values and sanctity of national culture in order to avoid its being subsumed by the process of globalization. To effectively localize Chinese culture, Chinese scholars have put forward a number of suggestions.

First, Chinese people must consciously take care of their national culture, recognizing that Chinese culture is facing serious challenges from Western culture during the era of globalization. Chinese people must recognize this challenge and assume responsibility for the preservation and further development of Chinese culture. The defense of national culture is essential to the existence of a nation. Chinese culture has lasted for more than five thousand years; arguably no other culture can bear comparison with its deep tradition and robust vitality. Therefore, faced with the challenge of globalization, Chinese culture's vitality should not be overestimated or taken for granted, but instead must be constantly defended and renewed.

Second, Chinese people should actively preserve the Chinese culture. As some advocates of national culture point out, to preserve the nationality of culture does not mean cultural nationalism. Its aim is not to refuse the excellent elements of foreign cultures but to consciously sustain the nationality and independence of Chinese culture and to carry forward its meritorious traditions and values in the process of cultural globalization: "Faced with cultural globalization, we must place top priority on preserving the nationality of Chinese culture and highlight its characteristics. The more national one's culture is, the more global it will be. To keep the nationality of culture is to push Chinese culture out to the world through absorbing and extending the common values of the whole world."[30]

When discussing how to sustain nationality and preserve culture, some scholars have imported discursive constructs from the realms of politics and economics. For example, in Feng Ziyi's view, Chinese people should pay urgent attention to the protection of cultural sovereignty and security. He argued that cultural security will not make sense without cultural sovereignty, while cultural preservation will be impossible without cultural security.[31] Feng has proposed several suggestions for protecting cultural sovereignty: First, one should maintain one's consciousness of being a cultural subject, that is, one should adopt the principle of "taking myself as the dominant actor" and "making foreign things serve our purposes" in the process of cultural exchanges. Second, one should adopt an appropriate cultural strategy so as to develop one's national culture and withstand the influence of foreign cultures. Third, the state should protect and develop its culture industry, withstanding the "colonization strategy" of some Western culture industry actors.[32]

Last, a culture can remain vital only by retaining its merits. This is as true of Chinese culture as it is of any other culture. Therefore, in the localization and nationalization of Chinese culture, the most important task is to construct an advanced culture with Chinese characteristics. Such an advanced culture would include a national spirit, a value system, a knowledge system, literature, and arts that are compatible with China's socialist market economy and democratic politics, as well as with national conditions.

How can the Chinese people and the Chinese nation best construct an advanced culture with Chinese characteristics? To answer this question, Chinese scholars have put forward many suggestions. These can be divided into four categories. First, China should retain and carry forward the essence of traditional culture. Second, China should persist in its strategy of opening up and engaging actively in cultural globalization. Chinese people must be good at learning and absorbing advanced ideas, values, and knowledge from foreign cultures and must excel at integrating them into Chinese culture. Third, one should accomplish the renovation and transformation of Chinese culture by retaining the essence of traditional culture while absorbing the best elements of Western culture. Finally, one should spread Chinese culture and help it "go out." This involves integrating the essence of Chinese culture into global culture. By so doing, Chinese culture will become an organic constituent of global culture.

Concluding Thoughts

There have been heated debates about culture among Chinese intellectual circles since the early 1980s. By aiming at the political, economic, and social modernization of China, the reform and opening-up policy China has been in some ways consistent with China's Westernization movement of the mid-nineteenth century. However, the historical context of modernization in China since the 1980s has changed greatly. The world has entered a new era of globalization. The links between modernization and globalization are crucial to any understanding of the social transformation of China since 1978.

From this perspective, the culture debates China has seen since the early 1980s are actually a response by the Chinese nation to the twin pressures of modernization and globalization, and a logical consequence of the transformation of traditional Chinese culture under these pressures. The aim of these cultural debates has been to accomplish the goals that the May Fourth movement failed to achieve, and in this sense the debates could fairly be regarded as a continuation of that movement. To be sure, they share a similar logic and arguments, focusing on problems such as tradition versus modernity, Sinification versus Westernization, Chinese substance versus Western function, radical versus conservative, advanced versus backward, and other such tropes.[33] The culture debates of the 1980s onward have aimed to establish a set of values and a knowledge system compatible with universal human values. On the one hand, some universal values will be absorbed into Chinese culture in this process; on the other hand, some elements of Chinese culture will become components of global culture.

The on-going cultural debates exhibit extreme complexity. Some support the modernization of tradition while others advocate cultural globalization; some make an appeal for cultural localization while others criticize it as cultural nationalism; some focus on the innovation of traditional culture while others seek its revival; some engage in global cultural exchanges while others plead for the preservation of national culture; some worry about the erosion of national identity while others are thrilled by more cosmopolitan values; some decry the backwardness of traditional culture while others proudly announce that the twenty-first century will be the century of Chinese culture.

If one examines these contradictory cultural phenomena more closely, however, it becomes both simple and clear: the Westernization movement of the mid-nineteenth century marked the beginning of the modernization process of China. Since then, two themes have prevailed. One has been the effort to accomplish modernization so as to resolve China's economic and cultural backwardness; the other trend has been to gain independence and break the "semicolonization" of Western dominance. In other words, modernization and national independence have been the two basic tasks of modern Chinese history.[34] Basically speaking, these two themes account for the contradictions between values such as modern versus tradition, progressive versus conservative, and Sinification versus Westernization.

Generally speaking, modern civilization refers to industrial civilization, which originated in the West. Modern industrial machinery, resources, energy, chemistry, medicine, and telecommunications were first established in the West. If modernization is narrowly defined as industrialization, then it will be necessary to learn from the advanced science, technology, manufacturing skills, and management institutions of the West in order to achieve modernization. In this sense, the more contact with and learning from the West China undertakes, the more modern and progressive a society it will be. From this perspective, it is not surprising that many Chinese scholars have equated modernization with Westernization.

This perspective on modernization would also, logically, lead one to conclude that the more unwilling a society is to learn from the West, the more backward it will be. In the particular context of modern China, the West was regarded as the embodiment of advanced culture while Chinese tradition was often seen as the symbol of backwardness. As a result, the conflict between progressive and reactionary forces in China's modern history often appeared to take shape as a conflict between Westernization and Sinification, between advanced values and backward values, and between modern and traditional worldviews. Reactionary forces were seen to be the representatives of vested interest groups. They strongly objected to China's reforms and to learning from the West by putting forward arguments about "the degeneracy of Western culture," "the incompatibility of Western culture with Chinese conditions," "the excellence of Chinese traditional culture," and other such notions. These arguments, as the philosopher Ai Siqi once pointed out, are common rhetorical tactics among all conservative and reactionary forces in China's modern history. Ignoring the universal logic of the human experience, they seek a "closed-door policy."[35]

Apart from accomplishing modernization through learning from the West, the other task of China's modern history has been to achieve national independence. These two tasks are to some extent contradictory. One question that has haunted Chinese intellectuals and politicians for many years has been how to deal with the relationship between Westernization and Sinification, or, more precisely, how to balance the necessity of learning from the West with the imperative of maintaining the independence of the Chinese nation. The semicolonization of modern China was caused by the West. To achieve independence, the Chinese nation had to get out from under the control and influence of the West, even while modernization necessitated learning from the West. This dilemma made Chinese intellectuals and politicians very sensitive about learning from the West and fearful that any attempt to do so might end in China's total colonization. As a result, Chinese thinkers have sought to emphasize the necessity of "making Chinese" or "nationalizing" those elements of Western culture that they feel compelled to adopt. Although China's politics, economy, and culture all changed fundamentally between 1949 and the end of the 1970s, China still lagged far behind Western countries. To achieve modernization, China's leaders realized that they had to swallow their concerns and undertake to learn from the Western capitalist countries in earnest. As such, the Chinese Communist Party, led by Deng Xiaoping, carried out bold and resolute reforms of the traditional socialist planned economy. One of these reforms was to reshape the strategy of modernization. Advocating that "development is the basic principle," China opened up once more to the West. In so doing, China learned about the most advanced scientific and technological developments and management experiences of the West, absorbed Western investment, and intensified exchanges as well as cooperation with Western countries. With the opening-up policy, concerns about Westernization versus Sinification, tradition versus modernity, and advanced versus backward cultural values reemerged. On one hand, China has had to learn from the West; on the other hand, China has had to strive to maintain its national autonomy. In this context, the long-standing questions of how to preclude foreign control while learning from the West and how to retain independence while embracing elements of Western culture reemerged as well.

Even compared with other Western countries, the United States enjoys superiority in both comprehensive national power as well as the fields of science and technology. It is fair to say that the United States is the leading force in the development of material civilization and spiritual civilization among Western countries and represents the highest development level of modern Western culture. With respect to the developing countries (including China), the United States undoubtedly exerts more influence than any other Western country. It might even be fair to argue that, with respect to any country in the world, the influence of American culture is to some extent irresistible. Not only are the developing countries facing the challenge of Americanization, other Western countries are to some extent suffering from this headache as well. In some sense then, Sinification versus Westernization is essentially a stand-in for Sinification versus Americanization.

The world entered the era of globalization beginning in the 1980s and 1990s. As the leading trend in current world history, globalization is fast becoming an unavoidable reality. As long as a country opens its doors to the outside world, it is drawn into a process of globalization—China is no exception. Although globalization is dominated by Western countries (led by the United States) that determine the rules as well as processes of globalization, no country, not even the United States, can control the process of globalization completely. In the future, the developing countries, represented by China, will definitely come to enjoy more and more weight in the process of globalization. Globalization is a double-edged sword for developed as well as developing countries. Both developed and developing countries benefit from and suffer harm from globalization. The modernization and globalization of Chinese culture proceed hand in hand.[36]

Globalization is a process characterized by intrinsic contradictions. It organically incorporates integration and fragmentation, universality and diversity, and cosmopolitanism as well as parochialism. The primary driver of globalization is economic integration. Economic globalization inevitably exerts profound influences on political, cultural, and social life as well. Deng Xiaoping, the chief architect of China's modernization strategy, incorporated both domestic reforms and opening up to the outside world into one seamless policy package. In responding to the adoption of this far-sighted strategy, some intellectuals supported cultural globalization while others appealed to cultural localization; some played up cultural uniqueness while others were attracted to cultural diversity; some advocated cultural nationalism while others appealed for cultural universalism; some emphasized national identity while others advocated emphasizing global identity. There are even some who advocate both values at the same time.

Every scholar or politician, as long as he or she cares about the modernization of China, will inevitably encounter—and will have to address directly or indirectly—the challenges outlined above. Some pay more attention to the significance of development and globalization. In their view, economic development as well as universal values are vital to the protection of national dignity, and culture and national identity are basically compatible with globalization. These scholars believe that there are many excellent elements in Western culture that can be shared collectively by humanity as a whole. As such, they place the focus on learning from Western culture and expect Chinese people to enjoy the same modern civilization as Westerners. They prefer to place their emphasis on learning from Western culture and on adapting to globalization, rather than prioritizing the advancement of traditional Chinese culture. Other analysts uphold the importance of independence and nationality. In this view, maintaining the purity and independence of national culture is more essential than even economic development. These scholars fear that China might lose its autonomy in the process of globalization and become subordinate to Western countries. They prefer to carry the banner of Chinese culture rather than adapting to cultural globalization.

It is easy for the two sides to go to extremes, especially when they talk past each other. The former school tends to label the latter as "conservatives" while the latter label the former as "radicals" or "complete Westernizers." Taking a holistic view of the cultural debates among the Chinese intelligentsia since the 1980s, one can identify several general trends. First, new discursive tropes such as globalization versus localization, cosmopolitanism versus nationalism, and "an identity based on our common humanity versus a national identity" are replacing earlier distinctions such as Sinification versus Westernization. Second, the cultural transformation that originated with the May Fourth movement is now coming to its end. In its place, a new kind of Chinese culture has been forming that represents neither the simple renaissance of traditional culture nor a carbon copy of Western values. This new Chinese culture has its roots in Chinese tradition but absorbs the best elements of other civilizations as well. It combines tradition and modernity while emphasizing both national identity and our common humanity. Third, even as global cultural values are entering into China, Chinese culture is spreading outward into the world. Chinese culture is becoming an important constituent of the mainstream of global culture, while global values such as freedom, equality, and human dignity are being incorporated into Chinese culture. In short, globalization is the abstraction of modern civilization on a global level. From the perspective of globalization, it is irrelevant whether modern civilization originated from the East or from the West. Indeed, just as learning from contemporary Eastern culture does not by necessity constitute "Easternization," learning from the West does not necessarily entail "Westernization."

CHAPTER NINE

CHINA'S ECONOMIC MODERNIZATION AND SUSTAINABILITY

C hina has fundamentally reformed its traditional socialist planned economy since the end of the 1980s.[1] The idea of a market economy with Chinese characteristics (also known as the socialist market economy) replaced the previous planned economy model, with multiple forms of ownership replacing the public-only model of property ownership. The state-owned enterprises lost their monopoly positions in the national economy while private and foreign-owned enterprises grew rapidly. As a result of these changes, China's economy has grown so rapidly that some have called it a miracle.

The average annual growth rate of China's gross domestic product (GDP) from 1978 to 2000 was over 9.0 percent. In the year 2000 China's total GDP was 8.94 trillion yuan, whereas in 1978 it was a mere 359 billion yuan. The gross national product (GNP) per capita in 2000 amounted to 7,078 yuan (about $800); the comparable statistic for 1978 was a mere 375 yuan. As a result, China has moved off of the list of low-income countries. The living standards of urban and rural households have continued to improve and are today rising toward the level of moderate prosperity for the country as a whole. At the same time, however, income disparities between urban and rural dwellers are growing. The annual per capita disposable income of urban households was 6,280 yuan in 2000 and the per capita net income of rural households was 2,253 yuan in the same year.

China's economic achievements resulted mainly from the performance of the market economy, where strategies of "prioritizing efficiency" and "prioritizing development" came to predominate. However, such development approaches to growth are like two-sided swords, particularly given that China had long practiced a traditional socialist planned economy model of growth. The process of social transition driven by market forces has brought Chinese people both pleasure and pain. China has paid high costs for its tremendous economic achievements partly because the Chinese public was mentally unprepared for some of the requirements of a market economy. Besides environmental degradation (discussed in chapter 10), China has paid huge costs in several key areas.

Unemployment and the Social Security System

According to official statistics, by the end of 2000, the number of people employed in China totaled 711.5 million. In the same year, the number of workers laid off from state-owned enterprises was 6.57 million. The urban unemployment rate was 3.1 percent, according to unemployment registration figures. However, unofficial estimates of unemployment are much higher than the official figure would suggest. Some scholars estimate that about 20 million people in urban areas are unemployed and that 100 million people in rural areas are potentially unemployed; these are the so-called surplus laborers.

All urban dwellers and many rural dwellers had at least some form of social security coverage under the traditional planned economy, even despite the extremely low personal income levels associated with that period. The previous system of providing social security collapsed during the reform era as policymakers reoriented growth toward the market economy without putting in place a new social security system adapted to the demands of a market economy. Thus, a huge number of citizens, especially those living in rural areas, have for the first time in their lives no access to any form of social security.

Economic Disparity and Corruption

The Chinese government encouraged some people to become rich faster than others. In fact, some people have become rich because of the market economy. A relatively uneven distribution system gradually replaced the previous egalitarian distribution system. The Gini coefficient of China's overall income distribution reached 0.445 in the 1990s, whereas it was between 0.2 and 0.24 before the reform era. On the one hand, there were more than 1 million millionaires, while on the other hand, as of 1997 for example, more than 80 million people were living under the poverty line of about 200 yuan a year. The food consumption of the families of this poor group accounts for more than 60 percent of their income.

Meanwhile, many cadres seem to view their official position as a "private good" and an opportunity to engage in rent-seeking behavior. Every day cases are reported in the Chinese press of high officials across the country who have been caught or punished for corruption. The phenomenon is widespread and appears to be growing in size, with reports of corrupt officials who have embezzled millions and even tens of millions of yuan becoming increasingly common. There are so many corrupt officials in China today that some people joke that "if we ordered all the cadres to line up and killed every other person in the line, sure there would be some innocents among them; but if we killed every other person in the queue, there must be a lot of corrupt officials who would have escaped punishment." The situation is truly serious. In one notable instance of corruption, about two hundred officials were arrested in the Xiamen smuggling case of the late 1990s, including almost all of the leading cadres of the Xiamen government and party.

Emerging Social Problems

China's social problems are increasing alongside the country's wealth. Before the reforms, Chinese were proud of having eliminated the "four pests" of drug abuse, prostitution, gambling, and secret societies throughout the country. Unfortunately, all of these have come back under the reforms. In the border areas of Yunnan and Guangxi provinces, for example, the number of drug users is on the rise. Even though prostitution is illegal in China, prostitutes are increasingly common, especially in the economically developed areas. Hainan Island, for example, was once famous for its "Red Women Army," a special team of women soldiers who fought for the Communist Party during the Revolution. Today, it is well known for its "Yellow Women Army," the local slang used to refer to the island's ubiquitous prostitutes. Gambling is terribly popular in the cities and countryside. The rate of crime in the country has risen dramatically in recent years. Furthermore, organized criminal groups and secret societies are spreading from the South to the North.

In the early years of the reforms, China adopted a strategy of "prioritizing development over governance" and neglected the social and natural environments. However, after recognizing the very high costs of its rapid economic growth, China changed its strategy to "balancing development and governance of the natural and social environments." Additionally, China has begun to pursue harmonious development between human beings, society, the economy, and the environment. Increasingly, Chinese people have seen the benefits of improving social and environmental governance as the Chinese government and nongovernmental organizations have come to focus more and more on these issues.

Government Responses

By the end of 2000, 667 cities and 1,682 counties had set up programs to support minimal living standards, and at least 3.8 million urban residents had obtained subsidies through these programs. The central government has contributed special funds to urban inhabitants in poor areas in northern and western China since 1999.

NEW INSURANCE SYSTEM

By the end of 2000, some 104.1 million workers were enrolled in the government's unemployment insurance program, and a total of 1.4 million people were receiving monthly unemployment insurance. Some 103.7 million workers, as well as more than 31.7 million retirees, were participating in the basic retirement security program, while 43.3 million workers were participating in the basic health care program. By the second half of 2000, twenty provinces and province-level cities (about three-fifths of all province-level administrative units) had developed their own medical services systems, and 80 percent of counties had met the goals of the National Primary Health Program.

SUSTAINABLE DEVELOPMENT STRATEGY

By the end of 2000, 128,000 people worked for environmental protection agencies in China. New achievements were made in the protection of nature, illustrated by the establishment of 213 environmental demonstration zones. China also established 1,227 protected nature zones (including 155 national protected nature zones) covering 98.2 million hectares, or 9.9 percent of the total land area of the country. The deterioration caused by environmental pollution has thus been brought under control, and the total emission of major pollutants into the atmosphere has begun to decline in these areas. By the end of 2000, over 90 percent of the 238,000 pollution-discharging enterprises met the country's environmental standards. Among the forty-six key environmental protection cities, the surface water quality in thirty-three cities and the air quality in twenty-two cities met the standards. Apart from those eighteen cities where both air and surface water quality reached national standards, the rest of the cities were close to the standards. As a major step to prevent the deterioration of urban environment, all major cities have released data on air quality to the public since June 2001.

POVERTY ALLEVIATION PROJECT

The number of people living in poverty has declined noticeably, from 160 million at the beginning of the 1980s to 60 million at the end of the 1990s. Progress was made in part through the implementation of reemployment projects. By the end of 2000, the number of laid-off workers from state-owned enterprises was 6.57 million, of which about 3.61 million found new jobs. The government has been increasing its spending on education, and had invested approximately 335 billion yuan in schooling through 1999, a figure that is the equivalent of about 2.79 percent of GDP. The nine-year compulsory education program today covers 85 percent of the total population, and the illiteracy rate among youths and the middle-aged is less than 5 percent. It is particularly worth noting that civil society organizations have, in recent years, taken on an increasingly important role in poverty alleviation, reemployment, and the promotion of nine-year compulsory education. For example, the Hope Project, which has helped millions of children go to school, was launched by the China Youth and Children Foundation, a major nongovernmental civil society group.

Foreign capital has also helped to resolve the problems of environmental degradation, unemployment, and poverty alleviation. In 1999 alone, the contracted foreign direct investment was $52.7 billion, including $10.2 billion in foreign debt relief. Foreign debt, for the most part, has been invested in environmental protection, poverty alleviation, and developmental education. For instance, one-third of World Bank loans to China have gone into improving environmental governance. For China's development, foreign investment has been mostly a help rather than a hindrance, in part because China has had $190 billion in foreign exchange reserves since August 2001.

Policy Initiatives for the Future

China's government and civil society have been making great efforts to promote harmonious development in the fields of the natural environment, society, and the economy and have made astonishing achievements. Nonetheless, China confronts a host of serious challenges and has a long way to go to achieve real harmony between development and sustainability. Environmental and ecological degradation, fundamentally speaking, have not been effectively controlled, and the problem of resource shortages has not been resolved.

China's future development will depend on its capacity and decisions with respect to the following measures on the way toward "harmony between man and nature": raising the rate of per capita natural resources; strengthening citizens' levels of awareness of the need for environmental protection and sustainable development; increasing investments into environmental governance; encouraging civil society to take a more active role in achieving sustainable development; improving the legal system; and eradicating local protectionism across the country.

CHAPTER TEN

HARMONY BETWEEN MAN AND NATURE

China's Environmental Practices and Challenges

Since Deng Xiaoping initiated the policy of economic reform in 1978, China has achieved meteoric economic growth.[1] The living standards of both urban and rural households have continually improved, and today China as a whole has almost reached a level of moderate prosperity.[2] Despite these economic advances, however, an astonishing number of people are not satisfied with the status quo even though they find themselves economically much better off than they once were. One of the main reasons for this surprising phenomenon is the very high price China has paid for its rapid economic growth, especially in the areas of ecological degradation and environmental pollution.

Air and water pollution in China's cities, for example, is astonishingly bad. Nationally, China's air has some of the highest concentrations of sulfur dioxide in the world. Every year, it is estimated, at least 200,000 people die and 11 million people fall ill from air pollution. During the 1990s, the average rate of economic growth was over 9 percent a year, while the estimated losses caused by air and water pollution amounted to 3–10 percent of GDP a year.[3] The township and village enterprises (TVEs), which some have called the "engine" of China's rural economic growth, are some of the largest sources of pollution and contamination in the country. In general, where township and village enterprises are more developed, one tends to find serious air and water pollution, industrial dust pollution, radioactive contamination, and noise pollution. Because illness ratios are increasing among the populations of these areas, some inhabitants of TVEs have begun to argue that, increases in personal income notwithstanding, they cannot afford the increased medical expenses they incur because of local pollution.

The high costs China has paid for its economic modernization and the awful situation the country is facing have led the government and the people to return to the ancient Chinese doctrine of "man and nature in harmony" (*Tianren heyi*). Over two thousand years ago, the doctrine was emphasized by famous thinkers such as Lao Tzu and Zhuang Tzu as the ideal relationship between human beings and nature. According to such Chinese classics, the needs of man and of the environment cannot be calculated in isolation from each other but must be given equal consideration. Human development must be carried out in harmony with nature. Obviously, this doctrine in many ways reflects the same concepts that underlie Western notions of sustainable development, while at the same time appealing to the trend among Chinese intellectuals to find culturally "authentic" models of development. With the adoption of the Rio Declaration on the Environment and Development, Agenda 21, and other important documents by the United Nations Conference on Environment and Development in 1992, the Chinese government and Chinese intellectuals have increasingly come to realize the importance of the concept of sustainable development, which has been gaining popularity among Chinese intellectual circles in recent years.

Sustainable Development

What is sustainable development? There are at least two influential views among Chinese scholars. First, in accord with the Rio Declaration, some people emphasize the fit between economic growth and the environment. In their view, sustainable development means that human economic development cannot overspend natural resources and exceed ecological and environmental carrying capacities. Social and economic development must meet not only existing needs but also the needs of the future, and the current generation must never satisfy its demands at the expense of its children's future.[4] The second view is deeply affected by traditional Chinese philosophy, which emphasizes the necessity of harmony between man and nature; sustainable development thus implies striking a harmonious balance between human beings, society, and nature. Sustainable development, according to this so-called "holistic development view," means not only harmony between economic development, environmental protection, population size, natural resources use, and ecological balance, but also coordination between man, society, economy, politics, culture, education, and the natural environment.[5]

However, most debates focus on the strategies for achieving sustainable development rather than the definitions of it. Among the major questions: Which is the higher priority—economic growth or environmental protection—if the two are in tension? What is the most effective path to sustainable development—state intervention or reliance on markets? What roles should the government and civil society play in achieving harmony between sustainability and development? What is the best way to mediate conflicts between different areas and departments with respect to development? And how does one best assess the quality of environmental governance of an administrative region or society as a whole? Various alternative strategies are available, but the dominant view seems to be that there is no time to delay in pursuing harmony between economic growth and sustainability. At the same time, however, there are those who argue that the highest priority should still be given to economic development. For those who hew to this approach, the most important consideration is China's status as a developing country because, as Deng Xiaoping argued, "the hard logic of (economic) development" means there can be no sustainable development without economic growth. This view previously served as the guiding principle of the country's official developmental strategy.

The Chinese leadership, however, has been attaching increasing importance to sustainable development and has compiled a number of achievements since the Rio Summit Conference, including:

—*Establishing administrative departments responsible for environmental protection above the county level and setting up coordinating committees that are working on China's implementation of the Agenda 21 goals.* In August 1992, only two months after the Rio Summit, the Chinese government set up a leading committee, an administrative center, and a standing office for China Agenda 21, a center consisting of fifty-two different departments. So far, twenty-five provincial and metropolitan governments have set up local leading committees of China Agenda 21.[6]

—*Implementing China Agenda 21.* In July 1992, only one month after the Rio Summit, China began working out China Agenda 21, the first draft of which was finished in April 1993, with the final version promulgated in 1994. On the basis of China Agenda 21, the government formulated the "Priority Program for China's Agenda 21," which includes eighty-two projects covering nine priority areas: capacity building for sustainable development; sustainable agriculture; cleaner production and environmental protection industries; clean energy and transportation; conservation and sustainable utilization of natural resources; environmental pollution controls; poverty alleviation and regional development; population, health, and human settlements; and global climate change and biodiversity conservation. Since then, various departments of the central and local governments have promulgated their own action plans. For example, Beijing municipality formulated the China Agenda 21: Beijing Action Plan in 1995, and the Ministry of Agriculture completed its China Agenda 21: Agricultural Action Plan around the same time.

—*Redefining sustainable development as one of two basic state policies.* Since the 1990s the Chinese government has officially identified population control and sustainable development as the two principles guiding China's medium- and long-term development. These ideals are enshrined in the Ninth and Tenth Five-Year Plans of National Economic and Social Development and the Outline for China's Long-term Objectives in 2010 and 2015. The central government has requested that all local governments incorporate these strategies into their planning efforts.

—*Improving legislation and the functioning of the legal system as they relate to sustainable development.* China has enacted over fifty national laws related to sustainable development since 1996, including important laws dealing with environmental protection, protection of wildlife, agriculture, and forestry. The State Council has promulgated and enforced over sixty environmental regulations and more than eight hundred environmental standards. Local governments at various levels have also promulgated laws and regulations related to environmental protection. As such, a preliminary legal system on environmental protection and sustainable development has been established.[7]

—*Prioritizing and increasing investment in environmental protection and sustainable development.* Between 1996 and 2004, China invested 952 billion yuan in environmental protection, amounting to 1 percent of total GDP.

—*Controlling efficiently the growth of the population.* In 1998 the growth in the birth rate was 9.53 percent, the first time it had fallen below 10 percent since 1949. In 2005 the growth in the rate of birth fell even further, to 5.89 percent.

—*Significantly reducing environmental pollution.* The Chinese government has taken measures to improve environmental governance, including closing about 84,000 small factories and mines that were heavy polluters between 1996 to 2004. For example, compared with 1996, in 2005 the proportion of cities with air quality reaching grade 2 (on a four-grade ranking system adopted by the Chinese government for the evaluation of air quality) increased by 31 percent, while that of cities with air quality lower than grade 3 decreased by 39 percent.

—*Promoting forestation.* New forests have reached over 6.7 million hectares every year since 2002. In recent years the total forested area and the amount of forest reserves have increased rapidly; the age and the form of forest have become more scientifically assessed and rationalized, and the quality of forests is improving, achieving a historic turn from a downward to an upward trend. Currently the national forest acreage is 175 million hectares, the forest covers 18.2 percent of China's land, and the forest reserves equal 12.5 billion cubic meters. By the end of 2005, planted grass covered 13 million hectares. The Chinese government has deemed the establishment of nature reserves as an important step to protect the environment. By the end of 2005, there were 2,349 nature reserves of various kinds and levels in China, covering 1.5 million square kilometers, the equivalent of about 15 percent of the country's territory. These nature reserves offer some protection for roughly 85 percent of the country's ecosystems, 85 percent of its wildlife species, and 65 percent of its natural plant types.[8]

The Role of Civil Society Organizations

The Chinese government has played a key role in achieving the goals of China Agenda 21. At the same time, one has to acknowledge that the achievements in sustainable development owe something to China's emerging civil society as well. After the Chinese Communist Party came to power in 1949, it implemented socialist public ownership and a planned economy, achieved through a highly centralized administrative system under the leadership of the party. Almost all civic organizations that had emerged before 1949 disappeared. As discussed in the section on civil society in this volume, China's civil society organizations (CSOs) began growing rapidly during the 1980s. In 1997 social associations at and above county level totaled more than 180,000 throughout the country, including 21,404 provincial ones and 1,848 national ones. There was no formal statistical data about the various organizations below the county level, but some scholars have estimated that these totaled more than 3 million.

China's CSOs are increasingly exerting influence in the areas of environmental protection and sustainable development. These groups have enhanced their impact on public policy by persuading the government to make reasonable laws and regulations and providing professional advice in environmental governance; supervising government and enterprise behaviors and urging them to avoid programs that are highly polluting or ecologically devastating; raising awareness about the importance of environmental protection and sustainable development and strengthening citizens' consciousness of the importance of protecting the environment; participating, with the government, in the execution of laws and regulations related to environmental governance; and raising funds from civil society to invest in environmental protection. In Beijing there are four well-known CSOs for environmental protection, the "four big green parties"—the Friends of Nature, the Global Village, the Green Home, and the Shannuo Society. These groups conduct publicity about environmental protection, criticize actions that damage the environment, and offer suggestions for how to better pursue environmental protection. In part because of their influence, the issue of environmental protection became a central topic for discussion at the annual meeting of the National People's Congress.

Nevertheless, it must be admitted that CSOs have played a limited role in achieving sustainable development in China. First, only a small number of CSOs specialize in environmental protection. Second, CSOs, including those whose focus is on environmental protection, are too weak to launch big programs related to environmental improvement. Finally, generally speaking, CSOs have little ability to directly affect the policymaking of the government or enterprises, and the attitudes and actions of the Chinese government remain the overwhelming factors determining China's approach to sustainable development.

China has made astonishing progress toward environmental governance while at the same time facing severe difficulties and challenges:

—*Soil erosion and desertification are worsening.* In recent years China has lost at least 36.7 million hectares, or 38 percent of the total area of the country, due to soil erosion, and the pace of such erosion is increasing at a rate of 1 million hectares a year. The area of salinized grasslands is currently 13.5 million hectares, and it is increasing at a rate of 2 million hectares per year. China has 26.2 million hectares of desertified land, and this area is expanding. Water quality in China's lakes and streams has been deteriorating, and there have been red tides in almost all of China's major inland bodies of water.[9]

—*Natural resources are under terrible stress.* Perhaps China's most serious environmental challenge is its shortage of water. Over one hundred cities have experienced water shortages in recent years. Cultivated land is being lost to expanding urban and industrial areas, and the area of cultivated land is only 9.3 acres per person, about half of the global average. Natural forest coverage per capita is also declining, to roughly one-fifth of the global average. China's biodiversity resources are in rapid decline as well. The area of grasslands under distress because of China's ubiquitous small mining industry has already reached 4 million hectares.[10]

— *Environmental pollution remains very serious.* Air and water pollution are threatening the livelihoods of vast numbers of Chinese citizens. China produced 0.78 billion tons of industrial waste and 0.15 billion tons of biomass waste in 2005, most of which has not been dealt with properly. Acid rain typically falls over one-third of the country; half of China's seven major water systems are deemed to be extremely polluted; the explosive growth of motor vehicles presents a significant new source of air pollution; and among China's 522 major cities, only 4.4 percent meet national air quality standards.[11]

Concluding Thoughts

To sum up, as a recent World Bank report on China's sustainable development points out, among comparable developing nations, China is unquestionably in the front rank, but it cannot become complacent. China's challenges are unprecedented. It needs to measure its performance against the developed countries, not against the most underdeveloped countries in the world.[12] By this standard, China still has a long way to go. It has to work harder on legal and administrative measures, on increasing investment in environmental governance, on getting the fundamentals of development policy rights and on human resources development. Most important, for the sake of harmony in economic growth, social development, and ecological protection, it has to move the concept of environmentally sustainable development onto the front page of all policy documents and achieve greater cooperation between the government, corporations, and nongovernmental organizations in protecting the natural environment.

PART IV

GLOBALIZATION AND GOVERNANCE

PRESERVING CHINA'S AUTONOMY IN THE ERA OF GLOBALIZATION

China represents a fascinating story about globalization and globalization studies, both in theory and in practice.[1] In the early half of the 1990s, the word "globalization" itself was so politically sensitive that Chinese scholars avoided mentioning it in articles and books. Today, by contrast, the notion of globalization has become so fashionable that almost everyone uses it, whether he or she accepts or rejects it. On a practical level, globalization was long regarded as synonymous with capitalist development, a fact that explains the previous ideological sensitivities it carried.[2] More recently, however, both inside the country and out, China has come to be seen as one of the biggest winners from globalization.

Globalization Studies in China

As noted above, before the mid-1990s the concept of globalization was perceived as a synonym for capitalism. For those few Chinese scholars writing about globalization, the term was used strictly in its economic sense. In this period, a journal editor would routinely add the adjective *economic* to the noun *globalization* when an author submitted an article on the subject. In 1998 Jiang Zemin, then president and general secretary of the Chinese Communist Party (CCP), spoke for the first time about "economic globalization" as "an objective trend of world economic development."[3] The top leader's recognition of globalization gave a great boost to scholars and analysts engaged in studies of globalization, making it a hot issue among Chinese intellectuals. A number of essays on globalization have since been published and huge numbers of foreign books and essays on globalization have been translated into Chinese and published in China. I was very lucky to chair the first national conference specifically on globalization, held in 1997 in Shenzhen, one of China's original special economic zones, and to edit the first *Globalization Studies Series* in Chinese. It includes seven books published in 1998. The *Globalization Translation Series,* which I have also organized, has published over thirty books, all by the same publishing house—the Chinese Social Sciences and Documentation Publishing House.

Currently Chinese scholars are focusing on several important dimensions of globalization, including definitions of the concept, articulation of a useful typology, the Chinese experience of globalization and the implications of globalization for China, and globalization's advantages and disadvantages for China. In each of these areas, Chinese scholars' views on globalization have tended to cluster around six paradoxes:

—*Is globalization fact or fiction?* Some people think that globalization is a fact—that it has an objective existence that deeply affects human development. They see humankind as entering into a global age. Others insist that globalization is simply a fiction promoted by Western scholars as ideological cover for a new wave of imperialism. In this latter view, globalization is argued to be a myth because the great diversity of human societies, economies, and cultures can never be globalized.

—*Is globalization inherently capitalist or potentially socialist?* Many Chinese intellectuals believe that globalization is the necessary consequence of capitalist development and an inherent goal of capitalism. Globalization represents the extension of capitalist modes of production across the planet and signifies that capitalism has entered a new stage of its development. Globalization, in this view, is simply global capitalism. In contrast, some scholars argue that globalization is ideologically neutral despite its origins in advanced capitalist countries. By its nature, globalization is neither capitalist nor socialist. Like the market economy, it can be combined with both capitalism and socialism.

—*Apart from economic globalization, are there political or cultural forms of globalization?* For many Chinese scholars, globalization is seen as little more than economic integration of capital, products, market, technology, production, and communication on a planetary scale. These scholars view globalization as being strictly limited to economics and refuse to accept definitions that extend the concept into other domains of human experience. Other scholars, however, believe that the concept of globalization extends beyond economics even though it originates in economic processes of integration. A process of political and cultural globalization, they argue, is under way at the same time as economic integration is occurring. In their view, globalization has not only economic implications but also political and cultural ones. Thus, globalization is an overall process of social change, including economic, political, and cultural processes.

—*Is globalization, on balance, advantageous or harmful for developing countries?* Some intellectuals believe that the superior economic and geopolitical influence of the developed countries allows them to dominate and control the process of globalization to the disadvantage of less developed countries. They thus suggest that developed, rather than developing, countries are the true winners of globalization. Other scholars have argued that globalization is not a zero-sum game and that all players can be winners. What matters for these analysts are the strategies that governments choose to employ in responding to the challenges posed by globalization. China is a good example of a country poised to benefit from globalization.

—*Is globalization anything more than modernization, Westernization, or Americanization?* Many analysts believe that globalization implies Westernization, and above all, Americanization, for China. Such a development is equated with the loss of autonomy and cultural dignity. In this view, the international standards, regimes, and regulations that govern globalization were designed to serve the values and interests of Western countries. Other analysts disagree, holding that globalization is different from Westernization or Americanization. For these scholars, globalization is fundamentally a process of modernization, irrespective of the fact that this process originated in the West.

—*Is there a path toward modernization in the global age that is specifically appropriate for China?* Some analysts answer this question with a resounding yes, arguing that there exists a specifically Chinese model for development, complete with its own special characteristics. Some analysts even take this view one step further, arguing that the Chinese experience can serve as the basis for a "Beijing Consensus" on how developing countries can best pursue modernization, an idea first noted by the American scholar Joshua Cooper Ramo.[4] Others, however, firmly reject this argument, holding that there is no specifically Chinese way to modernization, only a path that adopts either more or fewer of the basic features of capitalism. For some in this latter group, the only model China should adopt as it pursues development should be the so-called Washington Consensus, rather than any purported Beijing Consensus.

Given these debates, it is not surprising that intellectuals in China, much as those abroad, generally divide themselves into two camps. Some are advocates of globalization while others are opponents of it. The former see globalization as a blessing and warmly welcome it, while the latter resist globalization, viewing it as a disaster. Some Chinese scholars see globalization as the pathway to a Chinese renaissance. For these thinkers, China's future, including democracy and economic prosperity, depends largely on its successfully adapting to the challenges of globalization. Other people, however, see globalization as a trap and regard supporters of globalization as traitors.

Adaptation under the Pressures of Globalization

Many people believe that China is one of the biggest winners from globalization. From 1978 to 2003, the Chinese gross national product increased from 362.4 billion yuan ($44.2 billion) to 11.7 trillion yuan ($1.4 trillion). In constant yuan (and dollars), it has increased nearly eight and a half times, with an average yearly growth rate of over 9 percent. This growth rate is much higher than the 2.5 percent average GNP growth rate of the developed countries, the 5 percent growth rate of developing countries, and the 3 percent average world growth rate during the same period. In this period China has registered the fastest economic growth rate of any major country in the world. High-speed economic growth has been accompanied by a twenty-two-fold expansion in the scale of foreign trade over the past two decades. At the same time, China successfully protected itself from the shocks of the Asian financial crisis in the late 1990s and, after fifteen years of negotiation, realized its goal of entering the World Trade Organization (WTO).[5]

A primary reason China has become one of the biggest winners from globalization is the policy strategy that the Chinese government has followed in addressing the challenges of globalization. This basic policy has two pillars: actively opening up to the world while making great efforts to preserve the country's autonomy. Among the key measures that the Chinese government adopted in actively pursuing globalization were:

—*An independent globalization strategy.* With a good understanding of the processes of globalization, China has adopted an active and independent globalization strategy. China's politics are highly influenced by ideology, but in recent years ideological considerations have been consciously set aside in the pursuit of globalization. While many Chinese scholars were debating globalization, Chinese leaders made their own judgments about the nature of globalization, including its advantages and disadvantages. They adopted an active strategy and appropriate actions to take full advantage of globalization. For example, China made tireless efforts to join the WTO, expanded international cooperation and exchanges, actively participated in global governance and global actions to counter international terrorism, established the Shanghai Cooperation Organization, pushed forward negotiations to eliminate nuclear weapons in the Korean Peninsula, and proposed a strategy of "peaceful development."

—*Leadership development.* China has worked assiduously to improve the qualifications of government officials, to select and promote knowledge elites who are more cosmopolitan and who favor more international economic integration for leadership positions, and to train officials to be familiar with the knowledge economy and problems of globalization. Currently there are 672,531 officials above the county level, and 90 percent of them have academic degrees equal to or above the associate college degree level, up from 16 percent in 1981. According to central government statistics, 25,000 officials above the level of county or division were trained from 2001 to 2005, and about 2,000 of these were officials at the provincial or ministerial level.[6] This group of new leaders is professionally competent and increasingly skilled at conducting international cooperation and exchange activities. In short, these officials are set to become the core of the Chinese government in dealing with the process of globalization.

—*Adaptive capability and flexibility.* The Chinese government has developed a flexible system and set of governing mechanisms with strong adaptive capability. Participation in the global game means abiding by international regimes, but international regimes conflict with domestic regimes in a number of areas. How to deal with the relationships and potential conflicts between domestic and international regimes is an issue that the Chinese government has had to face. After a careful assessment of the advantages and disadvantages of globalization, Chinese leaders made the painful but correct choice to adapt domestic regulations to conform to international norms and rules and to revise domestic regimes that are not consistent with international regimes. Consequently, the government bypassed traditional forbidden zones and signed a series of international treaties covering a wide range of issues from political rights, to international security and trade, to environmental protection. It also revised domestic laws in accordance with relevant international treaties. In the process of negotiating terms for WTO membership, and subsequent to joining the WTO, the State Council required up to thirty ministries and departments in 2002 to clean up nearly 2,300 relevant laws and regulations. About half of the laws and regulations were eliminated or revised as a result. In addition, more than 100,000 local laws and regulations were revised or eliminated by various provinces and autonomous regions.[7]

—*Peaceful development.* The Chinese government has striven to engage in international cooperation and create a favorable international environment. China needs a peaceful international environment in order to focus on development, a need that is especially important in an era of globalization. In adapting to the challenges of globalization, the Chinese government proposed an international strategy of "peaceful development." The main elements of this strategy are to insist on the diplomatic principles of independence, self-reliance, and peaceful co-existence; to abide by the guiding ideology of "being peaceful and different"; and to strive for a new notion of security with "mutual trust, mutual benefits, equality, and cooperation." With these as its core guiding principles, the Chinese government has sought to promote global democratic governance and multilateralism. It has sought to engage in international cooperation more actively in all spheres and has pursued reciprocal benefits in peaceful coexistence and cooperation.

In following this approach, the Chinese government rose above ideological differences and developed bilateral and multilateral relations with various countries and regions in the areas of politics, the economy, and culture. Within just five years, from 1998 to 2002, it signed more than 1,056 bilateral and multilateral treaties. Over the same period the Chinese government encouraged foreign exchange and cooperation activities conducted by local governments, individuals, and civil society groups. In 2002 the number of foreign citizen arrivals was close to 13.5 million, while 16.3 million Chinese left China to visit other countries. In the past five years, the number of entries and departures has increased more than 10 percent a year on average. As of 2002, 296 Chinese cities had established partnership relationships with 847 foreign cities.[8]

Preserving Autonomy under the Pressure of Globalization

At the same time as China has participated extensively in globalization, it has taken several important steps to protect its autonomy. These have included:

—*Remaining aware of globalization's negative effects.* Generally speaking, the negative effects of globalization for China are threefold. First, globalization threatens domestic economic security. Foreign corporate control of majority stakes in major companies, and the threat that foreign actors might gain a monopoly on crucial technologies, threatens the prospects for upgrading the country's industrial infrastructure. Excessive debt owed to foreign entities may bring potentially enormous risks, and increased reliance on foreign capital and trade may weaken China's capacity to protect its economy and its citizens from fluctuations in the world economy. The large-scale opening of financial markets may also greatly increase financial risks. Second, globalization weakens state sovereignty. One of the basic conditions for participating in globalization is to abide by existing international rules, international treaties, and agreements. Most of these international regimes have been established in accordance with the interests and standards of advanced Western countries. To gain the economic benefits brought by globalization, developing countries usually have to make some concessions in administrative jurisdiction, thus weakening their sovereignty. Third, globalization threatens domestic political and cultural values, leading to possible loss of control over social order and increased risks to domestic governance. With advanced Western countries controlling the course of globalization and constructing global regimes, it is inevitable that they will seek also to export their worldviews and value systems along with their capital, technology, and products. These worldviews and value systems may clash with Chinese cultural traditions and political order, creating a potential for social and political instability.

—*Prevention of foreign capital control in key sectors.* On the one hand, China has done everything possible to attract foreign investment. Such investment is usually encouraged by favorable policies on taxes, land, and license permits. On the other hand, foreign investment is greeted with considerable caution when it comes to the most important economic sectors of the economy, such as energy, communications, finance, education, and mass media.

—*Controlling the speed of change.* The Chinese government has effectively achieved its goal of entering the world economy. At the same time, it has taken many measures to prevent the country from entering too quickly into the process of globalization and thereby destabilizing political and social order.

—*Retaining dominance of economic development for core national interests.* China has not given up its dominance of economic development for core national interests, even at the cost of slowing down overall economic growth. For example, China has revalued its currency at its own pace, regardless of the great pressures it has been under from the United States and other developed countries to appreciate the value of the yuan more quickly.

—*Emphasis on national sovereignty.* Unlike some Western political leaders who downplay state sovereignty in the global age, Chinese leaders make sovereignty the basis upon which all political and economic activities take place, including economic globalization.

—*Advocating national cultural values.* Since the period of reform began, the government has also encouraged a revival of traditional Chinese values.

In this respect, the opening up to the world has been complemented by an unprecedented promotion of long-standing cultural forms. Traditional clothing, cuisine, festivals, operas, and arts are becoming newly fashionable at the same time as McDonald's, the Internet, Mickey Mouse, and the NBA are gaining in popularity.

—*Vigilance against Westernization and Americanization.* In the view of many Chinese, there is a real risk that globalization will lead to Westernization or even Americanization. The government has developed many strategies to prevent this. For instance, Chinese leaders do not wish to imitate a capitalist economic model, and they refuse to adopt Western political systems and core political values.

Conclusion

China is no different from most Western countries in engaging in a broad set of debates and discussions about the advantages and disadvantages of globalization. Some believe that the disadvantages outweigh the advantages. Others, including many in the government, have come to believe that the advantages are potentially much more significant than the disadvantages. In acting on this belief, the Chinese government has entered into a wide range of international and regional cooperation arrangements, including becoming a member of the WTO. It has developed a conscious strategy to draw maximum advantage from globalization by improving the education and skills of its officials and promoting its own research and development policies. While China has engaged fully with globalization, it has also thought strategically about how best to preserve its economic, political, and cultural autonomy. It has protected core economic sectors, retained a political system that fits its needs and society well, and countered cultural globalization by promoting the revival of long-standing ideas, values, and cultural practices.

CHAPTER TWELVE

FEDERALISM IN MODERN CHINA
Concepts and Experiments

F or over four thousand years, from the Xia dynasty in 2205 BC to the
end of the Qing dynasty in 1911, China practiced a form of despotism
in which all power was concentrated in the hands of the emperor.[1] The
emperor appointed and removed not only the major officials of the central
government but also all the leading officials above the level of the county
government. The absolutist nature of this form of despotism was described
vividly by the traditional saying "there are no other people on Earth than the
subjects of the emperor, and there are no other lands on Earth other than the
lands of the emperor."[2] As a result, China never experienced federalism, and
did not know what federalism or any other political system other than their
own was, until the middle of the nineteenth century.

China's Early Advocates for Federalism

The Chinese idea of federalism originated in the middle of the nineteenth
century when China was forced to open up to the outside world after Britain
defeated China in the Opium War (1840–42). Afterward, the first generation of Chinese intellectuals who went abroad brought back knowledge
about foreign countries. The Chinese gradually began to awaken from the
delusion of being "the only power in the world" to the reality that there
existed political systems other than the Chinese dynastic system, such as federalism and democracy, and that some states that practiced these systems
were now more powerful than China. The pioneers of the Westernization
movement were the first to introduce Western knowledge to China. For

instance, Wei Yuan edited and published in 1842 his *Introduction to Overseas Countries,* which was the first systematic book to look at foreign politics, economies, and cultures. He initially described the federalist system as practiced in the United States positively:

> There is no king or emperor in the United States of America, [a country] that consists of twenty-seven states and millions of citizens. . . . The twenty-seven states were divided into two areas, West and East, and elected a person called a president. The president is not hereditary and has to be changed in a term of four years. Such a political system is fundamentally different from the one in our history while all American people give their consent to it. Why don't we think it is all right?[3]

Books published shortly thereafter, such as *Records of the Countries around the Sea* by Xu Jishe and *Talking about the United States* by Liang Tingnan, gave similar introductions to Western federalism. These early books played an important part in shaping Chinese intellectuals' early ideas about the Western experience of federalism, although their knowledge of how that system worked in practice seems very rough today.

Around the turn of the century, Chinese intellectuals began to deepen their analyses and assessments of federalism. Some divergent views emerged about the features, strengths, and weaknesses of federalism and its applicability to China. This round of debates climaxed in the 1920s.

By the end of the Qing dynasty and the founding of the Republican era, a number of intellectuals were already advocating learning from the West, and many, including Liang Qichao, Feng Ziyou, and Jiang Zhiyou, were calling for adoption of a federal system. Liang Qichao for instance, in his "Studies on Rousseau," praised the Swiss model of federal democracy, arguing that Switzerland was rich thanks to its adoption of these political systems and was therefore an example worth learning from. Liang emphasized that China was well positioned to reorganize along federal lines, arguing that China already had a number of long-standing traditions compatible with federalism:

> China has the very popular tradition of autonomy in civil society. This comes closest to approximating the ideal state in Rousseau's mind. Our country could become a model for other countries if we were to introduce good local systems from civilized countries, making the state, provincial, and county levels of government into autonomous units, making different laws according to each state or province, and making different decisions in accordance with different demands in each state or province.[4]

Feng Ziyou, a revolutionary spokesman, advanced more clearly a conception of federalism based on democratic republican government, which Feng argued was the political ideal for China: "What is a democratic republic? It is federalism. Isn't a democratic republic our political goal? Our political goal is to change the Chinese political system into the French republic system and American federalism."[5]

The Republic of China founded after the Revolution of 1911 was led by Dr. Sun Yat-sen, who overthrew the Qing dynasty and put an end to the Chinese system of imperialism. In the wake of the revolution, Chinese intellectuals' interest in studying and evaluating federalism experienced a new upsurge. Among the leading advocates of federalism during this period were Zhang Dongsun, Ding Foyan, Li Jiangnong, and Zhang Shizhao, all well-known professors of universities in Beijing.

Zhang Dongsun believed that there was a big gap between China and the advanced Western countries. In his view, China had to reform its unitary political system and transform itself along federalist lines (though it might not necessarily use the term *federalism*) if it wanted to become a rich and powerful country like those of the West. "China will not survive and become a powerful country without adopting the British and American systems," Zhang argued. Furthermore, he noted, "the spirit of federalism lies in its [support for] autonomy. We could adopt only its autonomy without the name of federalism."[6] Ding Foyan took a similar position. It was a Chinese characteristic, he pointed out, that "the country became strong so long as the will of the nation consists of the will of the local and that we would have good governance [only] so long as we put the central government under supervision of the local." In Ding's view, China should practice federalism with a high degree of local autonomy and should draft a new constitution based on federal principles that would define the power of both the central and the local in such a way as to limit central power while broadening the local power.[7]

Zhang Shizhao may have been the most active and radical federalist of the time. In a series of articles on federalism published in *Jiayin Magazine,* including his well-known "Essay on Federalism" and "Theory of Federalism," Zhang analyzed federalism in detail and offered powerful critiques of antifederalist views. Zhang was among the first group of Chinese public intellectuals to define the content of the concept of federalism for Chinese audiences. In criticizing some misconceptions of federalism prevalent in Chinese intellectual circles, Zhang argued that the fundamental difference between China's ancient feudal separatist system and Western variants of federalism was that federalism operated on the basis of a separation between power and autonomy. He defined federalism by citing Pierre-Joseph Proudhon's statement:

> Federalism is a system under which the central government is based on universal local interests that are the only ties by which the central and the local connect with each other. Local governments enjoy autonomy on the basis of the local interests. In short, federalism means a high degree of separation of power between the central and the local, and between the legislature and the executive.[8]

Zhang Shizhao's particular emphasis was that the basis of state power under federalism was not the nation or the province, but the people. Liang Qichao examined the main federalist countries in the world at that time, including Britain, the United States, Switzerland, Germany, Venezuela, Argentina, Mexico, and Brazil. He disagreed with the prevailing view that federalism must be realized by revolution and must coincide with the founding of the state. Instead, Liang argued that some federalist countries had evolved out of unitary systems and that therefore revolution was not the only route to federalism. China could and should use nonrevolutionary and peaceful methods to introduce federalism. Although there were allegations at the time that Liang only talked about general theories of federalism, not about its applicability to China, his political intention was very clear. In his eyes, almost all of the powerful countries in the world were federalist, and China would have to evolve in this direction too if it were to become rich and powerful.

Movement of Self-Government by United Provinces

With the 1911 Revolution, interest in federalism spread beyond intellectual circles to include political leaders, a broadening that helped move the discussion from the realm of theory to practice. For instance, Shandong Province made eight demands of the Qing dynasty in its declaration of independence from the central government in 1911, among which were four articles that posed federalist claims: "Article 5: The constitution must stipulate that China carries out federalism"; "Article 6: All officials and taxes inside the Province must be decided finally by the Province itself and the central government has no right to interfere;" "Article 7: The Chapter of the Provincial Consulting Bureau is the constitution regarding provincial matters, which cannot be revised without its intervention from the central government regime"; and "Article 8: The Province has the right to defend [its] freedom by recruiting troops."[9]

Federalist theory and practice in China climaxed during the 1920s in the movement known as Self-Government by the United Provinces. Self-government meant that each province made its own provincial constitution; organized its own provincial government; and created its own provincial executive, legislative, and judicial organs without intervention by the central government. It was on the basis of this movement that a national conference of the "United Provinces" took place to draft a National Constitution of the United Provinces to unite the nation. The conference issued a remarkable paper in the history of Chinese constitutionalism. As a result, the movement survived for six years from 1920 to 1926, with fifteen provinces responding to calls to participate in it.

The self-government movement originated in Hunan Province. On July 22, 1920, Tan Yankai, governor and chief commander of the province, declared that Hunan would practice self-government and that the governor would no longer be appointed by the central government but be elected by Hunan's own citizens. The constitution of Hunan was proclaimed not long after Tan's declaration, and Hunan's declaration of independence was followed by similar declarations from the provinces of Sichuan, Guizhou, Yunnan, Guangdong, Guangxi, Zhejiang, Jiangxi, Fengtian, Fujian, Shanxi, Jiangsu, and Hubei, each of which declared its approval of, and desire to participate in, the movement. At the same time, a number of civil society organizations also published their support for self-government by province, and a number of new organizations organized on the basis of the movement, such as the United Association of Self-Government by Province, the United Office of Self-Government, and the Promoting Association of Self-Government, among others. The movement itself was greatly weakened by the Nationalist army during the Northern Expedition in 1926, and the movement went bankrupt in 1927 around the time of the triumph of the Northern Expedition.

"Self-Government by the United Provinces" was a federalist effort that was clearly reflected in the provincial constitutions proclaimed during the movement. For example, there were similar articles in the draft constitution of Zhejiang Province, issued on September 9, 1921; the draft constitution of Guangdong Province, issued in December 1921; and the constitution of Hunan Province, issued on January 1, 1922. These documents made the following claims: the province has the power to make its own constitution independently; the chief executive, the legislature, and the judiciary will each be elected by the province without any interference from the central government; the national republic must be founded on the basis of self-government by province; the national congress must consist of representatives from all of the provinces; and central power and local power must be clearly defined, with the former dealing only with national affairs and the latter responsible for local affairs.

The federalist effort was not only reflected in provincial constitutions, but also in the national constitutions drafted by spokesmen from new political forces. The constitution of the National Assembly, issued in August 1922, and the constitution of the People's Republic, issued on October 10, 1923, for instance, had particular articles specifying "the power of the nation" and "the power of the province." The first article of the draft constitution of the Republic of China held that "the Republic of China will always be a democratic republic," an assertion that was explained by one of the document's main drafters as entailing nothing less than a full-fledged commitment to a federalist model.[10]

The Federalist Perspectives

Modern Chinese federalists advocated for federalism on the basis of its advantages and feasibility. The advantages of federalism seemed obvious to many Chinese federalists. In their eyes, federalism could avoid the despotism they associated with centralized power and unitary rule, while promoting democracy in China. In addition, federalism could put an end to the constant civil war among the provinces for control of the center, thereby producing a stable society. Furthermore, it could encourage people's enthusiasm for contributing to building the nation and thereby hasten the development of a rich and powerful country. In the view of Tang Dechang, a leading advocate of federalism at the time, federalism offered several advantages: it had the ability to unify the country; central despotism could be avoided while citizens' freedom could be protected; citizens' enthusiasm for participation in politics could be stirred; and local governance could be improved.[11]

It seemed imperative to Chinese federalists in the 1920s that China adopt federalism without delay. In their view, federalism was necessary to unite a China that had broken up into a number of private fiefdoms dominated by warlords. In the words of Sun Jiyi, a proponent of federalism writing in 1922:

"China now is divided by warlords and the central government has lost its power over the country. . . . Liaoning is a small country while Jilin and Helongjiang are its dependencies; Hebei is a big country while

Shandong and Henan are small countries. Simply put, each province has become its own country. The Republic of China is just an empty title and the real situation is that every province is like its own country with its own king. China can become one united country again only if it adopts a federalist constitution."[12]

Second, Chinese federalists argued that federalism was necessary for the establishment of democracy, a popular goal. In the eyes of Chinese proponents of federalism at this time, despotism had declined very little after the Qing dynasty ended and in some ways had even grown. Some intellectuals believed that the unitary system was the fundamental cornerstone of despotism and saw federalism as the main weapon by which despotism could be eliminated. Bemoaning the shortcomings of the federalist project some years later, one federalist scholar, Zhi Wei, was moved to write that the introduction of the republican regime following the Revolution of 1911 was expected to result in good governance, but unfortunately the warlords' rule was even worse than the Qing dynasty, the illegal activities of local governments were much worse than before, and the conflicts between the central and the local had deepened as well.[13]

Federalism would improve China's stability and help bring about an end to the country's internecine war, in the view of many Chinese federalist theoreticians. According to this view, the Chinese people had plunged into an abyss of misery in the 1920s not as a result of federalism but as a result of the warlords' in-fighting. Saying that "federalism is the solution by which China could stop the conflicts among its provinces and realize unification," Tang Dechang wrote that "the governor of each province would not dare to move troops against neighboring provinces if China were to adopt a federalist constitution according to which governors of provinces would no longer be appointed by the central authorities but elected by the people."[14]

The modern federalists were deeply confident in the prospect of federalism for China. They conceded that the Chinese had no experience with federalism but insisted that China's vast territory, huge population, and economic and cultural conditions were well suited to federalism. Tang Dechang tried to prove this by arguing, first, that federalism is a desirable political system for China because China has a vast territory with very weak communication infrastructure, which results in long distances between the central and the local, meaning that most provinces have underdeveloped industries. Second, he said, the reason why vast numbers of Chinese people are indifferent to politics is that people have scarce opportunities to participate in political life under the central government, which is both a reflection of and a cause of the great distance, both physical and perceptual, between citizens and the government. People would be much more interested in political participation if they were living under a federalist system that shortened the distance between citizens and government. Third, China was already practicing many of the elements of federalism even though it had never formally adopted federalism. The situation before the Revolution of 1911 was somewhat similar to federalism. In addition, he argued, there is not much difference between the process of building the Republic of China and the process whereby the United States achieved its independence from Britain.[15]

The Warlord Period and the Failure of Federalism in China

The naive ideals of modern Chinese federalists unfortunately ran up against the harsh realities of Chinese warlord politics in the 1920s. The movement of Self-Government by the United Provinces failed after just six years. Federalist politics were never truly realized in the Western sense even in the provinces where provincial constitutions were issued during the movement, and in the end the movement proved to be little more than a means by which local warlords tried to extricate themselves from the control of the central government.

The sovereignty of the Republic of China founded by the revolution was not in the hands of the Nationalist Party but rather in the hands of Yuan Shikai, the greatest of the so-called Northern Warlords. In 1916 Yuan attempted to restore the dynastic system, proclaiming himself the Hongxian emperor. Yuan's actions met great resistance among the people and led the Nationalists into a rebellion that forced Yuan to abandon his ambitions. Yuan's death on June 6, 1916, led to the collapse of the warlord coalition that had governed China since the fall of the Qing. In short order, local warlords emerged in large numbers. By the early 1920s, all of China was ruled by warlords, all of whom sought legitimate excuses for separating themselves from the central government and establishing their own regimes. In this context, the intellectual cover provided by China's profederalist intellectuals and the movement of Self-Government by the United Provinces were ideal justifications for actions that served the warlords' own private political interests.

For instance, Zhao Hengti, a warlord in Hunan Province and a pioneer of the self-government movement, clearly used the movement as an excuse to resist the incursions of other warlords from the north as well as the attacks from the south by the Nationalist armies. Zhao's plan to turn Hunan into an independent kingdom was quickly unmasked as a separatist plot; indeed, all the other warlords who answered Zhao's call to found a self-government movement had the same ambitions as Zhao. Even more transparent were the motives of Zhang Zuolin, the leading warlord in northeastern China, who initially opposed the self-government movement but then became one of its most fervent advocates after his troops were defeated in battle.[16]

In this setting, the federalist constitution proved little more than a paper that served to befuddle public opinion and was never truly put into effect. Zhejiang Province was a good example in this respect. Lu Yongqiang, the general commander of the province, declared the founding of an autonomous Zhejiang provincial self-government on June 4, 1911, and issued the first Zhejiang provincial constitution on September 9, 1911, the so-called Double-Nine Constitution. But Lu never put the constitution into practice. He issued three different drafts, one after another, which came to be known as the Tri-Color Constitution because of the red, yellow and white colors used to mark up the drafts. However, these draft constitutions were never approved for implementation. As Li Jiangnong pointed out,

> All of the constitutions issued in Zhejiang failed to be put into practice without exception. The reason was not that the people of Zhejiang had no enthusiasm for these constitutions but that Lu Yongqiang lacked the sincerity to implement them. He feared he would lose the freedom to practice his own particular brand of authoritarian rule in Zhejiang if the constitution was put into effect. His decision to promulgate provincial constitutions was a strategy to resist the northern warlords and nothing more. Besides Zhejiang, Sichuan and Guangdong also founded special committees to draft their own constitutions. The authorities in Yunnan, Guangxi, Guizhou, Shanxi, Jiangsu, Jiangxi, Hubei, Fujian, Liaoning, and Hebei also declared their intent to make their own constitutions and engage in self-government. The movement of Self-Government by the United Provinces spread across the whole country. But these purportedly federal constitutions were not put into effect by any of the warlords at this time.[17]

Chinese advocates of federalism believed that the self-government movement would help bring an end to the civil war and cause peace to break out in China. In fact, however, the movement helped fuel the continuation of the warlord era by giving it intellectual cover—numerous wars, both big and small, took place during the movement era, and these plunged the country into a state of chaos and darkness. As Li Jiangnong witnessed, "The voice of the movement of 'Self-Government by the United Provinces' was drowned out by [the] boom of bombardment. There were at least three national wars that occurred between 1911 and 1912, . . . the Hubei War in central China, the Hebei vs. Liaoning War in north China, and the Sun vs. Cheng War in south China, not to mention a number of local wars."[18]

The Causes of the Failure of Modern Chinese Federalism

With the failure of the self-government movement, the idea of federalism disappeared quietly in China. Indeed, the movement failed so spectacularly that it left most modern Chinese intellectuals bitter toward the profederalists, unable to recall why these individuals once held out hope for the notion of federalism, and reluctant to analyze the idea again. In retrospect, several factors probably foreordained the failure of the federalist dream.

First, modern Chinese advocates of federalism seriously misunderstood how it was practiced in Western countries, especially with regard to its nature and form and its social, political, and cultural conditions. For example, almost all of these scholars argued that democracy could be realized in China only by adopting a federal model of government. Today, most scholars believe that there is no necessary direct link between democracy and federalism. The former Soviet Union carried out federalism while maintaining a system of government in which the centralization of power was much higher than in some unitary countries. By contrast, France is a unitary state where the extent of decentralization is much higher than in some federal countries.

Second, the profederalists made a mistake when they thought that Chinese tradition was well suited to the adoption of federalism. China has been a highly unitary state for several thousand years and the country has little experience with a high degree of decentralization. The unitary idea is deeply rooted in both elite and popular consciousness, to the exclusion of federalist solutions, and as a result federalism is widely regarded as an intellectual cover for separatism. Such a political culture and traditions are, fundamentally speaking, heavily weighted against federalism.

Third, modern Chinese federalists did not sufficiently grasp the ambitions of the politicians who advocated on behalf of the self-government movement. No politician or warlord who supported the movement actually struggled for China's democracy, peace, or unification—quite the contrary, each did so for his own separate interests. Chen Duxiu, one of the founders of the Chinese Communist Party, acknowledged this clearly, pointing out that "the situation in China now is one of local despotism under which we need not advocate federalism. . . . The movement of 'Self-Government by the United Provinces' is not a good medicine with which China can be saved, and will bring nothing good but the warlords' separatist regimes."[19]

Nevertheless, the debate about federalism in modern China played a positive role in the sense that it enriched Chinese political thought. The failure of the federalist project in modern China teaches one very important lesson: anyone attempting to advocate on behalf of federalism in China, where the unitary tradition is deeply rooted, must be very careful.

CHAPTER THIRTEEN

A Harmonious World and Global Governance

A Chinese Perspective

C hina's foreign policy and global strategy have recently experienced some notable changes, one of which is the rise of the concept of a "harmonious world."[1] Officially put forward by President Hu Jintao, the idea of a harmonious world reflects China's basic judgment and value orientation toward the current international situation, as well as toward the common fate and ideal objectives of global humanity. As the latest development in China's foreign strategy, it is also the reflection of domestic political developments. This chapter first elaborates the concept of a harmonious world, then focuses on China's new global strategy based on that concept. The final part examines the concept of "harmonious diplomacy" as well as its significance for global governance.

Harmonious Society and Harmonious World

At the summit meeting of the Association of Southeast Asian Nations held in Jakarta on April 22, 2005, President Hu for the first time put forward the objective of "jointly constructing a harmonious world." Afterward, he elaborated on the idea of "building a harmonious world with sustained peace and common prosperity" at the celebration of the sixtieth anniversary of the United Nations on September 15, 2005.[2] The idea of "harmonious society" expresses a long-coveted dream of humankind: that at a time of risk, conflict, and fragmentation, humankind should strive to build a new international political and economic order featured by peace, tranquility, justice, mutual respect, and common prosperity. The quest for a harmonious world has always been the pursuit of human beings. As a new facet of the ancient Chinese dream of "great harmony in the world" (*Tianxia datong*), it is also the ultimate objective of China's strategy of peaceful development. The essence of the policy is to realize harmonious coexistence between nations as well as between nature and human beings.

The aim of constructing a harmonious world is the natural extension of China's domestic strategy of constructing a harmonious society. Hence to better understand China's vision of a harmonious world, one must first grasp the connotations of its domestic harmonious society strategy. In 2003 the political report of the Sixteenth National Congress of the Chinese Communist Party put forward the objective of constructing a harmonious society. In 2004, at the Fourth Plenary Session of the Sixteenth CCP Central Committee, "the construction of a harmonious socialist society" was formally incorporated into a fourfold strategic objective of China's social development program, together with economic development, political democracy, and cultural advancement. The issues associated with constructing a harmonious socialist society were put at the top of the agenda of the Sixth Plenary Session of the Sixteenth CCP Central Committee in 2006. The most important achievement of the session was the Resolution on Some Important Issues in Constructing a Harmonious Socialist Society.

The construction of a harmonious socialist society is the most important strategic objective in China today. In a speech entitled "Enhancing Our Ability to Construct a Harmonious Socialist Society," President Hu in June 2005 pointed out that this objective is not only based on domestic demands for reform and development but is also influenced by the contemporary international situation. Domestically, China's process of modernization has entered a new phase characterized by the emergence of new kinds of conflicts and problems. It urgently requires reconciling different interests and maintaining social harmony in order to achieve a society in which everyone is well off (*xiaokang shehui*). Internationally, the Chinese government will confront many external challenges and risks under volatile international situations in the years ahead.

Furthermore, President Hu defined the construction of a harmonious society in a systematic and concrete way. He pointed out:

We are constructing a harmonious socialist society, which should feature democracy, the rule of law, equity, justice, sincerity, amity, vitality, and orderliness as well as the harmonious coexistence of people and nature. "Democracy and the rule of law" mean that socialist democracy should be consciously carried forward, the strategy of governing the country by law should be implemented, and all positive forces should be fully motivated. "Equity and justice" mean different interests should be reconciled properly, the contradictions among the people and other social conflicts as well should be handled correctly, and social justice should be maintained consciously. "Sincerity and amity" mean that the social atmosphere is accommodating, faithful, affectionate, and harmonious. "Vitality" means any progressive and innovative idea should be respected, any creative activity should be supported, people's talent and creativity should be given full scope, and creative achievement should be encouraged. "Orderliness" means the organizing institutions of society should be intact, social management should be improved, social order should be maintained, people should live and work in peace and contentment, and society should be stable and unified. The "harmonious coexistence of people and nature" means that production, development, and prosperity should be pursued in a way that is not detrimental to the environment. The aforementioned basic features of a harmonious socialist society are interrelated with one another, and should be understood and implemented against the backdrop of constructing a well-off society.[3]

Harmonious society, therefore, is a concept with profound connotations. Basically speaking, it requires the harmonious coexistence of all kinds of social factors and relationships. Covering economic, political, and cultural interactions, as well as the daily life of the people, it involves a multilevel relationship between people and people, people and society, citizen and government, and humans and nature. The CCP Central Committee and President Hu Jintao himself have offered an authoritative interpretation of harmonious society that could be best described as follows:

—*A harmonious society is not a phased target but an ideal objective.* It is humanity's basic value and a long-term ideal objective to make society more harmonious. Thus, a harmonious society cannot be realized within a given period.

—*A harmonious society is not a unitary society but a plural society.* The diversity of interests is the reason why people should coexist harmoniously. The diversity of people should be maintained in a harmonious society. People should be "harmonious but different" in such a society.

—A harmonious society is one with democracy and good governance. To put it differently, a harmonious society should be a society with maximized public interests, exhibiting a high degree of cooperation between the citizenry and the government, and characterized by active political participation as well as high political transparency.

—A harmonious society is a society governed by the rule of law and order. A stable political environment and good social order are the preconditions for a harmonious society.

—A harmonious society is a society with tolerance, solidarity, accommodation, and cooperation. In a harmonious society, public virtues such as tolerance, modesty, and consideration should be common, and social solidarity and cooperation as well as harmonious interpersonal relationships should be the norm.

—A harmonious society is a society with equity and justice. One important basis of a harmonious society is the reasonable and equal distribution of political and economic interests among the citizenry.

—A harmonious society is a society with sincerity. Without sincerity, cooperation, and social solidarity, shared identity as well as social harmony will be groundless.

—A harmonious society requires sustainable development. In a harmonious society, the relationship between economic growth and environmental protection must be balanced. This means that the population, resources, environmental and ecological systems, as well as the economy, politics, culture, and education should all work together and not at cross purposes.[4]

Diplomacy is often viewed as an extension of domestic politics. The idea of a harmonious world is to some extent the extension of the domestic idea of a harmonious society. Although they should not be seen as completely synonymous, domestic politics and diplomacy share some common elements in value orientation and political logic, which are exemplified by the relationship between the ideas of a harmonious society and a harmonious world. As Li Jingzhi, a Chinese scholar of international relations, has pointed out, "'harmonious society' and 'harmonious world' are interlinked and complementary to each other. They are the two cornerstones of the overall development strategy of China."[5]

The goal of seeking to build a harmonious world is to construct a new order of international politics and economics based on democracy, justice, and equity and to realize sustained peace and common prosperity for all the people of the world. Just like China's domestic goal of building a harmonious society, its ideal of seeking a harmonious world entails working toward a planet that is populated by nations that are credible, cooperative, accommodating, and pursuing sustainable economic development. China holds that a "harmonious world should be democratic, harmonious, just, and tolerant."[6]

At a seminar entitled "The Chinese Dream and the Harmonious World," held in Beijing in 2006, China's vice minister of foreign affairs Zhang Yesui made clear his interpretation of what a harmonious world entails—a peaceful and stable world, in which nations trust each other and coexist harmoniously and in which the peace and security of the world are maintained through fair and effective security mechanisms. It should be a democratic and just world, in which every nation shares equal sovereignty, in which international relations are based on laws and multilateralism, and in which global issues are resolved through negotiation. It should be characterized by reciprocity and cooperation, in which economic globalization and the advancement of science and technology should contribute to the common development of the international community, particularly the economic growth of developing countries. It should be an open and inclusive world, in which different civilizations hold talks and learn from each other, and different social systems and development models coexist with each other and make progress together.[7]

In my opinion, another aspect of the goal of building a harmonious world should also be clarified, with the goal of constructing a sustainable world and harmonizing the relationship between human society and the earth. In a harmonious world, such values as "we share a common earth" or "we are one human family" should be shared globally. Based on these values, the global ecology and environment should be consciously protected, the resources of the earth should be reasonably explored, and the relationship between people and nature should be respectful.

The objective of constructing a harmonious society is based not only on China's judgment of its own domestic situation, but also on its judgment of the international situation in which China finds itself. This judgment comprises two core convictions. First, it is an objective goal for humans to build a harmonious world. Second, it is possible to construct a harmonious world because some necessary preconditions have already been achieved. Peace and development are the two themes of our age, and they are also the main objectives of a harmonious world. In an era of globalization, ties among nations are intensifying, national interests are growing ever more interdependent, and human societies increasingly share a common fate. As such, world peace and global cooperation are becoming ever more important. Nations should be "harmonious but different," tolerating, respecting, and coexisting with each other.

How should nations seek to construct a harmonious world? In his address to the sixtieth anniversary of the United Nations, President Hu Jintao proposed four answers to this question.

First, the international community should uphold multilateralism and realize common security. All countries should join hands in coping with global threats. By getting rid of cold war thinking, nations should establish a new conception of security defined by mutual confidence, mutual benefits, equality, and cooperation. A fair and effective collective security mechanism should be established in order to prevent conflict and war while maintaining world peace and security.

Second, the international community should engage in mutually beneficial cooperation so as to achieve common prosperity. Not only is development in the interests of all people in the world, but it is also a way to eliminate many global security threats. Without common development and prosperity, world peace will be impossible. Economic globalization should benefit all countries (especially developing countries) instead of just wealthy countries.

Third, to build a harmonious world, countries around the globe should adopt a spirit of inclusiveness. The diversity of world civilization is a basic feature of human society and an important driving force behind human progress. To construct a harmonious world, the social institutions and development models a country chooses to adopt should be decided by its own people and not be forced upon it by outsiders. Dialogue and communication among different civilizations should be enhanced, and the diversity of civilizations should be maintained as the very basis of equality and openness, while international relations should be democratized.

Finally, UN reforms should be conducted in an active but prudent manner. To enhance the organization's ability to handle new threats and challenges, the United Nations should be endowed with more authority, strength, and efficiency.[8]

The idea of a harmonious world as presented by President Hu is not only the continuation and development of the international strategic thought of Deng Xiaoping and Jiang Zemin, but also the goal of China's new global strategy at the beginning of a new era. The following section explains the significance of the concept of the harmonious world and the transformation of China's global strategy in a more historical context.

A Harmonious World and the Transformation of China's Global Strategy

The reform and opening-up strategy, initiated by Deng Xiaoping in the late 1970s, entailed an overall transformation of Chinese society and resulted in earthshaking changes in politics and economics, including both the domestic and foreign policies of China. Based on insightful judgments about China's domestic situation and global trends, Deng organically combined domestic reform with opening to the outside world, thereby forming the basic reform strategy of the CCP and the Chinese government. With the implementation of the opening-up policy, foreign policy has come to play a more critical role in Chinese political life while the boundary between domestic politics and diplomacy has been dramatically blurred. The transformation of China's foreign strategy came on the heels of broad-gauge domestic political and economic reforms. In line with its domestic political and economic strategy, China's international strategy has gradually taken shape. The idea of seeking to promote a harmonious world best summarizes China's new global strategy.

Today's Chinese government still adheres to many principles and guidelines of the traditional foreign strategy established by Mao Zedong and Zhou Enlai and implemented from 1949 to 1978. Such principles and guidelines include the principle of independence and self-reliance, the Five Principles of Peaceful Coexistence (that is, mutual respect for sovereignty and territorial integrity, mutual nonaggression, noninterference in each other's internal affairs, equality and mutual benefit, and peaceful coexistence), firmly resisting imperialism and hegemonism, insistence on no first use of nuclear weapons, and the active attitude that "China should contribute to humanity." Hence, the idea of a harmonious world as presented by Hu Jintao is in line with Deng Xiaoping and Jiang Zemin's international strategic thought. As the Chinese scholar Li Jingzhi has stated, "The idea of a 'harmonious world' exhibits the good will of the Chinese people to cherish peace and harmoniously coexist with other countries. It also demonstrates the consistent stand of the Chinese government to adhere to an independent foreign policy of peace as defined by 'the Five Principles of Peaceful Coexistence.'"[9]

The reform and opening-up strategy, however, made great adjustments to, and even some reform measures contrary to, the traditional socialist system established by Mao Zedong. These changes, for example, have included reorienting the work focus of the party and state from class struggle to economic development, the transformation from a traditional socialist planned economy to a socialist market economy, and the transformation from a system of public ownership to a mixed ownership economy.

Similarly, China's international strategy experienced a sharp transformation in two respects. First, the Chinese leaders shifted their basic judgments of the international situation. To Mao Zedong, the main themes of the world were revolution and war. He believed that the danger of world war was great while revolution was the major impetus for global development. By contrast, Deng Xiaoping defined peace and development as the two themes of the contemporary period. Hu Jintao adopted Deng Xiaoping's assessment in this regard, setting it as the cornerstone of his harmonious world idea.

Second, great changes occurred in the philosophy underlying China's foreign policy. The theoretical basis of China's traditional international strategy was Mao Zedong's philosophy of class struggle as well as the "supremacy of ideology."[10] The theoretical basis of China's current international strategy is cooperation, as well as the principle of the "supremacy of national interests." Because of these differences in foreign policy, fundamental changes occurred in the philosophy and judgment about the main themes of the current era following the initiation of reform and opening up of China's foreign strategy. For example, there have been shifts from a closed-door policy to an opening-up policy, from a philosophy of struggle to a focus on cooperation, and from a zero-sum approach to world politics to an emphasis on seeking win-win outcomes, as well as a shift from passive response to active engagement with the world community.

Cai Tuo, a scholar who has conducted a comparative analysis of China's foreign strategies before and after the reform and opening up, has concluded that China's foreign strategy experienced a sharp transformation as a result of these shifts. In Cai's view, the idea of a harmonious world initiated by Hu Jintao is "the crowning achievement of China's reorientation of its foreign strategy against the backdrop of globalization, and it epitomizes the transformation of China's foreign strategy." Such a process, Cai continued, was defined by several transformations: from the "supremacy of ideology" to an approach characterized as "bypassing ideology"; from a repudiator, revolutionist, and peripheral actor in the current international order to one that recognizes, engages with, and is increasingly an important actor in that order; from a doubter and dissenter of international regimes and multilateralism to an active advocate and engaged actor with these; from a focus on absolute "state centralism" to "transnationalism"; from only underscoring the particularity of society to gradually recognizing the universality of society; and from the philosophy of struggle to the philosophy of cooperation and coexistence.[11]

Since the end of the 1970s, both China and the world have experienced enormous changes. In China the CCP has transformed from a revolutionary party into a ruling party. A reform-oriented ideology has replaced the previous class struggle–oriented one, and China's political and economic systems have experienced fundamental changes. With the rapid economic growth, China strikingly developed its comprehensive national power and advanced its international position. At the same time, the cold war disappeared with the collapse of the Soviet Union. The era of globalization and the "information age" have arrived. Such tremendous changes pose a number of new issues for China concerning its global strategy, which did not exist before the reform and opening up. These changes also added new elements to the current foreign strategy of China. Such new elements include actively engaging in globalization and the establishment of global norms; helping to shape global political, economic, and cultural cooperation; playing a more active role in international affairs; striving to maintain the multipolar international structure and the diversity of national cultures; advocating the democratization of international relations and a new international political and economic order; and supporting multilateralism and multilateral diplomacy.

China's new global strategy highlights its attitude towards global governance. China's diplomacy, based on its new global strategy, is a kind of "harmonious diplomacy."

Harmonious Diplomacy and Global Governance

We have entered an era of globalization that calls for global governance. In addition to economic integration, globalization also entails tremendous social and historical transformations defined by increasingly intense interconnections throughout the world.[12] With the arrival of the era of globalization, the fates of all nations are interlinked to an unprecedented degree. Only through global governance can the diverse problems confronting human society be resolved and a new global order be established. The emergence of global governance not only highlights humankind's shared problems and destiny but also reflects people's efforts to pursue a world of sustained peace and common prosperity.

So far, there is no clear and universally accepted definition of global governance. Generally speaking, global governance could be defined as the attempt to resolve such problems as conflict, environmental degradation, the defense of human rights, international migration, drug-smuggling, and infectious diseases through international regimes with binding force so as to maintain international political and economic order. Anthony McGrew, a British expert on international affairs, has argued that global governance means not only formal institutions and organizations (government institutions or intergovernmental cooperation, for example), whose aim is to formulate and maintain the rules and regulations of the world, but also other types of organizations and pressure groups (such as multinational companies, transnational social campaigns, and numerous nongovernmental organizations), whose targets and goals are to exert influence both on transnational norms and authority systems.[13]

The idea of a harmonious world has much in common with popular theories of global governance in that these all focus on the destiny of humankind, object to unilateralism and hegemonism, oppose a "Pax Americana" while insisting on strengthening the role of the UN, advocate resolving global problems through international cooperation, and devote themselves to establishing international political and economic order. As Chinese scholar Pang Zhongying has argued, the idea of a harmonious world puts forth a new approach to how to meet the challenges of globalization and how to manage globalization from the perspective of global governance.[14] The effort to build a harmonious world is China's proposal for producing global governance as well as its view of the situation and main tendencies in the world today. This scholar also made the following five points.

First, China favors peaceful, fair, effective, and democratic multilateralism. Such multilateralism is, in China's perspective, substantial rather than empty. China advocates the idea of common security and insists on the UN's core role as a mechanism for maintaining global security. Second, China is devoted to the promotion of common development through an open, fair, and nondiscriminatory multilateral trade mechanism. Third, China insists that different civilizations and social systems should be free to communicate with each other in the spirit of mutual respect, toleration, and understanding. Fourth, China supports strengthening the UN through reform. The UN plays an essential role in meeting global challenges and will be able to cope with global threats more effectively after it undergoes proper reforms. Fifth, China advocates "protecting human rights" and "ensuring that everyone enjoys equal opportunities and rights for all-round development."[15]

The idea of a harmonious world epitomizes the Chinese government's standpoint on international affairs and global governance. It also highlights China's global strategy at the beginning of the twenty-first century, which is premised on a harmonious diplomacy with the following components:

—*A value orientation and basic objectives.* The basic objectives of harmonious diplomacy include realizing sustained peace by firmly rejecting war of any kind, opposing terrorism, wiping out violent crime, and resolving conflicts among nations through dialogue and cooperation; realizing common prosperity in the world through the development of all countries, narrowing the gap between North and South, eliminating poverty, improving human rights, and enhancing the welfare of everyone so all share in the achievements of human civilization; advancing the democratization of international relations, which entails establishing democratic, just, and rational international political and economic orders through dialogue, deliberation, negotiation, and cooperation, and ensuring that all nations can participate equally in international affairs; and harmonizing relations between human society and nature by using precious natural resources efficiently and economically, protecting the environment, reducing pollution, and realizing the sustainable development of the world.

—*International regimes.* Harmonious diplomacy gives great weight to international regimes, particularly the role of the UN in maintaining global security and establishing new orders for international political and economic affairs. From the perspective of the Chinese government, as President Hu said, "sovereignty, territory integrity, as well as the freedom to choose one's own social system and development model should be fully respected. This principle is not only an important cornerstone of the UN Charter, but is also the guiding principle for countries with different social systems and development levels seeking to establish and advance bilateral relations."[16] The authority of the United Nations charter as well as UN resolutions must be maintained and strengthened, because these provide the basic code of conduct for the functioning of the international community and represent the expressed will of the majority of the international community. "The objectives and principles established by the UN play an essential role in maintaining world peace and security. They have been recognized as the basic rules of international relations and therefore must be abided by continuously," President Hu stressed.[17]

—*Main actors.* The main actors of harmonious diplomacy include sovereign states and international organizations. From the perspective of the Chinese government, every sovereign state should enjoy equal rights in international affairs as well as shoulder inescapable responsibilities for maintaining world peace and development. The developed countries and great powers, however, should take on more responsibilities for sustained peace and common prosperity. The Chinese government insists that the UN plays a core role in maintaining world peace and establishing a new world order. As the cornerstone of collective security in an era of globalization, the UN must be strengthened. In the absence of permission from the UN, any action will lack legitimacy. As a specialized agent in maintaining world peace and security, the Security Council is endowed with special responsibilities. But this does not mean the UN should be left unchanged. As President Hu said, "the reform of the UN is a comprehensive process. In the spirit of 'putting what is easy before what is difficult,' UN reform should be carried out steadily and step by step. UN reform should enhance the UN's ability to devote more resources to the field of development. By so doing, the basic objectives and principles of the UN would be maintained and the solidarity among member states would be strengthened."[18]

—*Key fields.* The key fields of harmonious diplomacy include regional and global security, which are the preconditions of a harmonious world and without which a harmonious world will be impossible; international cooperation, as it is only through cooperation that the common interests of different countries and the common prosperity of the world can be realized; protection of universal human rights, since it is the responsibility of the international community as a whole to protect human rights such as the right to exist and the right of development; global environmental protection, since the degradation of the ecology and the environment threatens the existence of all human beings; global risk management, since many of the threats to domestic political and economic orders have been globalized in recent years, including financial crises, disease, and communication challenges, which must be met through mutual cooperation; and confronting transnational criminal activity, since crimes such as terrorism, smuggling, and drug trafficking have been internationalized in recent years. Only through cooperation will the international community be able to crack down on these crimes.

—*Important strategies.* The strategies of harmonious diplomacy center on dialogue and negotiation, win-win outcomes achieved through cooperation, finding commonalities while reserving differences, and promoting an environment characterized by inclusion and openness. To reach maximum consensus, harmonious diplomacy requires equal, friendly, and sincere dialogue and negotiation, and mutual trust as well as mutual respect. To realize win-win outcomes, harmonious diplomacy calls for equal and reciprocal cooperation and the maximization of common interests. Harmonious diplomacy aims to reduce the differing interests among countries by promoting consensus. Strong conflicts of interest that prove impossible to bridge in the near term should be handled according to the principle of shelving disputes and looking forward. Harmonious diplomacy accepts the diversity of civilizations and national cultures. It encourages countries to tolerate different political, economic, and cultural patterns while condemning such behaviors as imposing one country's culture, values, and institutions on another country.

Concluding Thoughts

China's strategy of pursuing a harmonious world not only embodies the universal values and aspirations of human beings in the era of globalization, but also epitomizes the political, economic, and cultural characteristics of China. As the biggest developing country, China is making every effort to develop itself by sticking to the road of modernization with Chinese characteristics. At the same time, to maintain the diversity of world civilizations as well as to promote comprehensive progress in the international community, China is actively participating in international affairs with a strong sense of responsibility. In traditional Chinese culture, the notion of "harmonious but different" is a highly valued concept. China's new global strategy incorporates this traditional philosophy and endows it with new elements appropriate to the era of globalization.

Notes

Introduction

1. Richard Madsen, "China in the American Imagination," *Dissent* (Winter 1998): 54.

2. President Woodrow Wilson used these words in his appeal to the U.S. Congress on February 3, 1917, to ratify his call for a declaration of war on Germany.

3. For a representative work in this school of thought, see James Mann, *The China Fantasy: Why Capitalism Will Not Bring Democracy to China* (New York: Penguin, 2008). An earlier, hardcover version is entitled *The China Fantasy: How Our Leaders Explain away Chinese Repression* (New York: Viking, 2007).

4. David Shambaugh, "Let a Thousand Democracies Bloom," *International Herald Tribune,* July 6, 2007.

5. Tang Shiping, "Coming Intellectual Power," *China Security* vol. 4, no. 2 (Spring 2008): 14–15.

6. Yu Keping, "Minzhu shige haodongxi" [Democracy Is a Good Thing], in *Minzhu shige haodongxi,* edited by Yan Jian (Beijing: Social Sciences Academic Press of China [Shehui kexue wenxian chubanshe], 2006).

7. See www.chinanews.com.cn/gn/news/2008/01-01/1120420.shtml (August 20, 2008).

8. *Nanfang Zhoumo* [Southern Weekend], December 12, 2007, p. 1; and *Nanfang Dushi Bao* [Southern Metropolis Daily], July 7, 2008, p. 7.

9. For a more comprehensive discussion of Yu's ideas about the democratic transition in China, see Yu Keping, *Zengliang Minzhu yu Shanzhi* [Incremental Democracy and Good Governance] (Beijing: Social Sciences Academic Press of China [Shehui kexue wenxian chubanshe], 2003); and Yu Keping, *Zhongguo gongmin shehui de xingqi yu zhili de bianqian* [The Emergence of Civil Society and Its Significance for Governance in Reform China] (Beijing: Social Sciences Academic Press of China [Shehui kexue wenxian chubanshe], 2002).

10. See www.hi.chinanews.com.cn/hnnew/2005-10-20/29705.html (August 20, 2008).

11. This discussion of Wen's meeting with the Brookings Institution delegation is based on John L. Thornton, "Assessing the Next Phase of a Rising China," memo, December 2006 (en.chinaelections.org/newsinfo.asp?newsid=14914); and "Riding the Dragon: Brookings Launches New Center with a Journey Across China," November 2007; as well as this author's notes.

12. For Wen's detailed remarks and more discussion of the definition of democracy, see Cheng Li, "Introduction: Assessing China's Political Development," in *China's Changing Political Landscape: Prospects for Democracy*, edited by Cheng Li (Brookings Institution Press, 2008), pp. 1–21.

13. Xie Maoshi, "Minzhu bushige huadongxi" [Democracy Is Not a Bad Thing], *Zhongguo jingji shibao* [China Economic Times], January 15, 2007, p. 4.

14. For Shi Tianjian's comments on Yu's argument about democracy, see www.westca.com/Forums/viewtopic/t=105658/lang=schinese.html (August 20, 2008).

15. See, for example, the popular website of China Elections and Governance, www.chinaelections.org/NewsInfo.asp?NewsID=100984 (August 20, 2008).

16. For more discussion of the role of the CCTB, see www.cctb.net/wjjj/2003103 00001.htm (August 20, 2008).

17. In Zheng Bijian's view, the theory of China's peaceful rise not only means that the country will become a major economic and cultural player in the world, but also requires a list of "won'ts"—China won't launch war to plunder the resources of other countries, won't export ideology, won't export economic development models to other countries, won't pursue an industrial development strategy that consumes a large amount of unsustainable resources, won't challenge the existing order of the international system, won't engage in large-scale emigration, and won't establish colonies overseas. For a more detailed discussion, see Zheng Bijian, *China's Peaceful Rise: Speeches of Zheng Bijian 1997–2005* (Brookings Institution Press, 2005).

18. For a more detailed discussion of the collective characteristics, see John Pomfret, *Chinese Lessons: Five Classmates and the Story of the New China* (New York: Henry Holt and Company, 2006); and Cheng Li, "China's Fifth Generation: Is Diversity a Source of Strength or Weakness?" *Asia Policy* no. 6 (July 2008): 53–93.

19. The other is Wang Puqu, presently vice president of the Macao Polytechnic Institute.

20. *Nanfang zhoumo*, December 27, 2007, p. 8.

21. This discussion is based on the laudation, which was delivered by Professor Thomas Heberer in the honorary degree ceremony at the University of Duisburg-Essen on May 20, 2008 (www.uni-duisburg-essen.de/oapol/Aktuelles_mit_en.shtml).

22. *Nanfang Zhoumo*, December 27, 2007, p. 8.

23. Shu Taifeng, "Yu Keping: Zhengfu chuangxin xuyao gengduo de kuanrong" [Yu Keping: Government Innovations Require Greater Tolerance], *Dongfang liaowang zhoukan* [Oriental Outlook Weekly], April 8, 2008.

24. China's Reform Institute (Hainan) conducted this survey. See chinanews.com, January 19, 2006.

25. *Zhongguo xinwen zhoukan* [China Newsweek], January 13, 2006; *Liaowang* [Outlook], December 5, 2005; and www.chinesenewsnet.com, December 12, 2005.

26. The other powerful interest groups include the monopoly industries such as telecommunications, oil, electricity, and automotive, all of which have a huge stake in government policies. See Sun Liping, "Zhongguo jinru liyi boyi de shidai" [China Is Entering the Era of a Conflict of Interests], www.chinesenewsnet.com, February 6, 2006.

27. Sun, "Zhongguo jinru liyi boyi de shidai."

28. Jin Sanyong, "Zhongyang difang cunzai mingxian boyi" [The Open Game that the Central and Local Governments Play], www.zisi.net, February 10, 2006.

29. *Shijie Ribao* [Shijie Daily], December 25, 2006, p. A3. Originally in *Beijing Ribao* [Beijing Daily], December 18, 2006.

30. This is based on Yu Keping, "Ideological Change and Incremental Democracy in Reform-Era China," in *China's Changing Political Landscape,* edited by Cheng, pp. 54–55.

31. Ibid.

32. For a more detailed discussion of Yu's argument about dynamic stability, see "Dongtai wending yu hexie shehui [Dynamic Stability and Harmonious Society], *Zhongguo tese shehuizhuyi yanjiu* [Studies on Socialism with Chinese Characteristics] no. 3 (2006): 25–28.

33. Xie Tao, "Zhiyou minzhu shehuizhuyi caineng jiu Zhongguo" [Only Democratic Socialism Can Save China], www.chinaelections.org/NewsInfo.asp?NewsID=100318 (August 20, 2008); also see Xie Tao, "Minzhu shehuizhuyi moshi yu Zhongguo de qiantu" [The Model of Democratic Socialism and the Prospects of China], *Yanhuang chunqiu* [Chinese History] no. 2 (2007).

34. Hu Ping, "Yu Keping fangmei jianghua xiaoyi" [Comments on Yu Keping's Speeches in the United States]. See hk.epochtimes.com/7/4/20/43430.htm, April 20, 2007.

35. See pkunews.pku.edu.cn/zdlm/2008-03/27/content_120756.htm, March 27, 2008.

36. The quote is from www.chinesenewsnet.com, April 25, 2006. For more discussion of Pan Wei's criticism of democratic worship and election obsession, see Pan Wei, "Toward a Consultative Rule of Law Regime in China," *Journal of Contemporary China* vol. 12, no. 34 (February 2003): 3–43; and also Suisheng Zhao, ed., *Debating Political Reform in China: Rule of Law vs. Democratization* (New York: M. E. Sharpe, 2006). It should be noted that criticism of Yu's thesis also comes from the "Old Left" scholars, in addition to the "New Right" and "New Left." According to the Old Left scholars, Yu's view on democracy not only advocates the Wesern liberal theory but also attempts to overthrow the Chinese Communist Party. See, for example, Cheng Mengyun, "*Bo Minzhu shige haodongxi* [Critical of Yu's "Democracy Is a Good Thing"], January 6, 2007 (www.zaobao.com/special/forum.pages5/forum_1x070106.html).

Chapter One

1. The original version of this chapter first appeared in Yu Keping, "Minzhu shige haodongxi" [Democracy Is a Good Thing], in *Minzhu shige haodongxi* [Democracy Is a Good Thing], edited by Yan Jian (Beijing: Social Sciences Academic Press of China [Shehui kexue wenxian chubanshe], 2006).

Chapter Two

1. The original version of this chapter first appeared in Chinese in Yu Keping, "Zhongguo Zhengzhixue de Jincheng" [The Development of Political Science in China], *Xueshu Yuekan* [Academic Monthly] 39, no. 11 (November 2007): 5–11. The section on the development of the discipline of public administration first appeared in Chinese in Yu Keping, "Quanqiuhua yu Zhongguo zhengfu de nengli" [Globalization and the Capacity of the Chinese Government], *Gonggong Guanli Xuebao* [Chinese Journal of Public Management] 1, no. 1 (February 2005).

2. Zhao Baoxu, "Century Progress of Chinese Political Science," *Academy of South East* 2 (2000): 39–40.

3. Deng Xiaoping, *Selections of Essays by Deng Xiaoping*, vol. 2 (Beijing: People's Press, 1994), p.180.

4. On the general development status of political science in China after reform and opening to the outside world, see Zhao Baoxu, "Century Progress of Chinese Political Science"; Liu Han and Yang Long, "Political Science in China in the Past 50 years," *Journal of Political Science Research* 4 (1999): 1–13; Lin Shangli, "Political Science and Political Development: Two Decades of Political Science Development in China," *Journal of Political Science Research* 2 (1998): 1–11; Yang Haijiao, "Characteristics and Development Trends of Political Science Research in China since the 1990s," *Zhejiang Journal of Social Science* 4 (2001): 19–28; and Han Xu, "Chinese Political Science in Development and the Development of Chinese Political Science," *Journal of Political Science Research* 3 (1998): 92–95.

5. For discussions in this matter, see Yu Jianxing, "Self-Examination of Political Science Development and Construction of Chinese Political Science," *Teaching and Research* 5 (2005): 16–23; Lin Shangli, "Scientific Political Science and Scientification of Political Science," *Journal of Political Science Research* 1 (1998): 18–20.

6. Xiao Tangbiao and Zheng Chuangui, "Topic, Category, and Norms: Status of Domestic Political Science Research—Statistical Analysis of Journal Articles from the 'Political Science' Volume of the Photocopied Material by Renmin University," *Journal of Beijing Institute of Public Administration* 2 (2005): 12–13.

7. The notion of the "three represents" was first developed by Jiang Zemin and then was adopted as a political ideology of the ruling party at the Sixteenth Party Congress in 2002. It asserts that the Chinese Communist Party should be representative of advanced social productive forces (namely entrepreneurs), advanced culture, and the interests of the overwhelming majority.

8. Xiao Tangbiao and Zheng Chuangui, "Topic, Category, and Norms."

9. For example, as recently reported by *China Youth Daily,* "in a class on politics in a higher education institute in Haidian District, Beijing, few among the over 100 students really listen to the teacher in class. Most of them are either sleeping or reading English books. Some are surfing on the Internet, downloading movies or chatting. Such an atmosphere in a class on politics is very common in higher education institutes." See "Investigation of the Status of the Class on Politics in some Higher Education Institutes: Students Not Interested, Teachers Feel Confused," *China Youth Daily,* April 23, 2007.

10. Feng Zhifeng. "Political Science Research Calling for Scientific Political Science Textbooks—A Research Report on an Investigation of 324 Political Science Textbooks," *Academic Journal of Qingdao University* 24, no. 1 (March 2007): 105.

11. Xiao Tangbiao and Zheng Chuangui, "Topic, Category and Norms."

12. Yu Keping, "Liberating Thought and Advancing Political Reality," *Theoretical Status* 20 (2007): 1–19.

13. In reviewing the development process of Chinese political science and looking forward to the future, Professor Zhao Baoxu from Beijing University and Professor Cao Peiling from Fudan University simultaneously put forward, by mere coincidence, "the three development directions." See Zhao Baoxu, "Century Progress of Chinese Political Science"; and Cao Peilin, "Three Development Directions of Chinese Political Science in the New Century," *Tianjin Social Science* 2 (2001): 13–16.

Chapter Three

1. The original, Chinese version of this chapter first appeared in Yu Keping, "Zhenggai hechu tupo?" [Political Reform: Where Is the breakthrough?], *Caijing* [Finance and Economics] 22 (October 2007): 88–92.

2. Hu Jintao, "Hold High the Great Banner of Socialism with Chinese Characteristics and Strive for New Victories in Building a Moderately Prosperous Society in All Respects—Report to the Seventeenth National Congress of the Communist Party of China on October 15, 2007" (Beijing: People's Publishing House, 2007), p. 28.

3. Ibid.

4. Ibid., p. 30.

5. Ibid., p. 29.

6. Ibid., p. 33.

7. Ibid., p. 33.

8. Ibid., p. 40.

9. Ibid., p. 32.

Chapter Four

1. The original, Chinese version of this chapter first appeared in Yu Keping, "Zhongguo Gongmin Shehui: Gainian Fenlei yu Zhidu Huanjing" [China's Civil Society: Conceptual Types and Institutional Environment], *Zhongguo Shehui Kexue* [Social Sciences in China] no. 1 (January 2006): 109–22.

2. Scholars are of different opinions on whether political parties and religious organizations should count as civil society organizations. On the basis of conditions in China, I adopt the definition of civic organizations given by Lester M. Salamon and others and do not count them as civil society organizations. See Lester M. Salamon, *The Emerging Sector* (Johns Hopkins University Press, 1994).

3. Douglass C. North, *Structure and Change in Economic History* (New York: Norton and Co., 1981), pp. 201–02.

4. Ibid., p. 17.

5. State Council publications, "Regulations Concerning the Registration and Supervision of Social Associations, Interim Regulations Concerning the Registration and Supervision of Privately Run, Non-Business Bodies, and Regulations Concerning the Supervision of Foundations" (www.mca.gov.cn/wjylzx).

6. Ibid.

7. Wu Zhongze, ed., *Managing Social Associations* (Beijing: China Social Press, 1996), p. 6.

8. Deng Guosheng, *Evaluation of Non-profit Organizations* (Beijing: Social Sciences Academic Press of China, 2001), pp. 5–6.

9. See, for example, Wang Ming and others, *Reform of China's Social Associations* (Beijing: Social Sciences Academic Press of China, 2001), p. 17; Wang Ying and others, *The Intermediate Level of Society* (Beijing: China Development Press, 1993), p. 70; CCP Research Group on Hangzhou's Civil Society Organizations, "Considerations on Strengthening Party-Building Work in Civil Organizations," *Research on Human Resource Management in Organizations* no. 3 (2003): 54–56; Wan Jianghong, Zhang Cui, and others, "Review of Research on China's Social Organizations during the Past Ten Years," *Jianghan Forum* no. 8 (2004): 125–27; and Wang Ying and Sun Bingyao, "Survey of the Development of China's Civil Organizations," in Yu Keping and others, *The Rise of China's Civil Society and Changes in Its Governance* (Beijing: Social Sciences Academic Press of China, 2002), pp. 4–5.

10. Xu Xiuli, "The Institutional Environment of Civil Organizations in the Republic of China (1912–1949)," a research report prepared for the project "Promoting an Enabling Environment for Civil Society Development in China," sponsored by the Ford Foundation, 2005.

11. Ibid.

12. Yu Keping and others, *The Rise of China's Civil Society.*

13. Ministry of Civil Affairs, *China Civil Affairs Yearbook 1999* (Beijing: China Social Press, 1999).

14. "Civil Government Statistical Data for the First Quarter of 2005" (www.mca.gov.cn/mztj/yuebao0503.html).

15. He Zengke,"Analysis of Factors Affecting the Institutional Environment of China's Civil Society," a research report prepared for the project "Promoting an Enabling Environment for Civil Society Development in China," sponsored by the Ford Foundation, 2005.

Chapter Five

1. The Chinese version of this chapter first appeared in Yu Keping, "Zhongguo Gongmin Shehui: Gainian Fenlei yu Zhidu Huanjing" [China's Civil Society: Conceputal Types and Institutional Environment], *Zhongguo Shehui Kexue* [Social Sciences in China] no. 1 (January 2006): 109–22.

2. Archival Department of Ming and Qing Dynasties in the Forbidden City, *Historical Archives on "Preparation for Constitutionalism" in the Late Qing Dynasty*, vol. 1 (Beijing: Chinese Publishing House, 1979), p. 59.

3. Cai Hongwu, *A Compilation of Laws in the Republic of China*, vol. 2 (Hefei: Huangshan Publishing House, 1999), pp. 1, 7, 8.

4. Renmin University of China, Law Department, ed., *Selected Readings in Chinese and Foreign Constitutions* (Beijing: People's Publishing House, 1982), pp. 21, 62.

5. Xie Zhenmin, ed., *History of Law in the Republic of China* (Beijing: China University of Political Science and Law Press, 2000).

6. Su Li and others, *Rules and Development: The Legal Environment of the Third Sector* (Hangzhou: Zhejiang People's Publishing House, 1996), pp. 26–27.

7. He Zengke, "Analysis of Factors Affecting the Institutional Environment of China's Civil Society," in *Institutional Environment of China's Civil Society,* edited by Yu Keping and others (Beijing: Peking University Press, 2006), pp. 121–65.

8. For more information, see www.mca.gov.cn/article/zwgk/fvfg/mjzzgl.

9. Xu Xiuli, "The Institutional Environment of Civil Organizations in the Republic of China (1912–1949)," a research report prepared for the project "Promoting an Enabling Environment for Civil Society Development in China," sponsored by the Ford Foundation, 2005.

10. "Decision of the CCP Central Committee Concerning Strengthening the Party's Governance Capacity" (Beijing: People's Publishing House, 2004), p. 25.

11. He Zengke, "Analysis of Factors Affecting the Institutional Environment of China's Civil Society."

12. Guo Jianmei, "The Existence and Development of Civil Organizations in China: The Example of the Women's Law and Research Center at Peking University," *Collection of Women's Studies* no. 5 (2000): 34.

13. Ibid., pp. 196–98.

14. See, for example, Legal Affairs Office of the CCP Central Committee General Office, Legal Affairs Office of the Central Commission for Discipline Inspection, and the General Office of the Organization Department of the Central Committee, eds., *Selected Laws and Regulations of the Chinese Communist Party* (Beijing: Law Press, 1997 and 2001); and Shandong Province Bureau for Supervising Civil Organizations, ed., *Collected Documents and Data Concerning the Supervision of Civil Organizations* (Jinan: Shandong University Press, 2005).

15. The State Council, "Regulations Concerning the Registration and Supervision of Social Associations," October 1998.

16. He Zengke, "Analysis of Factors Affecting the Institutional Environment of China's Civil Society."

17. Zhu Xiaoming, "A Study of the Legal Environment of the Existence and Development of Civil Organizations," *Zhejiang Social Sciences* no. 3 (2004): 204–25.

18. Yan Jian, "Survey of Rural Civil Organizations in Wenling, Zhejiang Province," a survey report prepared for the project "Promoting an Enabling Environment for Civil Society Development in China," sponsored by the Ford Foundation, 2005.

19. Wang Ming, "Speech at the Seventeenth Annual International Philanthropy Fellows in Philanthropy and Social Justice International Conference," July 11, 2005.

20. He Zengke, "Analysis of Factors Affecting the Institutional Environment of China's Civil Society."

21. Wang Ming, "Preface," *Tsinghua University NGO Research Studies* (Beijing: Tsinghua University Press, 2005).

22. Ministry of Civil Affairs, "Notice Concerning Issues Pertaining to Exemptions from Registration for Some Social Associations," M.F. no. [2000] 256, Beijing, December 2000.

23. Yan Jian, "Survey of Rural Civil Organizations in Wenling, Zhejiang Province."

Chapter Six

1. The original, Chinese version of this chapter first appeared in Yu Keping, "Zhongguo Gongmin Shehui: Gainian Fenlei yu Zhidu Huanjing" [China's Civil Society: Conceptual Types and Institutional Environment], *Zhongguo Shehui Kexue* [Social Sciences in China] no. 1 (January 2006): 109–22.

2. Li Jingpeng, "Comprehensive General Analytic Report on a Survey of Beijing and Zhejiang Province," working paper, Social Groups Research Center, Peking University. Respondents could choose more than more answer.

3. Wang Shaoguang and Wang Ming, "Policy Suggestions for Promoting the Development of China's NPOs," in *China's Nongovernmental Public Sector,* edited by Wang Ming (Beijing: Tsinghua University Press, 2004), p. 73.

4. He Zengke, "Analysis of Factors Affecting the Institutional Environment of China's Civil Society," in *Institutional Environment of China's Civil Society,* edited by Yu Keping and others (Beijing: Peking University Press, 2006), pp. 121–65.

5. Chen Sixi, "The State of Chinese Law Concerning Social Associations," *Global Law Review* (Summer 2002): 175–76.

6. For information on the International Treaty on Civil and Political Rights, see *The Human Rights Encyclopedia of China,* edited by Wang Jiafu and others (Beijing: Encyclopedia of China Publishing House, 1998), p. 790.

7. Bian Ganqun, Chen Chi, and Wei Hansong, "Supervision of Civil Organizations: Difficulties and Solutions," *China Civil Affairs* no. 9 (1999): 24.

8. Pu Wenzhong, "Flourishing Rural Civil Organizations," *China Reform* (rural edition) no. 5 (2003): 8.

9. See, for example, Wang Ming and Jia Xijin, "Theoretical Outline for Laws and

Policies Concerning Chinese NGOs," *Tsinghua University Journal* (Philosophy and Social Science Edition), additional issue, 2004; Wang Ming, "Speech at the Seventeenth Annual International Philanthropy Fellows in Philanthropy and Social Justice International Conference," July 11, 2005 (unpublished); and Jia Xijin, "Some Suggestions Concerning the System of Registration and Supervision of NPOs," Center of NGO Studies, Tsinghua University, Beijing.

10. Wang Ming, "Speech at the Twenty-First Century Forum," sponsored by the Chinese People's Political Consultative Conference in Beijing in September 2005.

11. See www.chinadevelopmentbrief.com.

12. Lu Jinfang, "An Analysis of Problems in the Regulation of Social Associations and Suggested Solutions," *Guangxi Auditing* no. 6 (2001): 40.

Chapter Seven

1. Part of this chapter appeared in the author's paper in the working papers series in Asian-Pacific Studies, Duke University, no. 2, 1994.

2. Chen Xujing, "Quanpan xihua de bianhu" [A Defense of Total Westernization], *Walking out of the East: Selected Collection of Chen Xujing's Thoughts on Culture,* edited by Tang Yijie (Beijing: China's Broadcasting Press, 1995), pp. 280–83.

3. Luo Rongqu, "Zhongguo jin bainian lai xiandaihua sichao yanbian de fansi" [Rethinking the Evolution of Thought on Modernization in China over the Last One Hundred Years], in *Cong xihua dao xiandaihua* [From Westernization to Modernization], edited by Luo Rongqu (Beijing: Peking University Press, 1990), pp. 13–14.

4. Chen Xujing, "Zhongguo wenhua de chulu" [The Way Out for Chinese Culture], in Luo, *From Westernization to Modernization,* pp. 389–90.

5. Xiong Mengfei, "Tan 'Zhongguo benwei wenhua' zhi xiantian" [Talking about 'Chinese Native Culture'], *Wenhua jianshe yuekan* [Cultural Construction Monthly] vol. 1, no. 9 (June 1935); also in Luo, *From Westernization to Modernization,* p. 524.

6. Lin Yutang, "Jiqi yu jingshen" [Machine and Spirit], *Zhongxuesheng* [Middle School Students] no. 2 (December 1929); also in Luo, *From Westernization to Modernization,* p. 199.

7. Ibid.

8. Hu Shi, "Women dui xiyang wenming de taidu" [Our Attitude toward Western Civilization], *Dongfang Zazhi* [Eastern Miscellany] vol. 23, no. 17 (July 1926); also in Luo, *From Westernization to Modernization,* p. 168.

9. Wu Shichang, "Zhongguo wenhua yu xiandaihua wenti" [Chinese Culture and Modernization], in Luo, *From Westernization to Modernization,* p. 351.

10. Chen Xujing, "The Way Out for Chinese Culture," pp. 371–72.

11. Hu Shi, "Our Attitude toward Western Civilization," p. 167.

12. Yan Jicheng, "'Women de zong dafu' shu hou" [A Comment on "Our General Answer"], *Dagong bao* [Takung Daily], May 22, 1936. Also in Luo, *From Westernization to Modernization,* p. 483.

13. Lin Yutang, "Machine and Spirit," p. 200.

14. Hu Shi, "Wenhua de chongtu" [Conflicts between Cultures], in Luo, *From Westernization to Modernization*, p. 362.

15. Ibid., p. 364.

16. Zhang Shenfu, "Lun zhongguohua" [On Sinification], *Zhanshi wenhua* [Wartime Culture] vol. 2, no. 2 (February 1939); also in Luo, *From Westernization to Modernization*, pp. 588–91.

17. Hu Qiuyuan, "Zhongguo wenhua fuxing lun" [On the Revival of Chinese Culture] (1939), in Luo, *From Westernization to Modernization*, p. 327.

18. Zhou Xiawen, "'Zhongguo chuantong sixiang' yu 'xiandaihua'" ['Traditional Chinese Thought' and 'Modernization'], *Xin zhonghua* [New China] vol. 2, no. 7 (July 1933). Also in Luo, *From Westernization to Modernization*, p. 347.

19. Yang Xinzhi, "Lun zhongguo xiandaihua" [On China's Modernization], *Shenbao yuekan* [Shenbao Monthly] vol. 2, no. 7 (July 1933); also in Luo, *From Westernization to Modernization*, p. 251.

20. Zhang Sumin, "Zhongguo xiandaihua zhi qianti yu fangshi" [On the Prerequisites and Methods of China's Modernization], *Shenbao yuekan* [Shenbao Monthly] vol. 2, no. 7 (July 1933); also in Luo, *From Westernization to Modernization*, p. 233.

21. Zhang Xiruo, "Quanpan xihua yu zhongguo benwei" [On Total Westernization and Chinese Nativism], *Guowen zhoubao* [News Weekly] vol. 12, no. 33 (April 1935); also in Luo, *From Westernization to Modernization*, p. 458.

22. Feng Youlan, "Zhongguo xiandai minzu yundong zhi zong fangxiang" [The General Direction of the Modern National Movement in China], *Shehuixue jie* [Sociological World] no. 9 (1936); also in Luo, *From Westernization to Modernization*, p. 322.

23. Liang Shuming, "Dong xi fang wenhua ji qi zhexue" [Eastern and Western Cultures and Their Philosophies] (1921), in Luo, *From Westernization to Modernization*, p. 71.

24. Xiong Mengfei, "Talking about 'Chinese Native Culture,'" p. 531.

25. Zhang Dongsun, "Xiandai de Zhongguo zenyang yao Kongzi" [How Does Modern China Need Confucius?], *Zhengfeng banyuekan* [Zhengfeng Semi-Monthly] no. 2 (January 1935); also in Luo, *From Westernization to Modernization*, p. 407.

26. Lu Yudao, "Kexue de wenhua jianshe" [Scientific Cultural Construction], *Kexue* [Science] vol. 19, no. 15 (May 1935); also in Luo, *From Westernization to Modernization*, p. 489.

27. Chen Shiquan, "Zhongguo wenhua jianshe de dongxiang" [The Trends of Chinese Cultural Construction], *Dagong bao* [Takung Daily], March 13–21, 1935; also in Luo, *From Westernization to Modernization*, p. 420.

28. Xiong Mengfei, "Talking about 'Chinese Native Culture,'" p. 531.

29. Wang Xinming and others, "Women de zong dafu" [Our General Answer], *Wenhua jianshe* [Cultural Construction] vol. 1, no. 8 (May 10, 1935); also in Luo, *From Westernization to Modernization*, p. 478.

30. Xiong Mengfei, "Talking about 'Chinese Native Culture,'" p. 517.

31. Ye Yin, "Xiandaihua de zhenglu yu qilu" [Right and Wrong Pathways to Modernization], *Shenbao yuekan* [Shenbao Monthly] vol. 2, no. 7 (1933); also in Luo, *From Westernization to Modernization*, p. 229.

32. As quoted in Yang Xinzhi, "On China's Modernization," p. 259.

33. Chen Gaoyun, "Zenyang shi Zhongguo wenhua xiandaihua" [How to Modernize Chinese Culture], *Shenbao yuekan* [Shenbao Monthly] vol. 2, no. 7 (1933); also in Luo, *From Westernization to Modernization*, p. 295.

34. Liang Qichao, "Ouzhou xinying lu" [Records of a European Tour] (1936), in Luo, *From Westernization to Modernization*, pp. 40, 47.

35. Hu Shi, "Chongfen shijiehua yu quanpan xihua" [Maximal Globalization and Total Westernization], *Dagong bao* [Takung Daily], June 21, 1935; also in Luo, *From Westernization to Modernization*, p. 553.

36. Liang Shiqiu, "Zixin li yu kuada kuang" [Confidence and Exaggeration], *Wenhua jianshe* [Cultural Construction] vol. 1, no. 10 (June 9, 1935); also in Luo, *From Westernization to Modernization*, p. 509.

37. Liang Qichao, "Records of a European Tour," p. 47.

38. Liang Shuming, "Eastern and Western Cultures and Their Philosophies," p. 74.

39. Karl Marx and Friedrich Engels, *The Communist Manifesto* (Oxford University Press, 1992), p. 7.

40. Liang Shuming, "Eastern and Western Cultures and Their Philosophies," pp. 49–50.

41. Hu Shi, "Bianji houji" [Editor's Comments], *Duli pinglun* [Independent Review] no. 142 (March 1935); also in Luo, *From Westernization to Modernization*, p. 424.

42. Feng Youlan, "The General Direction," p. 319.

43. Wu Jingchao, "Jianshe wenti yu dongxi wenhua" [The Problem of Construction and Eastern and Western Cultures] *Independent Commentary* no. 139 (February 1935); also in Luo, *From Westernization to Modernization*, p. 413.

44. Chen Xujing, "A Defense of Total Westernization," p. 561.

45. Chen Xujing, "Cong xihua wenti de taolun li qiu de yige gongtong xinyang" [Seeking a Common Belief from the Discussion on the Problem of Westernization], *Duli pinglun* [Independent Review] no. 149 (May 5,1935); also in Luo, *From Westernization to Modernization*, p. 463.

46. Ai Siqi, "Lun Zhongguo de teshuxing" [On China's Special Characteristics], *Chinese Culture* vol. 1 (1940); also in Luo, *From Westernization to Modernization*, pp. 592–93.

47. Wang Xinming and others, "Zhongguo benwei wenhua jianshe xuanyan" [A Declaration of Chinese Native Cultural Construction], *Wenhua jianshe* [Cultural Construction] vol. 1, no. 4 (January 10, 1935); also in Luo, *From Westernization to Modernization*, p. 399.

48. Ibid.

49. Wang Xinming and others, "Our General Answer," p. 478.

50. Zhang Xiruo, "On Total Westernization and Chinese Nativism," p. 458.

51. Hu Shi, "Shiping suowei 'Zhongguo benwei de wenhua jianshe'" [A Comment on the So-Called 'Chinese Native Cultural Construction'], *Duli pinglun* [Independent Review] no. 4 (March 31, 1935); also in Luo, *From Westernization to Modernization*, p. 425.

Chapter Eight

1. The original, Chinese version of this chapter first appeared in Yu Keping, "Xiandaihua yu quanqiuhua shuangchong bianzou xia de Zhongguo wenhua fazhan luoji" [The Developmental Logic of Chinese Culture under Modernization and Globalization], *Xueshu Yuekan* [Academic Monthly] vol. 38, no. 4 (August 2006): 14–24. A similar version of this article was published in English in *Boundary 2*, vol. 35, no. 2 (Summer 2008): 157–82.

2. Qi Zhenhai, "Chuantong wenhua yu xiandaihua" [Traditional Culture and Modernization], *Zhexue yanjiu* [Philosophical Research] no. 6 (1992): 54.

3. Minze, "Guanyu chuantong wenhua xiandaihua" [On the Modernization of Traditional Culture], *Zhexue yanjiu* no. 4 (1989): 20.

4. Li Shu, "Xiaomie fengjian canyu yingxiang shi Zhongguo xiandaihua de zhongyao tiaojian" [Eliminating the Influence of Feudal Remnants Is an Important Condition of China's Modernization], *Lishi yanjiu* [Historical Research] no. 1 (1979): 12.

5. Ibid.

6. Li Shenzhi, "Chinese Traditional Culture: No Democracy, No Science," in *Liberation Anthology (1978–1998)*, edited by Qiushi (Beijing: Economic Daily Press, 1998), pp.1118–24.

7. Fang Keli, *Xiandai xin ruxue yu Zhongguo xiandaihua* [Contemporary New Confucianism and China's Modernization] (Tianjin: Tianjin renmin chuban she, 1986).

8. Jiang Qing, "Zhongguo dalu fuxing ruxue de xianshi yiyi ji qi mianlin de wenti" [The Real Significance of Reviving Confucianism on the Mainland and Its Problems], *Ehu* [Goose Lake] nos. 170–71 (August-September 1989), quoted in Fang Keli, *Contemporary New Confucianism*, pp. 424–25.

9. Ibid.

10. Zhu Xueqin, "2005: Zhongguo wenhua zhi xingse" [2005: The Configuration of Chinese Culture], *Zhongguo qingnian bao [China Youth Daily]* vol. 9, January 4, 2005.

11. Liang Qichao, "Ouzhou xinying lu" [Records of a European Tour], *Yinbing shi heji* [Collection from an Ice Drinker's Studio] no. 23 (1936): 40.

12. Zhang Dainian, Ji Xianglin, and others. "Zhonghua wenhua fuxing xuanyan" [Manifesto of Chinese Cultural Renaissance] (http//www.column.bokee.com/77442.html).

13. Ibid.

14. Minze, "On the Modernization of Traditional Culture," p. 16.

15. Fei Xiaotong, "Guanyu 'wenhua zijue' de yixie zibai" [Notes on 'Cultural Self-Consciousness'], *Xueshu yanjiu* [Academic Research] no. 7 (2003): 5–7.

16. Ibid.

17. Wang Haiguang, "Xiandaihua yujing xia de wenhua zijue" [Cultural Self-Consciousness in the Context of Modernization], *Wenhui bao* [Wenhui Daily], September 14, 2004.

18. Gan Yang, "Wenhua zijue yu Zhongguo daxue de renwen jiaoyu" [Cultural Self-Consciousness and Humanities Education in Chinese Universities] (www.phoenixtv.com/phoenixtv).

19. Zhu Renqiu, "Quanqiuhua Beijing xia de rujia wenhua zijue" [Confucian Self-Consciousness against the Backdrop of Globalization], *Fujian shifan daxue xuebao* [Journal of Fujian Normal University] no. 5 (2004): 98.

20. Yue Daiyun, "Duoyuan wenhua yu wenhua zijue" [Cultural Pluralism and Cultural Self-Consciousness], speech at the Central Academy of Music, January 17, 2003 (www.ccmce.net/ShowArticle.asp).

21. Tang Yijie, "Guanyu wenhua wenti de jidian sikao" [Some Thoughts on the Question of Culture], *Xueshu Yuekan* [Academic Monthly] no. 9 (2002): 39.

22. Wang Heyu, "Wenhua quanqiu zhi yi-jingji quanqiuhua de wenhua sikao" [Doubts about "Cultural Globalization": Thoughts on the Cultural Effects of Economic Globalization], *Xi'an jiaotong daxue xuebao* [Journal of Xi'an Communications University] no. 3 (2001): 65–68.

23. Wang Ning, "Quanqiuhua shidai de wenhua lunzheng he wenhua duihua" [Cultural Debates and Cultural Dialogue in the Age of Globalization], in *Quanqiuhua: Xifanghua haishi Zhongguohua* [Globalization: Westernization or Sinification?], edited by Yu Keping (Beijing: Social Science Compilation Press, 2002), p. 267.

24. Li Shenzhi, "Quanqiuhua yu Zhongguo wenhua" [Globalization and Chinese Culture], excerpted from *Liberation Anthology (1978–1998),* edited by Qiushi (Beijing: Economic Daily Press, 1998), p. 880.

25. Li Zonggui, "Wenhua quanqiuhua yu dangdai Zhongguo wenhua jianshe" [Cultural Globalization and the Remaking of Chinese Culture], *Nankai daxue xuebao* [Nankai University Journal] no. 5 (2002): 4.

26. Li Shenzhi, "The Tendencies of Globalization and the Identification of its Values," in *Quanqiuhua de beilun* [Antinomies of Globalization], edited by Yu Keping (Beijing: Central Compilation and Translation Press, 1998), p. 16.

27. Feng Ziyi, "Quanqiuhua yu minzu wenhua" [Globalization and National Culture], *Zhexue yanjiu* [Philosophical Research] no. 3 (2001): 16.

28. Gong Qun, "Quanqiu wenhua yu bentu wenhua" [Global Culture and Indigenous Culture], *Nankai daxue xuebao* [Nankai University Journal] no. 5 (2002): 8.

29. Fang Shinan, "Quanqiuhua yu wenhua bentuhua de duoyuan bingcun yu shuangxing jiegou" [The Coexistence and Dual Structures of Globalization and Cultural Indigenization], *Makesi zhuyi yanjiu* [Marxism Research] no. 4 (2001): 64.

30. Lu Zhenhe, "Cultural Globalization and the Strategic Choice of Cultural Development," *Zhongyang dangxiao xiaobao* [Journal of the Central Party School] vol. 8, no. 4 (November 2004): 91.

31. Feng Ziyi, "Globalization and the Development of National Culture," p. 17.

32. Ibid.

33. Yu Keping, ed., *Zengliang Minzhu yu Shanzhi* [Incremental Democracy and Good Governance] (Beijing: Social Sciences Academic Press of China [Shehui kexue wenxian chubanshe], 2005), pp. 27–56.

34. Liu Danian, "Zhongguo jindai lishi yundong de zhuti" [Main Themes of Movements in Modern Chinese History], *Jindai shi yanjiu* [Modern History Research] no. 6 (1996).

35. Ai Siqi, "Lun Zhongguo de teshuxing" [On China's Particularity], in *Cong Xifanghua dao xiandaihua* [From Westernization to Modernization], edited by Luo Rongqu (Peking University Press, 1990), pp. 592–93.

36. Yu Keping, "Quanqiuhua: Meiguohua/Xifanghua huo Zhongguohua/xiandaihua? [Globalization: Americanization/Westernization or Sinification/Modernization?], in Yu, *Globalization: Westernization or Sinification?* pp. 1–27.

Chapter Nine

1. The original, Chinese version of this chapter first appeared in Yu Keping, "Zouxiang hexie de kechixu fazhan" [Toward Harmonious Sustainable Development], in *Zengliang Minzhu yu Shanzhi* [Incremental Democracy and Good Governance], edited by Yu Keping (Beijing: Social Sciences Academic Press of China [Shehui kexue wenxian chubanshe], 2005).

Chapter Ten

1. An earlier version of this chapter was presented during the plenary session of the Asienhaus conference Zukunftmusik: Nachhaltigkeit und Entwicklung im Duett, Arbeitnehmerzentrum Königswinter, November 2–4, 2001.

2. State Statistics Bureau, *China Statistical Yearbook 2006* (http://www.stats.gov.cn/tjsj/ndsj/2006/indexch.htm).

3. See www.chinanews.com.cn/other/news/2006/09-07/786348.shtml and www.gmw.cn/content/2007-03/19/content_574389.htm.

4. Liang Yanshun, "Institutions, Criteria and Models: A Study of Sustainable Development," *Macroeconomic Studies* no.1 (2001): 11.

5. Sun Liren, "Setting Up an Overall Outlook of Sustainable Development," *Journal of Yangzhou University* no. 1 (2001): 3.

6. See www.acca21.org.cn/local/other/contactus.htm.

7. State Council Information Office, *White Paper on China's Environmental Protection: 199—2005* (http://news.xinhuanet.com/newscenter/2006-06/05/content_464667 4_5.htm).

8. Ibid.

9. Gao Lihong, "Soil Erosion Is the Foremost Problem of Environmental Protection," *Newspaper on Water Conservancy and Irrigation Works,* July 8, 2001.

10. State Environmental Protection Administration of China, "The Bulletin of Environmental Protection 2005" (www.zhb.gov.cn/plan/zkgb/).

11. Ibid.

12. World Bank, *China: Air, Land and Water,* Washington, August 9, 2001 (www.worldbank.org.cn/english/content/china-environment.pdf).

Chapter Eleven

1. Part of this chapter was originally presented at the Fourth MCRI Globalization and Autonomy Team Meeting at the Munk Centre for International Studies, University of Toronto, September 23–25, 2005; it also appeared in Tian Yu Cao, ed., *The Chinese Model of Modern Development* (London: Taylor & Francis Group, 2005).

2. Yu Keping, "Introduction," in *Globalization: Westernization or Sinification?* edited by Yu Keping (Beijing: Social Sciences and Documentation Publishing House, 2002), pp. 1–28.

3. Jiang Zemin, "The Current International Situation and Our Diplomatic Work," in *Selected Works of Jiang Zemin* (Beijing: People's Publishing House, 2006).

4. Joshua Cooper Ramo, *The Beijing Consensus* (London: Foreign Policy Centre, 2004).

5. China Statistical Bureau, *China Statistical Yearbook: 2003* (Beijing: China Statistics Press, 2003); World Bank, *World Development Report: 2004* (Beijing: China Financial and Economic Press, 2004).

6. Department of Organization of the CCP, "The National Program of Cadre Training (2001–2005)" (http://news.eastday.com/).

7. Chinese Academy of International Trade and Economic Cooperation, Ministry of Commerce, "A One Year Review on China's Entry to WTO," *White Book of China's Foreign Economic Relations* (Beijing: CITIC Press, 2003), p. 68.

8. China Society of Urban Development, *China City Yearbook: 2003* (Beijing: China City Yearbook Press, 2003).

Chapter Twelve

1. The original, Chinese version of this chapter first appeared in Yu Keping, "Jindai Zhongguo dui Lianbangzhi de Sikao yu Changshi" [Ideas about and Experiments with Federalism in Modern China], in *Zengliang Minzhu yu Shanzhi* [Incremental Democracy and Good Governance], edited by Yu Keping (Beijing: Social Sciences Academic Press of China [Shehui kexue wenxian chubanshe], 2005).

2. *Shijing* [A compilation of poems in the Zhou dynasty] (http://www.ehappystudy. com/html/6/46/136/2006/5/ga24594052411915600219000-0.htm).

3. Wei Yuan, *Hai Guo Tu Zhi* [Introduction to Overseas Countries], vol. 59 (Gansu: Pingjing Qingju Dao, 1876).

4. Liang Qichao, "Studies on Rousseau," *Qingyi bao* [Independent Commentary] vol. 981100, 1901.

5. Feng Ziyou, "The People's Livelihood and the Future of the Chinese Revolution," Min Bao (*People's Newspaper)* no. 4, 1906.

6. Zhang Dongsun, "An Ultimate View of the Local System," *Chinese Magazine* no. 7 (July 1914): 1–13.

7. Ding Foyan, "An Evaluation of the Republic of China," *Chinese Magazine* no. 9 (August 1914).

8. Zhang Shizhao, "Theories of Federalism," in *Records of Jiayin* (Beijing: Commercial Press, 1922), p. 4.

9. Li Jiannong, *The Political History of China Thirty Years after the Reform Movement of 1898* (Beijing: Chinese Press, 1965), pp. 309–10.

10. Xu Mao, *The Political History of the Republic of China* (Shanghai: Shanghai People's Publishing House, 1992), pp. 113–14.

11. Tang Dechang, "The Movement of 'Self-Government by the United Provinces' and China Today," *Pacific Ocean* vol. 3, no. 7 (September 1922): 1–12.

12. Sun Jiyi, "The Movement of 'Self-Government by the United Provinces' and Federalism," *Gaizao* [Reform] vol. 3, no. 5 (January 1921).

13. Zhi Wei, "The Movement of 'Self-Government by the United Provinces' and China's Political Situation," *Pacific Ocean* vol 3, no. 7 (September 1922).

14. Tang Dechang, "The Movement of 'Self-Government by the United Provinces' and China Today."

15. Ibid.

16. Xu Zongmian, *Searching for Democracy* (Hefei: Anhui People's Publishing House, 1996), pp. 254–55.

17. Li Jiannong, *The Political History of China Thirty Years after the Reform Movement of 1898,* p. 315.

18. Ibid., p. 208.

19. Chen Duxiu, "The Movement of 'Self-Government by the United Provinces' and China's Political Situation," in *Selections of Chen Duxiu* (Shanghai: Shanlian Publishing House, 1984), p. 204.

Chapter Thirteen

1. The original, Chinese version of this chapter first appeared in Yu Keping, "Hexie shijie hexie waijiao yu quanqiu zhili" [Harmonious World, Harmonious Diplomacy and Global Governance], *Lilun Dongtai* [Theoretical Trends] no. 1737 (March 2007): 1–14.

2. Quoted in Hu Jintao, "Advancing with the Times, Carrying on the Past, and Constructing a New Strategic Partnership between Asia and Africa," *People's Daily,* April 23, 2005; and also Hu Jintao, "Striving to Construct a Harmonious World with Sustainable Peace and Common Prosperity," *People's Daily,* September 16, 2005, p. 1.

3. Quoted in Hu Jintao, "Enhance Our Ability to Construct a Harmonious Socialist Society," *People's Daily,* June 27, 2005, p. 1.

4. Yu Keping, "Aspects of Harmonious Society," *Marxism and Reality* no. 1 (2005): 1–6.

5. Li Jingzhi, "'Harmonious World': The New Development of China's International Strategy," *Scientific Socialism* no. 5 (2006): 23.

6. Information Office of the State Council of the People's Republic of China, "China's Peaceful Development Road," December 12, 2005 (www.china.org.cn/english/features/book/152684.htm).

7. Zhang Yesui, "The Connotations of Harmonious World" (www.china.org.cn/chinese/HIAW/1172233.htm).

8. Quoted in Hu Jintao, "Striving to Construct a Harmonious World."

9. Li Jingzhi, "'Harmonious World,'" p. 23.

10. These conditions changed in the last years of Mao Zedong's life, and the turning point was President Richard Nixon's visit to China. Generally speaking, however, the foreign policy of China was still dominated during this period by the principle of the "supremacy of ideology."

11. Cai Tuo, "'Harmonious World' and the Transformation of China's Foreign Strategy," *Journal of Jilin University* no. 9 (2006): 53–58.

12. Yu Keping, "Introduction to Theories of Global Governance," *Marxism and Reality* no. 1 (2002): 1.

13. David Held, Anthony McGrew, David Goldblatt, and Jonathan Perraton, *Global Transformations: Politics, Economics and Culture* (Chinese version) (Beijing: Social Sciences and Compilation Press, 2001), p. 70.

14. Pang Zhongying, "Chinese Perspectives on Global Governance," *International Herald Tribune,* December 29, 2005, pp. 60–62.

15. Ibid.

16. Hu Jintao, "Striving to Construct a Harmonious World," p. 1.

17. Ibid.

18. Ibid.

FURTHER READING
The Writings of Yu Keping

Books and Book Chapters

2008

China: The Road towards Democracy (Kamogawa, Japan: Kamogawa Publishing House, 2008).

Globalization and Changes in China's Governance (Leiden: Brill, 2008).

"Ideological Change and Incremental Democracy in Reform-Era China," in *China's Changing Political Landscape: Prospects for Democracy,* edited by Cheng Li (Brookings Institution Press, 2008), pp. 44–58.

Sixiang Jiefang yu Zhengzhi Jinbu [Liberation of Thoughts and Political Progress] (Beijing: China Social Sciences and Documents Publishing House, 2008).

Zhongguo Zhengfu Chuangxin Lanpishu 2007 [Blue Book of Chinese Government Innovations: 2007], ed. (Beijing: China Social Sciences and Documents Publishing House, 2008).

2007

"La sociedad civil en China hoy" [Chinese Civil Society], *Anuario ASIA PACIFIC,* CASA ASIA/ FUNDACIO C100B/. Real Instituto Elcano, Barcelona, 2007, pp. 347–54.

Shengtai Wenming Xilie Congshu [Series Research on Ecological Civilization], ed. (Beijing: Central Compilation and Translation Press, 2007).

Yifa Zhiguo yu Yifa Zhidang [Governing the Country and the Party by Law], ed. (Beijing: Central Compilation and Translation Press, 2007).

Zhongguo Difang Zhengfu Chuangxin Anli Yanjiu Baogao, 2005–2006 [Innovations and Excellence in Chinese Local Governance: Case Study Reports, 2005–2006], ed. (Beijing: Peking University Press, 2007).

2006

Dangdai Zhongguo Zhengzhi Tizhi [China's Present Political System], ed. (Beijing: Jiuzhou Publishing House, 2006).

"From the Discourse of 'Sino-West' to 'Globalization': Chinese Perspectives on Globalization," in *Asia and Europe in Globalization: Continents, Regions and Nations,* edited by Goran Therborn and Habibul Haque Khondker (Leiden: Brill Group, 2006), pp. 107–22.

Minzhu shige haodongxi [Democracy Is a Good Thing] (Beijing: China Social Sciences and Documents Publishing House, 2006).

Zhongguo Gongmin Shehui de Zhidu Huanjing [The Institutional Environment of Chinese Civil Society], coauthored with He Zengke, Xu Xiuli, and others (Beijing: Peking University Press, 2006).

Zhongguo Zhengfu Chuangxin Niandu Baogao 2006 [Annual Report of Chinese Governmental Innovations 2006], ed. (Beijing: Central Party Literature Press, 2006).

2005

Minzhu yu Tuoluo [Democracy and Top] (Beijing: Peking University Press, 2005).

Zhengfu Chuangxin de Lilun yu Shijian [The Theory and Practice of Government Innovations], coauthored with He Zengke and others (Hangzhou: Zhejiang People's Publishing House, 2005).

Zhongguo Difang Zhengfu Chuangxin Anli Yanjiu Baogao 2002–2004 [A Case Study Report of Chinese Government Innovations 2002–2004], ed. (Beijing: Peking University Press, 2005).

2004

Quanqiuhua yu Guojia Zhuquan [Globalization and Sovereignty] (Beijing: China Social Sciences and Documents Publishing House, 2004).

Zhongguo Nongcun Zhili de Lishi yu Xianzhuang: yi Dingxian, Zouping he Jiangning Weili [The Past and Present Condition of Chinese Rural Governance: Cases Studies of Dingxian, Zouping and Jiangning Counties], coauthored with Xu Xiuli (Beijing: China Social Sciences and Documents Publishing House, 2004).

2003

"Americanization, Westernization, Sinification: Modernization or Globalization in China," in *Global America? The Cultural Consequences of Globalization,* edited by Ulrich Beck, Natan Sznaider, and Rainer Winter (Liverpool University Press, 2003), pp. 134–52.

Difang Zhengfu Chuangxin yu Shanzhi: Anli Yanjiu [Case Studies of Local Governance Innovations], ed. (Beijing: China Social Sciences and Documents Publishing House, 2003).

Quanqiu Zhili [Global Governance], ed. (Beijing: China Social Sciences and Documents Publishing House, 2003).

Quanqiuhua yu Zhengzhi Fazhan [Globalization and Political Development] (Beijing: China Social Sciences and Documents Publishing House, 2003).

Zhengzhi yu Zhengzhixue [Politics and Political Science] (Beijing: China Social Sciences and Documents Publishing House, 2003).

Zengliang Minzhu yu Shanzhi [Incremental Democracy and Good Governance] (Beijing: China Social Sciences and Documents Publishing House, 2003).

2002

Quanqiuhua: Xifanghua Haishi Zhongguohua? [Globalization: Westernization or Sinification?], ed. (Beijing: China Social Sciences and Documents Publishing House, 2002).

Zhongguo Difang Zhengfu Chuangxin 2002 [Innovations in Local Chinese Governments 2002], ed. (Beijing: China Social Sciences and Documents Publishing House, 2002).

Zhongguo Gongmin Shehui de Xingqi yu Zhili de Bianqian [The Emergence of Civil Society and Its Significance for Governance], coauthored (Beijing: China Social Sciences and Documents Publishing House, 2002).

2000

Zhili yu Shanzhi [Governance and Good Governance], ed. (Beijing: China Social Sciences and Documents Publishing House, 2000).

1999

Gongyi Zhengzhi yu Quanli Zhengzhi? [Politics of Public Good or Politics of Rights?] (Beijing: China Social Sciences and Documents Publishing House, 1999).

1998

Dangdai Geguo Zhengzhi Tizhi: Zhongguo [China's Present Political System] (Lanzhou University Press, 1998).

Quanqiuhua de Beilun [Antinomies of Globalization], ed. (Beijing: Central Compilation and Translation Press, 1998).

Quanqiuhua Shidai de Shehui Zhuyi [Socialism in the Age of Globalization], ed. (Beijing: Central Compilation and Translation Press, 1998).

Shequn Zhuyi [A Comment on Communitarianism] (Beijing: Chinese Social Sciences and Documents Press, 1998).

Articles

2008

"Political Reform, Chinese Style," *Caijing* [Annual English Edition] (2008): 50–51.

"Zhongguo Zhili Bianqian Sanshi nian" [China's Governance Reform in the Last Three Decades], *Jilin Daxue Xuebao* [Journal of Jilin University] no. 3 (2008): 5–17.

2007

"Gongzheng yu Shanzheng" [Justice and Good Government], *Nanchang Daxue Xuebao* [Journal of Nanchang University] no. 4 (2007): 1–4.

"Hexie Shijie yu Quanqiu Zhili" [Harmonious World and Global Governance], *Tianjin Shiwei Dangxiao Xuebao* [Journal of the Party School of Tianjin Committee of CPC] no. 2 (2007): 5–10.

"Makesi Lun Minzhu de Yiban Gainian Pubian Jiazhi he Gongtong Xingshi" [Marx's Viewpoints on the General Concepts, Universal Values and Common Forms of Democracy], *Makesi Zhuyi yu Xianshi* [Marxism and Reality] no. 3 (2007): 4–13.

"Sixiang Jiefang yu Zhengzhi Jinbu" [Liberation of Thoughts and Political Reform in China], *Lilun Dongtai* [Theory Trend] no. 1749 (July 2007): 1–19.

"Zhenggai Hechu Tupo" [Political Reform: Where Is the Way Out?], *Caijing Zazhi* [Caijing Magazine] no. 22 (2007): 88–92.

"Zhenggai Zhongdian" [Priorities of Political Reform in China], *Caijing Niankan* [Annual Edition of Caijing Magazine] (2007).

"Zhongguo Zhengzhixue de Jincheng" [The Progression of Chinese Political Science], *Xueshu Yuekan* [Academic Monthly] no. 11 (2007): 5–11.

2006

"Chuangxinxing Guojia Xuyao Chuangxinxing Zhengfu" [Innovative Government: The Cornerstone of an Innovation-Oriented Country], *Jingji Shehui Tizhi Bijiao* [Comparative Economics and Social Systems] no. 2 (2006): 2–3.

"Dongdai Wending yu Hexie Shehui" [Dynamic Stability and Harmonious Society], *Zhongguo Tese Shehui Zhuyi* [Studies on the Socialism with Chinese Characteristics] no. 3 (2006): 25–28.

"Gaishan Woguo Gongmin Shehui Zhidu Huanjing de Ruogan Sikao [Suggestions on Improving the Institutional Environment of Chinese Civil Society], *Dangdai Shijie yu Shehui Zhuyi* [Contemporary World and Socialism] no. 1 (2006): 4–10.

"La logique du développement culturel chinois sous variation de la modernisation et la mondialisation," 1st ed. *Deux mille cinquante—2050*, 2006.

"Quanshijie Wuchanzhe Lianhe Qilai Haishi Quanshijie Laodongzhe Lianhe Qilai" [Proletarians of All Countries, Unite or Working Men of All Countries, Unite], *Makesi Zhuyi yu Xianshi* [Marxism and Reality] no. 3 (2006): 4–10.

"Xiandaihua yu Quanqiuhua Shuangchong Bianzou Xia de Zhongguo Wenhua Fazhan Luoji" [The Logic of Chinese Cultural Development under Various Forms of Modernization and Globalization], *Xueshu Yuekan* [Academic Monthly] no. 4 (2006): 14–24.

"Zhongguo Gongmin Shehui: Gainian Fenlei yu Zhidu Huanjing" [Chinese Civil Society: Concepts, Classification and Institutional Environment], *Zhongguo Shehui Kexue* [Social Sciences in China] no. 1 (2006): 109–22.

2005

"Hexie Shehui Mianmianguan" [Broad Overview of Harmonious Society], *Makesi Zhuyi yu Xianshi* [Marxism and Reality] no. 1 (2005): 4–5.

"Lun Zhengfu Chuangxin de Ruogan Jiben Wenti" [Principal Issues of Governmental Innovation], *Wen Shi Zhe* [Journal of Literature, History and Philosophy] no.4, (2005): 138–46.

"Quanqiuhua yu Xinde Siwei Xiangdu he Guancha Jiaodu [Globalization and New Thinking], *Shixue Lilun Yanjiu* [Research on Historical Theory] no. 1 (2005): 8–10.

"Quanqiuhua yu Zhongguo Zhengfu de Nengli" [Globalization and Capacity of Public Sectors: A Case Study of China], *Gonggong Guanli Xuebao* [Chinese Journal of Public Management] no. 1 (2005): 1–9.

"Zhengfu Chuangxin de Zhuyao Qushi" [Major Tendencies of Governmental Innovation], *Xuexi yu Tansuo* [Study and Exploration] no. 4 (2005): 2–5.

2004

"Dangdai Xifang Zhengzhi Sichao Gaishu" [Overview of Western Contemporary Political Thought], *Jiaoxue yu Yanjiu* [Teaching and Research] no. 6 (2004): 52–59.

"Lun Quanqiuhua yu Guojia Zhuquan" [Globalization and National Sovereignty], *Makesi Zhuyi yu Xianshi* [Marxism and Reality] no. 1 (2004): 4–21.

"Re Huati yu Leng Sikao: Guanyu Beijing Gongshi yu Zhongguo Fazhan Moshi de Duihua" [Hot Topic and Calm Thinking: Dialogue on 'Beijing Consensus' and 'China's Model'], *Dangdai Shijie yu Shehui Zhuyi* [Contemporary World and Socialism] no. 5 (2004): 4–9.

"Shanzheng: Zouxiang Shanzhi de Guanjian" [A Good Government: The Key to Good Governance], *Sixiang Lilun Dongtai Canyue* [Ideology Trends] no. 6 (2004): 2–5.

"Zengliang Zhengzhi Gaige yu Shehui Zhuyi Zhengzhi Wenming Jianshe" [Incremental Political Reform and the Construction of a Socialist Political Civilization], *Gonggong Guanli Xuebao* [Chinese Journal of Public Management] no. 1 (2004): 8–14.

"Zhongguo Nongcun Zhili de Lishi yu Xianzhuang" [Chinese Rural Governance: History and Present Condition], *Jingji Shehui Tizhi Bijiao* [Comparative Economics and Social Systems] nos. 2 and 3 (2004): 13–26; 22–42.

"Zhuanggui Zhong de Zhongguo Zhengzhi Zouxiang: Shanzhi yu Zengliang Minzhu" [Destination of Transitional Chinese Politics: Good Governance and Incremental Democracy], *Kexue Shehui Zhuyi* [Scientific Socialism] no. 1 (2004): 3–7.

2003

"The Emergence of China's Civil Society and Its Significance for Governance," *Focus Asien* no. 11 (2003): 1–34.

"Globalization and China's Political Development," *East Asia Survey* vol. 44 (2003): 7–25.

"Jiji Shixing Zengliang Zhengzhi Gaige Jiakuai Jianshe Shehui Zhuyi Zhengzhi Wenming" [Exercising Incremental Political Reform and Pushing Forward the Construction of Socialist Political Civilization], *Lilun Dongtai* [Theory Trend] (April 2003): 1–13.

"Juece Kexuehua Minzhuhua de Zhidu Jichu" [Institutional Basis for Scientific and Democratic Decisionmaking], *Hongqi Tongxun* [Red Flag Briefing] no. 4 (2003): 40–42.

"Quanqiuhua Shidai de Ziben Zhuyi" [Capitalism in the Age of Globalization], *Makesi Zhuyi yu Xianshi* [Marxism and Reality] no. 1 (2003): 4–22.

"Shehui Ziben yu Caogen Minzhu" [Social Capital and Grassroots Democracy], *Jingji Shehui Tizhi Bijiao* [Comparative Economics and Social Systems] no. 2 (2003): 21–25.

"Zhengzhixue de Gongli" [Axiom of Political Science], *Jiangsu Shehui Kexue* [Jiangsu Social Sciences] no. 5 (2003): 62–68.

"Zhongguo Difang Zhengfu de Gaige yu Chuangxin" [Excellence and Innovations in Local Chinese Governance], *Jingji Shehui Tizhi Bijiao* [Comparative Economics and Social Systems] no. 4 (2003): 31–34.

2002

"Quanqiu Zhili Yinlun" [An Essay on Global Governance], *Makesi Zhuyi yu Xianshi* [Marxism and Reality] no. 1 (2002): 20–32.

"Towards an Incremental Democracy and Governance: Chinese Theories and Assessment Criteria," *New Political Science* vol. 24, no. 2 (June 2002): 181–200.

2001

"Zhili he Shanzhi: Yizhong Xinde Zhengzhi Fenxi Kuangjia" [Governance and Good Governance: A New Political Analytical Framework], *Nanjing Shehui Kexue* [Nanjing Journal of Social Science] no. 9 (2001): 40–44.

2000

"Chuangxin: Shehui Jinbu de Dongliyuan [Innovations: The Dynamics of Social Progress], *Makesi Zhuyi yu Xianshi* [Marxism and Reality] no. 4 (2000): 31–34.

"Jingji Quanqiuhua yu Zhili de Bianqian" [Economic Globalization and Changes of Governance], *Zhexue Yanjiu* [Philosophical Studies] no. 10 (2000): 17–24.

"Rang Zhengzhixue Zai Xinshiji Zai Fang Guangcai [A Perspective on the Development of Political Science in the New Century], *Zhongguo Shehui Kexue* [Chinese Social Sciences] no. 1 (2000): 27–28.

"Zengliang Minzhu: Sanlun Liangpiaozhi Zhenzhang Xuanju de Zhengzhixue Yiyi" [Incremental Democracy and the Direct Election of Mayors at the Township Level], *Makesi Zhuyi yu Xianshi* [Marxism and Reality] no. 3 (2000): 27–28.

"Zhongguo Nongcun de Minjian Zuzhi yu Zhili: Yi Fujiansheng Zhangpuxian Changqiaozhen Dongshengcun Weili" [Civil Organizations and Governance in Rural China: A Case Study], *Zhongguo Shehui Kexue Jikan* [Chinese Social Sciences Quarterly] (Summer and Autumn, 2000): 85–96; 99–106.

1999

"Cong Lishi de Zhongguo Dao Xianshi de Zhongguo" [From a Historical China to a Realist China—Comments on Overseas Scholars' Studies of China], *Renmin Luntan* [People's Forum] no. 1 (1999): 24–26.

"Quanqiuhua Shidai de Zhengzhi Guanli Moshi" [On the Mode of Political Management in the Global Age], *Fangfa* [Method] no. 1 (1999): 34–35.

"Shilun Nongcun Minzhu Zhili de Jingji Jichu" [Elementary Comments on the Economic Foundation of Rural Democratic Governance], *Zhonggong Tianjin Shiwei Dangxiao Xuebao* [Journal of Tianjin Party School] no. 3 (1999): 49–52.

"Zhili yu Shanzhi Yinlun" [Introduction to Governance and Good Governance], *Makesi Zhuyi yu Xianshi* [Marxism and Reality] no. 5 (1999): 37–41.

"Zhongguo Gongmin Shehui de Xingqi yu Zhili de Bianqian" [The Emergence of Civil Society Organizations and Changing Governance in Reform-era China], *Zhongguo Shehui Kexue Jikan* [Chinese Social Sciences Quarterly] no. 3 (Autumn 1999): 105–18.

1998

"Dangdai Xifang Shequn Zhuyi Jiqi Gongyi Zhengzhixue Pingxi" [A Comment on the Current Debate between Communitarianism and Individualism], *Zhongguo Shehui Kexue* [Chinese Social Sciences] no. 3 (1998): 105–21.

"Zhengfu: Yingdang Zuo Shenme Bu Yingdang Zuo Shenme" [The Government: What It Should and Should Not Do], *Zhengzhixue Yanjiu* [CASS Journal of Political Science] no. 1 (1998): 71–78.

"Zhengzhi Zhidu Xuyao Yanjiu he Bijiao" [Political Systems Need Comparative Studies], *Jingji Shehui Tizhi Bijiao* [Comparative Economics and Social Systems] no. 1 (1998): 41–44.

Index

Administrative regulations and statutes, 52–62
Agenda *21*. *See* China Agenda *21*
Agricultural Action Plan, 143
Agricultural issues, 70–71, 81–82, 115, 143, 145
Ai Siqi, 110, 130
Americanization, 131, 151, 156. *See also* Westernization
Annual No. *1* Documents, 60
Anti-Japanese War (*1937*), 8
Aristotle, 14, 15
Asian financial crisis, 152
Asian tigers (Hong Kong, Singapore, South Korea, Taiwan), 116, 120, 122
Association of Southeast Asian Nations, 168
Associations, 47–48. *See also* Civil society; Organizations

Banks and banking, 71
Behavior and behavioralism, 10–11, 42
Beijing, 75, 145
Beijing Action Plan (*1995*), 143
"Bosses' Class." *See* Qianyuan National Studies Class

Bureau for Supervising Civic Organizations, 51

Cai Tuo, 175
Cao Jianming, xxiv
Cao Siyuan, xxviii
CASS. *See* Chinese Academy of Social Sciences
CCP. *See* Chinese Communist Party
CCTB. *See* Central Compilation and Translation Bureau
CCP. *See* Chinese Communist Party
CCYL. *See* Chinese Communist Youth League
Center for Chinese Government Innovations (Peking University), xxi
Central Committee. *See* Chinese Communist Party
Central Compilation and Translation Bureau (CCTB), xx–xxi, xxiv, 19
Central Executive Committee of the Nationalist Party, 58
Central Party School (CPS), xxi, xxiv, xxvi
Checks and balances, 31
Chen Duxiu, 96, 115, 166–67
Chen Xujing, 95, 96, 97–98, 109

Chen Zhiquan, 102
China. *See* People's Republic of China;
 Republic of China
China Agenda *21,* 141, 142–43
China Association for Science and Tech-
 nology, 40
China Center for Comparative Politics and
 Economics, xxi
China Democratic League, 49
China Disabled Persons' Federation, 40
China Federation of Writers and Artists, 40
China Local Government Innovation
 Awards, xxiv
China Women's Federation, 40
China Youth and Children Foundation,
 138
Chinese (language), 37–38
Chinese Academy of Social Sciences
 (CASS), 18, 19
Chinese Communist Party (CCP): Annual
 No. *1* Documents of, 60; Central
 Committee of, 56, 58, 49, 60–61, 64,
 72; civil society under, 49, 59, 63,
 67–68, 72–73, 78; constitutional
 authority and, 30; constitutional legitimacy of, 29; democracy and, 27, 59;
 dissemination of political knowledge
 and, 16; economic issues and, 49, 59;
 evolution of, 24, 176; focus of, 174–
 75; intraparty democracy and, 29;
 mass, national, and people's organizations and, 40, 56; membership of, 29;
 policymaking and, 30, 67; power and
 authority of, xxviii, 29, 31; reforms of,
 131; regulations and policies of, 58–60,
 144; rejection of Maoism, xxi; sociopolitical tensions and, xxvii–xxviii; system of checks and balances and, 31;
 theoreticians of, xxi. *See also* People's
 Republic of China; Political parties-
 China
Chinese Communist Party-Fifteenth Party
 Congress, 59
Chinese Communist Party-Seventeenth
 Party Congress: accountability and
 public oversight, 30–31; goals of, 27;

grassroots democracy and, 28, 29;
 intraparty democracy and, 29; people's
 democracy and, 27; policymaking
 reforms, 30; political reform agenda,
 28; reform of administrative system
 and, 33; reform of legislative and judicial systems and, 29; social management reforms and, 32–33
Chinese Communist Party-Sixteenth Party
 Congress: development of social organizations, 59; intraparty democracy and,
 27, 28–29; objective of a harmonious
 society, 169; reform of legislative and
 judicial systems and, 29; social management reforms and, 32
Chinese Community Youth League
 (CCYL), 40, 49
"Chinese Dream and the Harmonious
 World, The" (Zhang), 172
Chinese People's Political Consultative
 Congress (CPPCC), 33, 72
Chinese Social Sciences and Documenta-
 tion Publishing House, 150
Chinese written characters, 109–10, 111
Churchill, Winston, xvii
Citizens organizations, 41. *See also* Civil
 society organizations
Civic organizations, 38, 41
Civil Procedure Law, 54
Civil society: changes in, xxiii–xxiv, xxvi;
 civil society organizations, 39–40, 41;
 classification/categorization of civil
 organizations, 45; definition and concepts of, 38; institutional environment
 of, 42–43; laws and legislation and,
 53–54; political systems and, 53
Civil society—China: Chinese translations
 of English term for, 37–38; classifica-
 tion/categorization of civil organizations in, 43–47; civic organizations, 38,
 41, 53; clarification of key concepts,
 37–41; constitutional provisions for,
 53; development of, 37, 61, 62, 63,
 77–78; faith and trust in, 62; history of
 (*1912*–present), 47–51; institutional
 environment of, 42–43, 49, 52, 55, 56,

62–73, 75; judgment and attitudes toward, 77–79; laws and legislation and, 54, 55; political factors and, 47; poverty and education and, 138; problems of, 76–77; regulation and oversight of, 64–74. *See also* Regulations

Civil society organizations (CSOs)—China: actual and institutional space of, 71–73; China Agenda *21* and, 144–45; environmental protection and sustainable development and, 144–45; foreign CSOs, 86–87; funds, taxes, and financial management, 86–88; government and self-government and, 79, 161; history of, 47–50, 73–74; judgment and attitudes toward, 77–79; leadership, staffing, and administration of, 88–90; numbers of, 50–51, 71, 73, 144; present-day organizations, 50–51; problems and solutions of, 75–77, 79–81, 82–83, 84–85, 86–90; property ownership of, 87; provision of public services by, 86; registration of, 55, 60, 61, 64–66, 72–73, 76, 82–84, 85, 87; regulation and supervision of, 52–62, 64–74, 77, 79–82, 83, 84–85, 86–87; studies and surveys of, 75–76; sustainable development, 138–39; types of organizations, 39–41, 43–47. *See also* Civil society-China; Organizations

Class and class issues, 15–16

Classification of civil organizations in China (listing), 43–47

Cold war, 176

Commission for Restructuring the Economy, 5–6

Communism, 108

Confucianism and New Confucianism, 117, 120, 123

Congress (CCP). *See* Chinese Communist Party-Seventeenth Party Congress; Chinese Communist Party-Sixteenth Party Congress

Constitutions—China (*1922, 1923*): basic rights in, 63; Chinese Communist Party and, 29, 30; civil society organizations and, 63; Double-Nine Constitution, 165; federalism and, 162, 165; history and characteristics of, 52–53; provincial constitutions, 161–62, 165; Republic of China, 53, 162; Qing dynasty and, 48, 53; rule of law in, 68; Tri-Color Constitution, 165

Constitutions—provincial: Fengtian, 161; Fujian, 161, 165; Guangdong, 161–62, 165; Guangxi, 161, 165; Guizhou, 161, 165; Hebei, 165; Hubei, 161, 165; Hunan, 161–62; Jiangsu, 161, 165; Jiangxi, 161, 165; Liaoning, 165; Shandong, 160; Shanxi, 161, 165; Sichuan, 161, 165; Yunnan, 161, 165; Zhejiang, 161–62, 165

Constitutional issues, 42, 161–62

Corruption: dissemination of political knowledge and, 17; political transparency and, 31; power and, 31; professionalization of political science and, 20. *See also* Crime

Corruption—China: economic disparity and, 135–36; political reforms and, 28; political transparency and, 32; in the public sector, 25, 136; system of checks and balances and, 31; Xiamen smuggling case, 136. *See also* Crime

Cosmopolitanism. *See* Cultural issues

CPPCC. *See* Chinese People's Political Consultative Congress

CPS. *See* Central Party School

Crime, 136. *See also* Corruption

CSOs (civil society organizations). *See* Civil society—China

Cultural issues: American culture, 131; core and global principles of, 125; cultural localization and nationalization, 126–27; cultural pluralism and diversity, 127; functions of culture, 126; Western culture, 118, 119, 124, 125–26; world culture, 122. *See also* Globalization—cultural

Cultural issues—China: Confucianism and New Confucianism, 117, 120, 123; core values, 114, 115; cosmopolitanism,

96; cultural localization, 127–28; cultural modernization, 114–16, 133; cultural renaissance and revival, 116–20; cultural self-consciousness, 120–24; culture fever, 113, 116; democracy, 111, 115–16; Eastern civilization, 101; Europeanization, 95; feudal transitions, 115; intellectual debates about modernity, 93–94, 128–29, 132–33; material civilization, 98–99, 100, 101; modernization as Westernization, 94–99, 105–11, 130; modernization with Chinese characteristics, 99–111, 127–28, 180; morality, 97; national culture, 127; national studies approach, 117, 119–20; nativism, 110–11; obstacles and problems of modernization, 113, 118, 120, 169; politics of intellectual discourse on culture, 111–12; rule by/of law, 116; science, 115–16; social modernization, 115; spiritual values, 96–97, 98, 104; superiority of Chinese culture, 118, 127; *ti-yong* formula, 98, 111; traditional culture, 114, 115, 116–20, 121, 123, 127, 155–56, 166, 167, 180; values, 125, 129, 155–56; Western views of modernization in China, 108. *See also* Globalization—cultural; Intellectuals, scholars, and theorists; Social issues
Cultural Revolution (*1966–76*), xxviii, 56

"Declaration of Chinese Native Cultural Construction" (Sa, Tao, and others), 110–11
Decree *250* (*1998*), 56
Democracy: advantages and disadvantages of, 3–5; corruption in, 31; federalism and, 166; grassroots democracy, 28; implementation of, 4–5; incremental democracy, xxvii; intraparty democracy, xxvii; modernization and, 114; policy-making processes and, 30; power in, 31; price of, xxvi; requirements of, 5; universal values of, xviii–xx. *See also* "Democracy Is a Good Thing"

Democracy—China: arguments against, xxix; arguments for, xxvi; harmonious society and world and, 169–70; Chinese Communist Party and, 59, 63; Chinese socialism and, 5; civil society and, 78; cultural values and, 115; federalism and, 162, 163; grassroots democracy, 29; improving democracy at the grassroots level, 28; intraparty democracy, 27, 28–29; mapping a path to, xxv–xxix; modernization and, 115, 116; obstacles to, xxv; people's democracy, 27; rule of law in, 170; scholars participation in, xxviii, 111; social democracy, 28–29; views of Yu Keping, xviii–xx
"Democracy Is a Good Thing" (Yu), xvi–xvii, xxvi, 3–5
Democracy Wall Movement (Beijing; *1979*), xxviii
Deng Xiaoping: economic reforms of, xxi, 131, 132, 140; international strategic thought of, 173; reform and opening-up policies of, 50, 174, 175; revitalization of study of political science, 8; sustainable development and, 142; theory of, 16
Despotism, 157, 162, 163, 166–67
Developed countries, 125–26, 131
Developing countries, 122, 124, 131, 155
Ding Foyan, 159
Diplomacy, 171, 177–80
Dissidents, xxviii
Dynasties: Eastern Han, 47; Ming, 47; Qing, 7, 48, 53, 93, 111, 157, 158, 159, 160, 163, 164; Song, 47; Tang, 47; Xia, 157

Eastern and Western Cultures and their Philosophies: Indian, Greek, and Chinese (Liang), 101
Economic issues: capitalism, 108; cultural advantages, 125; democracy, 4, 5; modernization, 114; rules and regulations, 42; third and tertiary sectors, 40. *See also* Globalization

Economic issues—China: banks and banking, 71; business systems, 70–71; capitalism, 100, 106, 107, 108–09, 149, 150, 151; cultural modernization, 122; currency revaluation, 155; development of civil society, 77–78; economic disparity and corruption, 135–36; economic growth and development, xxvi, 40, 134–35, 136–37, 140, 152, 155, 176; economic modernization, 134–137, 141; economic reforms and restructuring, xxi, xxv, 24, 50, 63; employment and unemployment, 136, 137, 138; Five-Year Plans, 143; foreign investment, 138, 155; government responses to, 137–38; gross domestic and national product (GDP and GNP), 134, 152; living standards, per capita income, and poverty, 134, 135–36, 137, 138, 140, 142–43; market economy, 40, 50, 59, 61, 63, 73, 78, 106, 134, 174–75; nature and direction of modernity, 93; negative effects of globalization, 154–55; ownership, 50, 63, 87, 134, 144; planned economy, 63, 134, 135, 144, 174–75; real estate development, xxv–xxvi; social security, 135, 137; sustainability of development, 138–39, 141–44; trade, 152, 154–55; world civilization and, 122. See also Corruption—China; Environmental issues—China
Educational issues, 15, 44
Educational issues—China: college entrance exams, xxii; compulsory education program and illiteracy, 138; foreign academic exchange, 9; national studies courses, 119; private schools, 119; reform and readjustment of higher education, 8; spending on education, 138; teaching and study of political science, 7–14, 16–18; teaching and study of public administration, 23–24
Elections, xxix, 28
"Enhancing Our Ability to Construct a Harmonious Socialist Society" (Hu; speech), 169–70

Environmental issues—China: China Agenda 21, 142–45; civil society organizations, 144–45; development, 138–39; difficulties and challenges, 145–46; doctrine of man and nature in harmony, 141; economic factors, 140–41; environmental demonstration zones, 137; environmental governance, 137; environmental protection, 137–38; foreign direct investment, 138; forestation, 144, 145; "four big green parties," 145; in a harmonious world, 172; pollution, 137, 140, 143, 146; soil erosion, 145; sustainable development, 141–44; township and village enterprises (TVEs), 140–41; water shortages, 145–46
"Essay on Federalism" (Zhang), 159
Europeanization. See Cultural issues
Excellence Award Program for Innovations in Local Governance (PRC), 22

Family contract responsibility system, 70
FDI (Foreign direct investment). See Economic issues—China; Environmental issues—China
Federalism: definition of, 160; early advocates for, 157–60; failure of Chinese federalism, 164–67; movement of self-government by the provinces, 160–62; perspectives of, 162–64
Fei Xiaotong, 121
Fengtian province, 161
Feng Youlan, 101, 108
Feng Zhifeng, 19
Feng Ziyi, 127–28
Feng Ziyou, 158, 159
Feudal traditions, 115
Five Principles of Peaceful Coexistence, 174
Five-Year Plans of National Economic and Social Development, 143
Foreign direct investment (FDI). See Economic issues—China; Environmental issues—China
For-profit organizations, 39, 40, 87

Foundations, 43
France, 166
Friends of Nature, 145
Fujian province, 161

Gan Yang, 122
GDP (gross domestic product). *See* Economic issues—China
GNP (gross national product). *See* Economic issues—China
Gender issues, 115
General Principles of Civil Law, 54
General Rules of Civil Law, 82
Globalization: China's adaptation to, 152–56; China's global strategy and, 173, 174–76; contradictions, questions, and paradoxes of, 132, 150–52; globalization studies in China, 149–52; harmonious diplomacy and global governance, 176–80; negative effects of, 154; preserving autonomy and, 154–156; as an unavoidable reality, 131–32; United Nations and, 179
Globalization—cultural: competition and, 122; concepts and core principles of, xix, 124–25; cultural localization and, 126–27; cultural pluralism and, 127; effects of, 113, 121, 125–26, 155; modernization and, 128–33; national culture and, 127; social modernization and, 122; universal/global values and, 125
Globalization—economic: in China, 24, 107, 152–56; competition and, 122; effects of, 106, 113, 124, 132, 155; worldwide, 113
Globalization Studies Series, 150
Globalization Translation Series, 150
Global Village, 145
GONGOs. *See* Government-organized nongovernmental organizations
Government Administrative Council, 55
Government and governance issues: accountability and public oversight, 31;

civil society, 78; components of good governance, xxiv; democracy, 5, 28; harmonious diplomacy and global governance, 176–80; objective of government, xxiii–xxiv; results of good governance, xxviii. *See also* Democracy; Federalism
Government and governance issues— China: accountability and public oversight, 25, 30–31, 32; adaptive capability and flexibility, 153; administrative departmental regulations, 57; China Agenda *21,* 143; civil affairs departments, 65–67; civil society, 63–64, 73, 78, 79, 86, 145; country entries and departures, 154; dissemination of political knowledge, 17; faith and trust in, 62; federalism, 157–67; functions of government, 63–64; as a focus of the political process, 24; government regulations, 55–57; improving governance and government, 33; leadership development, 153; local governments, 57, 65, 68, 154, 160; NGOs, 39; peaceful development, 154; political reforms, 28, 50; retired officials of, 88; self-government, 160–62; service delivery, 25; social problems and, 136–37; state laws and party policies, 67–68; supervision by, 65–68; sustainable development, 143, 145. *See also* Public administration—China; Public sector— China; Regulations
Government-organized nongovernmental organizations (GONGOs), 39
Great Leap Forward, xxviii
Green Home, 145
Gross domestic product (GDP). *See* Economic issues—China
Gross national product (GNP). *See* Economic issues—China
Guangdong province, 161
Guangxi province, 136, 161
Guilds, 47
Guizhou province, 161

Harmonious society and world: concepts of, 168–73; key fields of, 179; harmonious diplomacy and global governance, 176–79; important strategies of, 179–80; transformation of China's global strategy and, 174–76
Hebei vs. Liaoning War, 166
He Weifang, xxviii
Holistic development view, 141
Hong Kong, 65, 116–17
Hope Project, 138
Hubei province, 161
Hubei War, 166
Hu Fuming, xxi
Hu Jintao: harmonious society and world and, 168, 169–70, 173, 174, 175, 178; importance of democracy and, xix, 5; importance of reforms and, 27; reform of the UN and, 179; theory of China's peaceful rise, xxi
Human rights issues, xxiii, 22
Hunan province, 161, 164–65
Hu Ping, xxviii–xxix
Hu Qiuyuan, 100
Hu Shi, 95, 96, 97, 98, 99, 101, 105, 107, 111–12, 115
Huxley, Thomas, 48

Ideological liberation campaign (1970s), 115
Institutions, 41–43
Intellectuals, scholars, and theorists: advocates for federalism, 157–60, 166; cultural globalization, 124; cultural localization, 126, 127–28; cultural modernization, 128; cultural renaissance, 118–20; cultural self-consciousness, 121–23; culture fever and, 113; federalism and, 162–64; globalization and, 132, 149–52, 156; modernization and, 94–112, 114–15, 119–21, 130–31, 132–33; reform and opening up and, 114; sustainable development and, 141; warlords, 164–65; Westernization versus Sinification, 130–31

Intellectuals, scholars, and theorists—specific: Ai Siqi, 110, 130; Cai Tuo, 175; Chen Duxiu, 96, 115; Chen Xujing, 95, 96, 97–98, 109; Chen Zhiquan, 102; Ding Foyan, 159; Fei Xiaotong, 121; Feng Youlan, 101, 108; Feng Ziyi, 127–28; Feng Ziyou, 158, 159; Gan Yang, 122; Hu Qiuyuan, 100; Hu Shi, 95, 96, 97, 98, 99, 101, 105, 107, 111–12, 115; Jiang Qing, 117–18; Jiang Zhiyou, 158; Ji Baocheng, 119; Ji Xianlin, 118–19; Lao Tzu, 141; Liang Qichao, 104, 105, 118, 158, 160; Liang Shiqiu, 105; Liang Shuming, 101, 105, 107, 117; Liang Tingnan, 158; Li Jiangnong, 159; Li Jingzhi, 171, 174; Lin Yutang, 96, 87, 101; Li Shenzhi, 115–16, 124–25; Li Shu, 115; Lu Yudao, 102; Lu Xun, 109, 115; Pang Zhongying, 177; Qu Qiubai, 104; Sa Mengwu, 110; Sheng Jiyi, 162–63; Tang Dechang, 162, 163–64; Tao Xisheng, 110; Wei Yuan, 158; Wu Jingchao, 108–09; Wu Shichang, 97; Xiong Mengfei, 101, 103; Xu Jishe, 158; Yang Xinzhi, 100; Yan Jicheng, 95, 98; Ye Yin, 103; Yue Daiyun, 123; Zhang Dainian, 118–19; Zhang Dongsun, 102, 159; Zhang Shenfu, 99; Zhang Shizhao, 159–60; Zhang Sumin, 100; Zhang Xirou, 101, 111; Zhang Zuolin, 165; Zhao Hengti, 164–65; Zhi Wei, 163; Zhou Xiawen, 100; Zhuang Tzu, 141
Intermediary organizations, 39–40
International Classification of Nonprofit Organizations, 44
International Standard Industrial Classification (UN), 44
International Treaty on Civil and Political Rights, 80
Introduction to Overseas Countries (Wei), 158

Jiang Qing, 117–18
Jiangsu province, 161

Jiangxi Province, 57, 161
Jiang Zemin, 149–50, 173
Jiang Zhiyou, 158
Jiayin Magazine, 159
Ji Baocheng, 119
Jingshi Daxue Tang (Metropolitan University), 7, 8
Ji Xianlin, 118–19
Johns Hopkins University Comparative Nonprofit Sector Project, 44

Kang Youwei, 48
KMT. *See* Kuomintang
Korean Peninsula, 153
Kuomintang (KMT), 58, 59, 93, 164

Lao Tzu, 141
Law of the PRC for Contributions to Public Service Institutions, 54
Laws, 54, 55. *See also* Legislative issues
Laws-specific: Civil Procedure Law, 54; General Principles of Civil Law, 54; Law of the PRC for Contributions to Public Service Institutions, 54; Organic Law of Neighborhood Committees, 54; Organic Law of Villagers' Committees, 54; Red Cross Law, 54; Trade Union Law, 54, 69
Legal issues: checks and balances and, 31; civil society, 53–54; institutional environment of civil society, 42; institutions, 42; political systems, 29; rule of law, 28. *See also* Legislation; Regulations
Legal issues—China: civil society, 49, 54; political reforms and governance, 33, 50; political transparency, 32; problems in the legal system, 29; reform of judicial systems, 29–30; rule by law, 116; rule of law, 33, 50, 63, 68, 82, 116, 170; sustainable development, 143
Legislative issues, 29, 31, 42. *See also* Regulations; Laws; Legal issues
Legislative issues—China: civil rights, 80; civil society organizations, 49, 80, 85; international treaties, 153; political transparency and, 32; reform of legisla-

tive systems, 29, 30; state laws and party policies, 67–68; sustainable development, 143
Leninism, 117, 118
Liang Qichao, 48, 104, 105, 118, 158, 160
Liang Shiqiu, 105
Liang Shuming, 101, 105, 107, 117
Liang Tingnan, 158
Li Cheng, xv–xxix
Li Jiangnong, 159
Li Jiannong, 165–66
Li Jingpeng, xxii
Li Jingzhi, 171, 174
Lin Yutang, 96, 87, 101
Li Shenzhi, 115–16, 124–25
Li Shu, 115
Lu Yongqiang, 165
Lu Yudao, 102
Lu Xun, 109, 115

"Machine and Spirit" (Lin), 96
Madsen, Richard, xv
Man and nature in harmony, doctrine of, 141
Manchu regime, 53
Maoism, xxi
Mao Zedong, 6, 16, 174, 175
Market organizations, 39
Marxism, 11, 16, 117, 118
Marx, Karl, 106
May Fourth movement (*1919*): culture debates and, 113, 115–16, 121, 129; modernization and, 93, 94, 96, 121; Westernization and, 95
McGrew, Anthony, 177
Medical science, 10
Metropolitan University. *See* Jingshi Daxue Tang
Mill, John Stuart, 7, 48
Ming dynasty. *See* Dynasties
Ministry of Agriculture, 143
Ministry of Civil Affairs: civil society groups and, 43, 51, 56, 57, 60, 61, 65, 68; national conferences and, 71; registration of social associations and, 72
Ministry of Internal Affairs, 55

Ministry of Social Affairs, 48
Modernity. *See* Cultural issues

National Conference on Developing
    Village Occupational Economic
    Associations, 71
National Conference on Theoretical
    Exchange and Discussion (*1979*), 8
National Constitution of the United
    Provinces, 161
Nationalism, 106, 107
Nationalist army, 161
Nationalist Party. *See* Kuomintang
National People's Congress, 145
National Primary Health Program, 137
National studies, 117, 119–20
National Studies Academy (Renmin Uni-
    versity), 119
National Studies Club, 119
Nativism, 110–11
Natural sciences, 12–13
New Culture movement, 113
New Left, xxix
New Right, xxix
Nongovernmental organizations (NGOs):
    as civil society organizations, 38–39,
    41; definition and concepts of, 39;
    international NGOs, 39; registration
    of, 71; role of, xxiii–xxiv
Nongovernmental organizations
    (NGOs)—China, 39–41
Nonprofit organizations, 39, 40, 43, 44,
    62, 71–72, 87
North, Douglass C., 41–42
Northern Expedition (*1926*), 161
Notice on Strictly Limiting the Establish-
    ment of National Organizations, 56
Nuclear weapons, 153

"On China's Special Characteristics" (Ai),
    110
"On Chinese Characteristics" (Zhang),
    99–100
"On Freedom of Speech" (Hu), xxviii
On Liberty (Mill), 7
Opening up. *See* Reforms and opening up

Opium War (*1840–42*), 157
Organic Law of Neighborhood Commit-
    tees, 54
Organic Law of Villagers' Committees, 54
Organizations: actual and institutional
    space of, 71; categorization/classifica-
    tion of civil organizations in (listing),
    43–47; government supervision of,
    64–73; informal rules and institutions
    and, 61–62; registration of, 55, 60, 61,
    64–66, 72–73, 76; supervision and
    oversight of, 64–67, 68–71, 77
Organizations—specific: academic organi-
    zations, 43; chambers of commerce, 72;
    citizens' organizations, 41; civic associa-
    tions, 42, 53; civic organizations, 41,
    64, 78; civilian non-enterprise bodies,
    68; cooperatives, 70–71; enterprise and
    non-enterprise economic organizations,
    70, 82–83; extralegal civil organiza-
    tions, 71–72; farmers' cooperative
    organizations, 70, 81–82; foreign proj-
    ect organizations, 72; foundations, 43,
    68, 86; grassroots organizations, 51,
    61; intermediary organizations, 39–40;
    mass organizations, 40, 48, 49–51,
    60–61; mutual assistance organizations,
    38, 46, 60, 70, 72; nonprofit organiza-
    tions, 39, 43; people's organizations,
    40, 72; political and political party
    organizations, 41, 47; professional
    organizations, 43; rural cooperative
    organizations, 60; social associations,
    41, 43, 51, 55–56, 60, 68, 69, 72, 144;
    third-sector organizations, 40–41; trade
    organizations, 43; village community
    development organizations, 72; village
    occupational economic associations, 71;
    voluntary organizations, 40, 41. *See also*
    Civil society organizations (CSOs)—
    China; Nongovernmental organizations
Outline for China's Long-term Objectives,
    143

Pang Zhongying, 177
Pan Wei, xxix

Peking University, xxiv, 7, 62, 75, 119, 121

People's Republic of China (PRC): constitutions of, 53; decade *1988–98* in, xxii; fifth generation of, xxii; founding of, 8; globalization and, 152–56; global and foreign strategies of, 173, 174–76, 177; mapping a path to democracy, xxv–xxix; national goals in, 22; national sovereignty of, 155; New Confucianism in, 117; peaceful development of, 154; political future of, xvi; politics in, 6; socialist transformation of, 93; state laws and regulations in, 59; U.S. views of, xv–xvi. *See also* Chinese Communist Party; Democracy— China; Harmonious society and world

Philosophy and philosophers, 7

Policymaking. *See* Political issues

Political issues: civic-association activities, 42; civil society, 53; class struggle, 11; decisionmaking, 30; goals of political reforms, 27; grassroots democracy, 28; in human history, 7, 14–15; incremental political development, xxvii; legislative and judicial systems, 29; peaceful development, 154; policymaking systems, 30, 31; political party organizations, 41; political systems, 15, 42, 53; political transparency, 31; practice of modern democratic politics, 10; rule of law, 68. *See also* Democracy; Government and governance

Political issues—China: crucial questions, xvi; establishment of a socialist state based on rule of law, 82; goals of political reforms, 27, 28; good governance, xxiii; mass and people's organizations, 40; modernization and, 112; new ideological factors, 22; New Left, xxix; New Right, xxix; policymaking systems, 30; political culture, 62; political development and reforms, xix–xx, xxv–xxvi, 21–22, 27–28, 50; political transparency, 32; politics of intellectual discourse on culture, 111–12

Political parties—China: civil society regulations and rules, 68, 73; party policy regulations, 58–61, 67; political and political party organizations, 41, 47; role of, 58; state laws and party policies, 67–68. *See also* Chinese Communist Party; Federalism; Government and governance—China

Political science: academic integrity and ethics in, 20; behavioralists and postbehavioralists in, 13; as a cause, 20–23; definition and concepts of, 7, 9–11, 13–14, 20; as knowledge, 14–18; as a profession, 18–20, 22–23; research methods in, 13; as a science, 10–14. *See also* Social science

Political science—China: as a cause, 21, 23; guidelines for development of, 23; importance and effects of, 6, 21–22; as a profession, 18–19; research in, 21; as a science, 11–14; teaching and study of, 7–14, 16–18, 21, 24. *See also* Public administration—China

Politicians, 4, 166–67

Population, 143

Poverty. *See* Economic issues—China

Power, 31–32

"Practice is the Sole Criterion for Testing Truth" (Hu), xxi

PRC. *See* People's Republic of China

Promoting Association of Self-Government, 161

Proudhon, Pierre-Joseph, 160

Provinces: China Agenda *21* committees, 142; federalism and, 157–67; medical services systems in, 137; movement of self-government by, 160–62

Provinces—specific: Fengtian, 161; Fujian, 161; Guangdong, 161; Guangxi, 161; Guizhou, 161; Hubei, 161; Hunan, 161, 164–65; Jiangsu, 161; Jiangxi, 161; Shandong, 160; Shanxi, 161; Sichuan, 161; Yunnan, 161; Zhejiang, 161, 165

Public administration, 23–26, 33. *See also* Government and governance issues— China

Public opinion polling, 75
Public sector—China, 24–25. *See also* Government and governance issues—China

Qianyuan National Studies Class (Peking University), 119
Qing dynasty. *See* Dynasties
Qu Qiubai, 104

Ramo, Joshua Cooper, 151
Realism, 11, 14
Records of the Countries around the Sea (Xu), 158
Red Cross Law, 54
"Red Women Army," 136
Reforms and opening up (*1978*–present): civil society and, 63, 73, 77, 78; cultural transformation and, 120; effects and changes of, 22, 50, 59, 118, 131, 174–75; foreign policy and, 174; political reforms and, 27, 28; response of intellectuals to, 114, 115; Westernization and, 128–29
Reform movement (*1898*), 121
Regulations: administrative statutes, 54–55; behavioral regulations, 42; for civil society organizations, 42, 68–73, 74; economic activity and, 42; globalization and, 153; implicit rules, 61; informal institutions, 61; as the institutional environment, 42–43, 68–71; institutional regulations, 42; norms and informal rules, 42; rules of conduct, 42; state laws and party policies, 67; statutory regulations, 42. *See also* Legal issues; Legislative issues
Regulations—China: administrative departments of the state regulations, 56–57, 64; central government regulations, 55–56, 64; for civil society and civic organizations, 59–61, 63–73, 79–82, 84–85; general laws, 54; informal rules and institutions in, 61; institutional environment and, 42–43; local government regulations, 57, 64, 66;

party policy regulations, 58–61; registration of social associations, 55–56, 60; regulatory bodies, 66–67, 68, 69
Regulations Concerning the Registration and Supervision of Social Associations, 55, 56, 64–66, 82
Regulations Concerning the Supervision of Civilian Non-enterprise Bodies, 64–66
Renmin University, 13, 19
Republic of China (*1912–49*): civil society organizations in, 47–49, 54, 55, 58; constitution of, 53, 162; sovereignty of, 164
Research and research methods, 11, 12–13, 45
Research and research methods—China, 21, 26
Resolution on Some Important Issues in Constructing a Harmonious Socialist Society, 169
Revolution of *1911*, 48, 159, 160
Rio Declaration on the Environment and Development, 141, 142
Rousseau, Jean-Jacques, 7, 158
Rule of law. *See* Legal issues
Rules and regulations. *See* Regulations

Sa Mengwu, 110
SARS. *See* Severe acute respiratory syndrome
School of Public Policy and Management (Tsinghua University), 44
Science, 13, 115–16. *See also* Natural science; Political science; Social science
Science and scientism, 10–14, 45, 95–96, 97, 106, 110, 111
Second Advanced Seminar on Sociology and Anthropology, 121
Self-Government by the United Provinces (movement), 161, 164, 165–66, 167
September *3* Society, 49
Severe acute respiratory syndrome (SARS), 62
Shambaugh, David, xvi
Shandong Province, 160
Shanxi province, 161
Shanghai, xxi, 57

Shanghai Cooperation Organization, 153
Shannuo Society, 145
Shenbao Monthly, 96, 100
Sheng Jiyi, 162–63
Shenzhen (economic zone), 150
Sichuan province, 161
Shi Tianjian, xx
Shixue Guan (Training Center for Government Officials), 7–8
Singapore, 116–17
Social Contract, The (Rousseau), 7
Social issues: class struggle, 11; grassroots democracy, 28; social management, 32–33; social development, 121; social progress and political science, 20–21. *See also* Cultural issues
Social issues—China: emerging social problems, 136–37; public sector, 24; social management, 32–33; social security system, 135
Social organizations, 43
Social science, xvi, 12, 13. *See also* Political science; Public administration
Social security, 135
South Korea, 116–17
Soviet Union, 168, 176
Stability: of civil society's administrative workforce, 89; democracy and, 3; federalism and, 163; social stability, 27, 30, 32, 79, 80, 155
State Commission for Restructuring the Economy, 60
State Council: civil society organizations and, 56–57, 60, 61, 64, 65, 68, 69; environmental regulations, 143; legislative cleanup and, 153; registration of civic organizations and, 72
"Statement of Chinese Cultural Renaissance, A" (Zhang, Ji, and others), 118–19
"Studies on Rousseau" (Liang), 158
Sun Liping, xxv–xxvi
Sun vs. Cheng War, 166
Sun Yat-sen, 159
Sustainable development strategy. *See* Economic issues—China

Taiwan and Taiwan people, 65, 116–17
Talking about the United States (Liang), 158
Tang Dechang, 162, 163–64
Tan Yankai, 161
Tao Xisheng, 110
Tax issues, 87
Third sector organization, 40–41
Theories: class-struggle theory, 11; Deng Xiaoping theory, 16; dependency theory, 107–08; Marxism-Leninism, 8; political theory, 16; theory of development, 16
"Theory of Federalism" (Zhang), 159
Ti-yong formula, 98, 111
Township and village enterprises (TVEs), 140
Trade Union Law, 54, 69
Training Center for Government Officials. *See* Shixue Guan
Treaties, 153, 154
Tsinghua University, 71, 75
TVEs. *See* Township and village enterprises

UN. *See* United Nations
United Association of Self-Government by Province, 161
United Nations (UN), 39, 168, 173, 177, 178–79
United Nations Conference on Environment and Development, 141
United Office of Self-Government, 161
United States, 117, 131, 132. *See also* Americanization; Western countries; Westernization

Voluntary organizations, 40, 41

Wang Huning, xxiv
Warlords, 162, 163, 164–66, 167
Washington Consensus, 151
Wei Yuan, 158
Welfare Donations Law, 87
Wen Jiabao, xix
Western countries: civil organizations in, 73–74, 86; cultural exportation by,

125–26, 155; federalism in, 166; globalization and, 132, 155; modernization as Westernization, 94–99, 105–11; sustainable development, 141; systems of checks and balances in, 31; United States and, 131; view of China's rise, 122. *See also* Americanization; Developed countries; Westernization; United States

Westernization, 94–99, 105–11, 157. *See also* Americanization

Wilson, Woodrow, xv

Women's Law Research and Assistance Center, 62

World Bank, 138, 146

World Trade Organization (WTO), 152, 153

WTO. *See* World Trade Organization

Wu Jingchao, 108–09

Wu Shichang, 97

Xia dynasty. *See* Dynasties

Xiao Tangbiao, 19

Xia Yong, xxiv

Xie Tao, xxviii

Xiong Mengfei, 101, 103

Xu Jishe, 158

Yang Xinzhi, 100

Yan Jicheng, 95, 98

"Yellow Women Army," 136

Ye Yin, 103

Yuan Shikai, 164

Yue Daiyun, 123

Yu Keping, xvi–xvii, xviii–xix, xx–xxix, 150

Yunnan province, 136, 161

Zhang Dainian, 118–19

Zhang Dongsun, 102, 159

Zhang Shenfu, 99

Zhang Shizhao, 159–60

Zhang Sumin, 100

Zhang Xirou, 101, 111

Zhang Yesui, 172

Zhang Zuolin, 165

Zhao Baoxu, xxii, 8

Zhao Hengti, 164–65

Zhejiang Province, 57, 75, 161, 165

Zheng Bijian, xxi

Zheng Chuangui, 19

Zhi Wei, 163

Zhou Enlai, 174

Zhou Ruijin, xxi

Zhou Xiawen, 100

Zhuang Tzu, 141